The Great Rat Race For Europe

The Great Rat Race For Europe

Stories of the 357th Fighter Group

Sortie Number One

Joey Maddox

To order additional copies of this book, contact:
Xlibris Corporation
1-888-795-4274
www.Xlibris.com
Orders@Xlibris.com
97244

Contents

Dedication

Mayor Clyde H. "Smokie" Maddox and Brigadier General Charles E. "Chuck" Yeager discuss the Captain Fletcher E. Adams 357th Fighter Group Museum in Ida, Louisiana, shortly before its dedication and grand opening (Photo by Bob McMillan)

This book is dedicated to the future of the Captain Fletcher E. Adams 357th Fighter Group Museum in Ida, Louisiana. I appreciate all of the hard work done by the mayor, the Town Council, and the citizens of the village of Ida in order to create this wonderful tribute to the brave men of the 357th Fighter Group. In addition to this, I hope that their good work will carry on and that the museum will continue to grow. It is my fondest wish to see the Captain Fletcher E. Adams 357th Fighter Group Museum moved out to Interstate 49 in Ida and for it to become a "world class" military aviation history museum one day. Thanks to all who have worked and continue to work toward this goal.

Joey Maddox

Acknowledgments

Special thanks to the following: Arch and Veronica Mooney; Jesse Frey; William "Bill" Overstreet; Werner Oeltjebruns; Hans-Peter Koller; Jane Ann Maddox; Mayor Clyde "Smokie" Maddox and the Town Council of Ida, Louisiana; Jim Anderson; C. E. "Bud" Anderson; Jay A. Stout; Will Foard; Pasquale Buzzeo; Joe Dempsey; Mary Jean Chester; Tim and Kerry Allen (two Christians that talk the talk *and* walk the walk); Damaris and Frank Boston (translator extraordinaire); Carol Krall; Michael Olmsted; Bob McMillan; Marshall Maddox (thanks for the smokes); Pam (the best-lookin' woman in Ida) Wright; Billy Shears; Larry McGuire; the Shipley Family; Lt. Col. Joseph "Joe" Shea (who shared this dream with me and worked so hard to make it become a reality); and especially to the *Spirit of Merle Olmsted* and all of the Yoxford Boys up there in that great *Pilot's Lounge in the Sky*!

Aviation Artist Len Krenzler

I would also like to thank world-class aviation artist Len Krenzler for the use of his artwork on the cover of this book. Please visit his website at *www.actionart. ca* or contact him at *len@actionart.ca* as his exceptional prints are for sale. In addition to this, I must also give *much* credit to Jim Anderson for allowing me to utilize the stories and photographs from his extraordinary website. To get in touch with Jim or to view his website, visit *www.cebudanderson.com* in order to relive World War II through the experiences of the Yoxford Boys.

Joey Maddox

Brigadier General Charles E. "Chuck" Yeager speaks to a crowd of 1,500 aviation and history enthusiasts at the dedication of the Captain Fletcher E. Adams 357th Fighter Group Museum in Ida, Louisiana, on July 24, 2010 (Photo by Joe Dempsey)

Introduction

On July 23, 2010, members of the 357th Fighter Group, their wives, and families all converged on the small village of Ida, Louisiana, to dedicate the Captain Fletcher E. Adams 357th Fighter Group Museum, the only museum in the United States dedicated solely to the preservation of the memory of this premier Mustang fighter outfit. One by one they arrived with their spouses, families, and friends and filed into Ida's Means Community Center where most of the population of the tiny village (278) had been busy all day preparing an honorary dinner and "meet and greet" for these heroes of WWII.

The last Yoxford Boy to enter the community center that night, his flight having been delayed in Dallas, was Brigadier General Charles E. "Chuck" Yeager, and as he walked through the doors at a little after 10:00 p.m. the entire crowd erupted into cheers and applause as they gave him a standing ovation. Grinning broadly, General Yeager seemed genuinely surprised and pleased with the reception he received that night, and he later told the press that arriving in Ida, he had felt as if he was "coming home again" due to the overwhelming expression of welcome lavished upon him by Ida's populace.

Understandably, Yeager was the only Yoxford Boy that the citizens of Ida could easily recognize that night, no doubt because of the fact that Chuck was arguably the most famous living fighter and test pilot in the world at the time. Some attendees that evening had been alive when Yeager stunned the world by becoming the "fastest man on earth" in 1947, having finally shattered the so-called sound barrier in the Bell X-1 rocket plane the *Glamorous Glennis*, and living to tell about it. Others had seen him before in his Delco battery commercials on television, and even the younger members of the crowd knew that actor Sam Sheppard had portrayed him in the movie *The Right Stuff*, although they probably were not aware that Yeager himself had appeared in an early scene in the film as the old drunk in Pauncho's Bar.

By the time Chuck Yeager and his wife Victoria sat down to eat a cold plate of fried catfish that had been saved for them (Yeager told me that it was the best catfish he had ever eaten in his life), most of the other pilots and crewmen of the 357th Fighter Group had gone back to their hotels to rest up for the dedication ceremony being held the next day. The Yeagers stayed and visited with the local villagers until nearly midnight and then, after the world-famous aviator had entertained the audience with several stories about Fletcher Adams and himself, the couple climbed back into their rental car and drove back to the Hilton Hotel in Shreveport.

Compared to their world-famous group mate, pilots Jesse Frey, Joe Shea, Will Foard, Frank Gailer, and crew chief Pasquale Buzzeo, who also attended the dedication dinner that Friday night, could not have seemed more anonymous. All of them were in their late eighties or early nineties, and unless one noticed the ever-present white 357th Fighter Group caps (designed by former Yoxford Boy Clarence E. "Bud" Anderson) on their heads, he or she might have mistaken them for any of the other elderly people in the room. But these men *were* different. They were fighter pilots from the first Eighth Air Force Mustang fighter group specifically charged with the responsibility of escorting Allied bombers deep into enemy territory and back again. As such, these men had flown and fought against the German Luftwaffe's best fighter pilots during the last two years of the war. Every one of these pilots had faced down the enemy (and death itself) miles above the earth over Germany, France, Poland, the Netherlands, and other occupied countries held by the Nazis during World War II, and because of this, the author considers them *all* true heroes. The fact that they are not as famous as Chuck Yeager and other members of the 357th Fighter Group has nothing to do with whether or not I respect these pilots as such. All of these men put their lives on the line for their country at a time when it was desperately needed. The fact that each and every one of them had the courage to fly into combat undoubtedly saved the lives of hundreds, perhaps thousands, of young members of the bomber crews they were responsible for protecting during the war. As they slugged it out day after day in the violent "rat races" with the Luftwaffe over Europe, these boys watched their friends as they were mutilated and/or killed during combat, but this never affected or diminished their commitment to see the war through and to do their duty. Because of this, they are all heroes in my eyes, to the last man, regardless of their victory tallies, the number of missions they flew, or the quality of the German pilots they faced toward the end of WWII.

For these reasons and others, these pilots and the crewmen who supported them have always been and will forever be my *personal* heroes. They all deserve to have their stories recorded in print in order that every generation of Americans can read about their history and never forget the sacrifices they made in order to ensure our freedom today. It is for these reasons that I wrote this book, and I hope that it serves its purpose.

By Joey Maddox

Dear Muff, So Long for Now, Walter

Whispers of the Dead
(A Prologue)

This book, its predecessor, and those that follow are all written for Muff, Hibbie, Butch, Arch, and all of the other children who lost their big brothers who gallantly flew and died with the 357th Fighter Group during the Second World War. They are written for the many fathers, mothers, sons, daughters, nephews, nieces, and other family members who have spent the rest of their lives paying loving tribute to the memory of *their* Yoxford Boy who never returned from the war.

Although some authors write books about the 357th Fighter Group purely for profit and professional or personal recognition, I hope to join the ranks of such writers as Merle Olmsted, Bud Anderson, Harve Mace, Leonard "Kit" Carson, and the others who have written books about the group in order to preserve its history and to document the brave, selfless deeds of the hundreds of pilots and their crews who helped to smite Hitler's murderous minions in Europe during World War II.

In early 2011 I received a telephone call from Joseph "Joe" Shea, a replacement pilot who joined the 357th Fighter Group's 362nd Fighter Squadron late in the war. Shea began by telling me that he had recently begun writing stories based on his memories of his experiences during the war. He went on to say that although many of the pilots and crewmen of the 357th had written stories that were later included in the dozens of books that had been written over the years about "the group," he was sure that many more stories were still floating around out there, and as "We," in Joe's words, "are dropping like flies nowadays, I think you and I should try to document these untold stories." Of course I agreed wholeheartedly, and several days later I received a package. [Author's note: The package arrived in Louisiana only after touring New York. Right, Joe? Or should I say, "Shaky"? But that's a private joke.] It contained twenty combat stories written by Shea that had never been published before, and all of them were interesting. It is funny how quickly a mundane, boring moment in a combat pilot's life may change into a hair-raising experience with the snap of a finger!

In a matter of weeks, Joe Shea and I had contacted many of the other living members of the group and they threw their support behind this project and began to send us stories of their own that had hitherto been undocumented. Bill Overstreet, Jesse Frey, Will Foard, Jim Anderson (the son of pilot Bud Anderson), and other members of the 357th and its extended family had soon provided Joe and I with a proverbial "ton" of material, enough to literally fill three volumes. This was the genesis for *The Great Rat Race for Europe: Stories of the 357th Fighter Group.*

Months, even years before this happened though, another reason for writing this trilogy of books percolated its way to the surface of my brain. Over the course of writing *Bleeding Sky: The Story of Captain Fletcher E. Adams and the 357th Fighter Group,* I had begun meeting and talking to family members of the pilots who had died during combat with the 357th, and I had noticed an underlying trait that ran through each and every one of them. This was, of course, their unending affection for these brave loved ones who had given the ultimate sacrifice for their families and their country. In addition to this, I noticed that they all, be they widows, siblings, nephews or nieces, etc., had spent the rest of their lives documenting as much as they could about their own Yoxford Boy and were extremely anxious to have these stories told and preserved in print. Some of them, like Aline Adams, the widow of 362nd Fighter Squadron pilot Captain Fletcher Adams who was brutally murdered by German civilians on the 30th of May 1944, had altered their entire lives due to these tragedies, and their future lives reflected this. For instance, Aline Adams never dated again or married and raised her and Fletcher's only child, Jerry, as a single mother, which was as difficult then as it is now. Even today, at the age of 88, Aline's home is a shrine to her late husband, and as I have told the press in subsequent interviews since I wrote the book about her husband, she is as in love with Fletcher today as she was the day they kissed goodbye and parted ways in Pocatello, Idaho in 1943.

Others like Captain Walter Perry's siblings Muff, Hibbie, and Butch Perry have continued to document the stories of their loved one's life by collecting books, documents, personal stories by fellow pilots, artifacts gleaned from the crash sites of the Mustangs, etc. And in the case of Walter Perry, Jr., they have passed this affection and devotion on to their children. Perry's nephew has produced two exceptionally wonderful documentaries about his uncle, both of which brought tears to this writer's eyes every time I watched them, and Walter's brother Gaston (Butch) Perry named his son Walter Perry III after his big brother.

Captain Bill Mooney's kid brother, Arch Mooney, found a book from Germany documenting the capture and murder of his brother by a Nazi thug, which had been written by amateur military aviation historian Hans-Peter Kollar, and with the author's help, translated and published an English version of the book so that Bill's story could be told here in America. And so the story is repeated over and over again. These people dedicated the remainder of their lives paying tribute to their long-lost brothers, fathers, husbands, uncles, and so forth, and this author found himself deeply affected by their devotion to these boys whose futures had been snuffed out in the prime of their youth.

So this book and the others that will surely follow are dedicated to you Muff, and Hibbie and Butch and Arch and Aline and Jerry, and on and on and on. Your loved ones will never be forgotten as long as I can hold a pen in my hand. I thank each and every one of you for allowing me to tell the stories of these heroic **Yoxford Boys.**

Joey Maddox

Dear Walter, I Love You

By Anna Mae Perry Beachem
(Muff)

Walter N. Perry was born June 8, 1923. He was the third child, first son, of eight children born to Annie and Walter N. Perry Sr., of Raleigh, North Carolina.

Walter Jr. grew up in Raleigh, graduated from Broughton Senior High School, and was attending North Carolina State College when he enlisted in the Army Air Force. He also spent some time working on his father's farm near Raleigh. He was twenty-one years old when his P-51 Mustang went down over Prum, Germany, on December 23, 1944. He died in the crash. He is buried in the American Military Cemetery at Hamm, Luxemburg in Europe.

Walter Jr. always loved airplanes and spent much time in his "shop" at home building gas powered model airplanes from balsa wood and tissue paper. I remember him sitting in that shop next to a large window with a huge sycamore tree outside and the sun streaming in on him. He was very good to his family and especially to his younger sisters and brother, and I can recall him taking me and my younger sister out to see the Christmas lights on Christmas Eve while someone else got "Santa Claus" items out of the attic! The last time I remember seeing him was before he left to go to Leiston Airfield in England. He was standing near our front door and looked so proud and handsome in his Army Air Force brown uniform with the Eight Air Force insignia on his sleeve and leather belt strapped tightly around his waist. Walter died when I was just ten years old.

Walter Jr. was much beloved by his entire family. None of us will ever stop loving him, nor will we ever forget him.

Thank God for all these wonderful men who served and sacrificed so much for their families, for their country, and for all of those suffering in Europe.

God bless them all!

To War with the Yoxford Boys!

(A Brief History of the 357th Fighter Group)

357th Fighter Group historian MSGT Merle C. Olmsted, Col. C. E. "Bud" Anderson, Margreth Olmsted, and William "Bill" Overstreet, Jr. in front of the current version of Anderson's P-51 Mustang *Old Crow*

The title of the first chapter of this book is borrowed from my personal "historian hero," Merle C. Olmsted, the official historian of the 357th Fighter Group, and I am extremely proud to say that he was a friend of mine. While researching my first book, *Bleeding Sky: The Story of Captain Fletcher E. Adams and the 357th Fighter Group*, Merle and I met by accident over the Internet. I had just discovered the superb video documentary about the Yoxford Boys entitled *Mustang Magic: War Chronicles of the 357th Fighter Group*, which had been produced by former Yoxford Boy Tom Beemer, Merle Olmsted, and other members of the 357th.

While singing the praises of this documentary over the Internet, I received an email from someone who called himself "Old Sarge," requesting that I send him a copy of the video. Immediately I smelled a rat and wondered if I was being set up in some sort of video pirating sting operation. (I have never denied that paranoia has always been a part of my psychological makeup!) Anyway, I replied to this mysterious *Old Sarge* that I would be happy to send him a copy of *Mustang Magic* as soon as I could locate Mr. Beemer and get written permission from him to copy his documentary. Of course I had no idea how to get in touch with Beemer, and I expected this to be the end of my email conversation with my newly found anonymous friend concerning the matter. To my surprise, within minutes of hitting the send key on my computer, a reply from Old Sarge popped up on my screen. I clicked on it and was amazed to find not only a description of the video and Mr. Beemer, but also his phone number and address along with the contact information for his wife and son! This was my first encounter with Master Sergeant Merle C. Olmsted of Paradise, California, and by the way, after dropping Merle's name, I was given permission by Tom Beemer's son to copy the documentary. (And I am very grateful to Mr. Beemer for that.)

Merle Olmsted on the wing of Robert Wallen's P-51B Mustang *Joan*

Over the next few years Olmsted and I worked closely together on my first book, and finally during the fall of 2007 I was able to meet him face to face at the Mustangs and Legends Air Show that was being held in Columbus, Ohio that year in conjunction with the United States Air Force's sixtieth anniversary celebration. The 357th Fighter Group members were the honored guests at the air show that week at Rickenbacker Field, and Olmsted was singled out and lauded for his exceptional historical work concerning the history of the Yoxford Boys and the 357th Fighter Group.

Unfortunately, very soon after this historic occasion Merle Olmsted's health began to fail him and sometime in 2008 I received a letter from his wife, Margreth, informing me of this bad news. In the same letter, Mrs. Olmsted told me that her husband had decided to leave all of his "357th stuff" to me and that I could come to get it in a few months after they had gotten settled into their new home. (The Olmsteds had just moved from Paradise, California, to their new home in Springfield, Missouri, where they would be closer to their son Michael and his family.) It was a very sad coincidence when I learned that Merle had passed away the very day I received this letter. His lovely wife Margreth would join him shortly after this, but in 2008 I attended Mr. Olmsted's memorial service. And after having tea with Margreth and Michael the day before, I was honored to receive a large collection of 357th Fighter Group memorabilia, art, photographs, and historical documents that MSGT Olmsted had collected over the years. I had promised Merle and his family that I would not rest until this collection was on display to the public, and during the summer of 2010, I made good on this pledge by opening (with the help of Ida's Mayor Clyde H. "Smokie" Maddox and the Town Council) the Captain Fletcher E. Adams 357th Fighter Group Museum in Adams's hometown of Ida, Louisiana.

**The official historian of the 357th Fighter Group and former member
of the 362nd Fighter Squadron Merle Olmsted at the Yoxford Boys
reunion held during the Mustangs and Legends Air Show in 2007
(Olmsted was singled out and honored, along with other members of the
357th Fighter Group, at the USAF's sixtieth anniversary celebration at
Rickenbacker Field for his historical work and the books he authored about
the 357th's accomplishments during WWII)**

During the time between Merle's passing and the opening of the museum dedicated to the 357th, I published the book about Fletcher Adams and the group. Then sometime around January of 2011 I received a call from Yoxford Boy Lt. Col. Joe Shea whom I had met previously at the Mustangs and Legends Air Show, and he suggested that I write a second book about the group. Shea had recently begun writing down stories of events that occurred during WWII while he was flying with the 357th Fighter Group as a replacement pilot in 1945. He told me that he was sure that there were many other undocumented stories of the Yoxford Boys' adventures "floating around out there" which had never appeared in books about the group before, and Joe wanted to know if I'd be interested in writing another book if he could track down the pilots who were still living and "wring" a few more tales out of them. Naturally I agreed, and this was the genesis for *The Great Rat Race for Europe: Stories of the 357th Fighter Group.*

The 357th Fighter Group was, arguably, the best group of fighter pilots ever produced by the United States Army Air Force during World War II, and the group's record certainly seems to prove it. The Yoxford Boys (their name was coined by German propagandist Lord Haw Haw the day they arrived at Leiston, England) arrived in the European Theater of Operations on November 29, 1943, after a six-day crossing of the Atlantic aboard the *Queen Elizabeth*. After a short stay at Raydon Wood, England, during which they were assigned to the Ninth Air Force, a deal was struck and the 357th Fighter Group was exchanged for a P-47 outfit based at Leiston, England. With this exchange, the group got a new base, Station AAF-373, or Leiston Field as it was known, and officially became part of the "Mighty" Eighth Air Force.

Shortly after they arrived at Leiston, some of the senior pilots from the 357th joined other fighter groups and flew indoctrination missions in order to familiarize themselves with combat flying, and it was during the first mission, on February 8, that the group lost its first member when Lloyd Hubbard was killed while strafing a German airfield. The 357th Fighter Group became officially operational on February 11, 1944, and on the very next day Lt. Col. Don Blakeslee of the Fourth Fighter Group led the Yoxford Boys on their first real mission, a bomber escort job over northern France that lasted just over two hours.

Starting on February 20th and ending on February 25th of 1944, Operation Argument, a large-scale attack on the German aircraft industry and related targets, was carried out by the Eighth Air Force. As a result of this the pilots of the 357th Fighter Group received their first real *baptism by fire*, losing eight pilots that week alone. The Yoxford Boys quickly recovered from this and went on to set quite a few records during World War II. By the time the war ended in Europe, the 357th Fighter Group was, indeed, destined for the record books and achieved the following:

1. **The 357th was the fastest scoring fighter group in the Army Air Force during the last year of the war.**
2. **The group produced more aces (forty-two) than any other Army Air Force fighter group during WWII, and this record still stands.**
3. **The Yoxford Boys also shot down more German jets than any other AAF group during the war.**
4. **The 357th Fighter Group set an all-time record in U. S. military aviation history when on January 14, 1945, a day the Yoxford Boys call "the Big Day" and "the Great Rat Race," the group shot down 55.5 enemy aircraft in a dogfight that lasted just over two hours.**

In addition to this illustrious record, the 357th Fighter Group was awarded two **Distinguished Unit Citations** (for action over Berlin on March 6, 1944, and over Derben on January 14, 1945) and the **Croix de Guerre with Palm** from France for their historic contributions to the war effort. In the decades following the end of World War II, many books have been written about the 357th Fighter

Group, and I plan to add more to that list over the next few years. Without a doubt, the best of these books chronicling the tremendous contributions to the Army Air Corps made by the Yoxford Boys were written by Merle C. Olmsted, and the reader would be well served to obtain and read a copy of his last book entitled *To War with the Yoxford Boys,* which is the *definitive* historical book about the 357th Fighter Group.

**The 357th Fighter Group shield featuring the
now famous winged fist brandishing a sword**

That said, this book, *The Great Rat Race for Europe: Stories of the 357th Fighter Group,* is meant to complement the work done by Olmsted over the years. The majority of the stories included here have never appeared in printed form before and even the ones that have been published previously were pulled from books that have long been out of print. Some of the stories included in the pages of this book were written by the author, but the vast majority were written by the pilots themselves, and it is for this reason that this collection of stories is unique.

It is imperative that I must give a tremendous amount of credit to Jim Anderson, the son of Yoxford Boy C. E. "Bud" Anderson, who graciously allowed me to have unlimited access to his collection of stories and photographs which are currently available to 357th Fighter Group enthusiasts on his website located on the Internet. Without the help of the Andersons, Lt. Col. Joe Shea, and Mr. Michael Olmsted, this book would have been impossible to write. In addition to this, I must inform the reader that all of the stories appearing in this book have been edited by this author. In my attempts to do this I have tried to be as *light-handed* as possible, and in most cases I have only corrected the misspellings and errors in grammar.

As for the order in which these stories appear here in this book, I have chosen to present them in a random manner, very much similar to the experience one would have while walking from table to table at a 357th Fighter Group reunion and listening to the stories being told by the pilots themselves. Although attempts were made, originally, to order the stories chronologically, it finally became apparent that this more random format was better.

That said, I hope to give the reader an experience very much like the one I had when I became "a fly on the wall" at my first Yoxford Boys reunion in 2007. Incidentally I tried to record all of the tales told by the pilots and crewmen at the hotel that night in Columbus, Ohio, but the participants were having such a good time that the background noise created by all of their mirth rendered the recording on my digital recorder unintelligible. Hopefully this book will allow the reader to enjoy the same tall tales and death-defying accounts of heroism in a much quieter format.

Joey Maddox

Front cover art by Len Krenzler: 357th Fighter Group ace Robert Winks achieves what most WWII fighter pilots do not in this computer graphics portrait entitled *Bolt from Above*. Flying his P-51D Mustang, *Trusty Rusty*, Winks shoots down a German Me-262 jet on January 15, 1945. He later described the remarkable event as follows:

> *I was at 15,000 feet near Munich when I saw a plane doing slow rolls on the deck-it was an Me-262. He had been flying away from what I later learned was the Schongau Airdrome. I dropped my wing gas tanks, and rolled over into an 80 degree dive with 5 degrees of diving flaps. He made a 180 degree turn and flew back toward me, just before I started my dive. I was diving at a point ahead of his aircraft, and I had to adjust my dive angle to about 60 degrees.*
>
> *I closed to within 500 yards above him, and scored multiple hits across, and on both sides of his canopy. It flamed at once, rolled over, and that is all I saw because I was going straight back to 15,000 feet of altitude. But, I had a problem. My engine had no power. It [the propeller] was wind milling! Ack-ack was coming up at me from all directions! The engine had no power!?! I had dropped the wing auxiliary tanks (which I was using), without turning the gas selector switch onto the internal wing tanks! If I had a vapor lock, which I probably had, my P-51 prop was turning so fast as a result of my near vertical dive, that it sucked it out and took off for 15,000 feet of altitude, which we made back, toot-sweet!*

The Great Rat Race

(January 14, 1945)
By Leonard "Kit" Carson

Kit Carson on the wing of his P-51K Mustang *Nooky Booky IV*
(This autographed photo now hangs in the Captain Fletcher E. Adams
357th Fighter Group Museum in Ida, Louisiana)

The 357th Fighter Group came to life by the clatter of the teleprinter machine in Group Operations, punching out Field Order 1515A from Eight Air Force Fighter Command, northwest of London, a hundred miles away.

The night watch at Group Ops scanned it and then the field phone and the one in our squadron orderly room buzzed lightly. The Charge of Quarters picked it up and heard, "Roust 'em, the briefing's in one hour." The C. Q. then knocked cautiously at our door, as if he knew the hostility inside to being roused at such an uncivilized hour. In the blackest part of the January night we groped our way to consciousness, pulled on cold boots, and stumbled to the mess hall through the half frozen mud that comprised the local real estate. The Nissen huts that were our homes looked like igloo-shaped freighters floating on a sea of mud. The freezing cold was the wet kind that permeates the soul. The only thing good about the morning was that the weather wasn't as rotten as it could have been.

No one bathed or shaved after getting up. Sleep was more important and if doing something didn't make the missions shorter, improve the weather or your chances, then why bother? All of the amenities, plus a combat ration of Bourbon or Scotch, administered by the Flight Surgeon, would come after the mission if you wanted it. [Author's note: In addition to the alcohol doled out to the fliers after their missions, chocolate bars and chewing gum were also distributed to the combat pilots. According to Captain Fletcher Adams, in his war diary and letters he sent home to his wife, the candy was a highly sought after commodity, and some pilots signed on for missions just for the sweets.] Many pilots ate nothing before a mission except for the usual "fighter pilot's breakfast," a cigarette and a cup of coffee. Some believed that having an empty stomach made them more alert. Some believed if they were "gut shot" in combat, the likelihood of peritonitis was less on an empty stomach, if they got back at all, which was unlikely in the event. However, I'll leave the medical truth of that belief to the experts. Who's going to argue with a man trying to shave the odds of survival in his favor?

Being a farm boy, I ate everything in sight, because I had learned about the need for food to generate body heat when you're going out to work in sub-zero temperatures. None of the misgivings had anything to do with the Luftwaffe per se. Most of the pilots believed, as I did, that with the superb fighting machine that we had in the Mustang, they couldn't lay a glove on us if we saw them coming. We made it our business to see them; that's what it was all about. Escort fighters were the "defensive linebackers," as in football, and you can't "clothesline" the opposition if you don't see them.

My first concern was of having to bail out or ditch in the North Sea in winter and dying of exposure. Nobody hates cold water more than I do. I've never taken a cold shower in my life if there was any choice. If you didn't get out of the water and into your dinghy within twenty minutes, death from exposure was almost certain. The near-freezing water would take the body heat from you that quickly. My second concern was bailing out and lying in a POW camp hospital with a broken back or gangrenous arm or leg with drugs and medical expertise in short supply, or non-existent. Third, was of being massacred by the civilian population if I went down in the area of a heavily bombed target. It happened to others. I had no illusions about my reception by a hostile, overwrought mob of bombed-out civilians, especially if I were standing next to a wrecked Mustang with 19 swastikas painted on its side. They weren't going to hand me any bouquets. The Geneva Convention and the Rules of War would be several light years removed. It could be a one-on-one gut level confrontation with a mob. That's the reason I carried my service-issue Colt .45 and two extra clips of ammo.

After bacon, pancakes, and coffee, the pilots took the dirt path that had been scuffed across a small meadow and walked, almost idly, in clumps of three or four to Group Operations for the briefing. Small talk, the latest jokes, a lot of bull, and some bitching passed back and forth, mostly about the weather. The Army was recouping the situation in the Battle of the Bulge in the Ardennes, during the worst weather that Europe had seen in thirty years. For the past two weeks, we tried to climb up through that crap, as much as 25,000 or 30,000 feet thick, picking up ice most of the way, only to have the mission scrubbed and for us to be ordered to return home. We lost thirteen pilots that month, at least six of the losses were directly attributable to the weather. The P-51 was a fine weather airplane, but if an inexperienced pilot panics, gets vertigo, or collides with someone in the muck, nobody can help him.

357th Fighter Group Briefing Room at Leiston Field

The pilots were fed up with the morning scramble to get to briefings only to find that the mission had been scrubbed, sometimes before the actual briefing started. Hurry up and wait. Attitudes on the morning of January 14, 1945, were no different. As the 66 pilots of the three squadrons filed into the Briefing Room they were watched by Doc Barker, our group flight surgeon, who was checking for red eyeballs, sniffles, and bronchial coughs. I walked in with John Sublett and my wingman, "Hot Shot Charlie" Duncan, both aces. Damned comforting to have an ace for a wingman. That kid's got his head screwed on real good and is as fine a shooter and rudder stomper as has ever come down the pike. "Is it scrubbed yet?" "Nope, still on." "'Fraid so, the B-17s have already taken off. I heard 'em forming up to the west as we came in."

The ominous red ribbon that marked our route and target ran eight feet across the large briefing map of Europe pasted to the wall at the rear of the speaker's stage.

"What's the target?" "Berlin." "Dammit, I can see that!" "Someone said Derben/Stendal, but for you and me, that's Berlin." "All I need is one more trip to Berlin to round out my career in aviation." "What's at Derben?" "Snow and sauerkraut."

Briefing time. Over six thousand kids, just out of their teens but in reality light years removed, and a few "old-timers" over thirty, in Mustangs and Fortresses, were converging for a single purpose. The bombers had indeed taken off and a corps of crew chiefs, armorers, and radiomen were in a last minute hustle to get the fighter escort off. The name of the village, Derben, at the end of the ribbon really didn't matter. It was Berlin in January.

Kit Carson with what appears to be *Nooky Booky III*

The chances of evading the enemy and walking out if you were shot down over Germany at this time of the year were zero. The nearest friendly territory was occupied Denmark, but even that was a 250 mile hike from the target area. The chances of being mobbed and cut down by angry civilians, the SS, or a trigger-happy private in the Wehrmacht were excellent. The chances of becoming a POW, with your skin in one piece, in that populated area were somewhere between mediocre and non-existent. The best bet was to put yourself into the hands of the Luftwaffe, if you could spot an airfield on the way down. Failing that, well, be sure and take "Mother's little helper" along in your shoulder holster. Wisely used, it could put some distance between you and any hostile parties on the ground and make the difference in staying alive.

"The target's probably a couple of forty pfennig outhouses." "Yeah, they'll think the sauerkraut backfired. It'll cause a national stampede!" "That's our secret weapon." Talk. Just idle, nervous, loose talk while you're standing by waiting for something to happen.

This was my ninety-ninth mission in a year, and the fourteenth to Berlin. No sweat. The vital characteristic of the whole group was that we all still had the "spirit of attack." If that spirit doesn't exist, we're out of business. The fundamental characteristic of fighter action was, at all times and in all places, to be *offensive*, because only the fighter pilot that attacks has the advantage. He must be the *hunter* to avoid being the *hunted*. If he or his airplane could not perform sufficiently well to do this, then neither had any reason to exist. The pilot was trained, and the aircraft was designed to carry the fight to the enemy. The cavalry had "sprouted wings."

We came to attention as the group commander Colonel Dregne arrived. He had planned and was leading the mission. A congenial and thoughtful man, Dregne would fly all day and then write papers on tactics at night and shoot them up to Fighter Command. He wasn't asking them, he was telling them how it was done.

Colonel Dregne

There had been no precedent for strategic escort against the Luftwaffe and we wrote the book, mission by mission, as we went along. Dregne had a strong intuition about how to put a fighter group in the right spot to clobber the opposition. This particular mission was to be a North Sea cruise over 300 miles of water to the coast of Denmark, avoiding landfall and flak until the last minute, and then turning southeast to Derben/Stendal just west of Berlin. The target was 180,000 tons of oil storage. The weather was clear over the target. The 357th was assigned the lead escort position for the Thirteenth Combat Wing of Fortresses which was leading the Third Air Division column of B-17s. Within the Thirteenth Combat Wing, the Ninety-fifth Bomb Group was leading the whole force, followed by the "Bloody" 100th and the 390th. All three of these veteran groups had participated in the Schweinfurt ball bearing plant raids in October 1943, and the Ninety-fifth had been the first group to bomb Berlin in March 1944. We were at Berlin that day too, as the first P-51 group assigned to General Doolittle's Eighth Air Force. Now we were to rendezvous again west of Denmark over the North Sea. The intelligence portion of the briefing centered upon the massed "company front" attacks by the Luftwaffe Fighter Command that could be expected. We were aware of this from previous missions but the reminder did no harm. In round numbers, they would probably attack in groups of forty or fifty FW-190s and/

or Me-109s, spread out in lines six to eight abreast and coming head on into the Forts in wave after wave. There might be a few of the Me-262 jet fighters which were 80 mph faster than our P-51s. They could be a problem. A general assessment of the air war did not reveal any tendency on the part of the Luftwaffe to ease up on their defenses. On Christmas Eve 1944, General Doolittle dispatched 2,034 heavy bombers and 1,000 plus fighters over Fortress Europe, probably the greatest air armada that history will ever record. While escorting a part of that force into central Germany, our Group destroyed thirty-one Luftwaffe fighters for a loss of three. On Christmas Day we went to Kassel, just east of the Ruhr, with no opposition in sight; five hours sitting on that rock-hard dinghy before pulling up to a government issue plate of turkey and cranberries. Riding the "point" position on escort today, we could expect to meet the first assault of the company front attack. Timing on our part was imperative. We had to be in position at the point of the column of Forts at all times. If the German fighters got into the column head on, there would be no getting them out—and they would most certainly be there. The weather was good over Germany and our line of flight was a clear threat to Berlin.

At the appointed time, sixty-six airplanes came to life around the perimeter of the field. To anyone standing at the Control Tower, it sounded as if two or three Merlin engines were being born every second. The sun cut itself on the edge of a cloud and a shaft of light bled down onto the field, giving some promise of relief in the weather. There's no chatter on the radio. There's nothing to talk about. The radio was for emergencies, enemy surprises, or if someone had to abort the mission; otherwise, stay off the air. Hotshot Charlie came puttering down the taxi strip and waited for me to pull out ahead of him. I was leading Blue flight so we were the ninth or tenth airplanes in sequence in takeoff position. Getting into position in the group gaggle of airplanes was easy. Once you're in the right sequence taxiing out, the chore of getting airborne into the right formation slot was only a matter of throttle and bending.

John Duncan

"Hot Shot Charlie" Duncan

Once airborne, we settled back for the two-hour haul to the rendezvous with the Fortresses. A few of our Mustangs called in to abort and returned to base. Landing gear won't retract, engine too rough, coolant hot. Once in a while someone had a slight case of flu that developed into stomach cramps. In that event, there's only one thing you can do: abort and hope to hell you make it back before the pressure overcomes your sphincter valve. There are no toilets in fighters. When you get the cramps two hours from home base, it's a crisis of will power. We did have relief tubes with a plastic funnel on the end to urinate in, but the residue would freeze and plug up the tube. The second time you relieved yourself on a long mission, you were stuck with a plastic funnel full of cold pee in your left hand while you flew with your right. After another crisis of will power, you drop it to the floor and hope that you don't have to get inverted in a dogfight anytime soon.

We came upon the Third Division column of B-17s with their red, black, and yellow rudders clearly visible. Tooling up front to the Thirteenth Combat Wing, we found our three bomb groups. Once again we rendezvoused on time as briefed. Our good reputation was maintained; we had never missed a rendezvous. Colonel Dregne, as "Judson Red Leader," put his lead squadron of escorts high over the Ninety-fifth Bomb Group at 30,000 feet; my squadron on the right flank at 26,000 feet; and the third squadron on the left flank at the same altitude. The division column of Forts was at 24,000 feet. Now for the wait. Everyone got their eyeballs focused into the distance, waiting for those tell-tale specks on the horizon or condensation trails to show. We could see for fifty miles in that air. We turned right and headed southeast toward Berlin. The Luftwaffe was tracking us and now they knew our intent. There was a Jagdgeschwader (literally translated, a "hunting group" consisting of about 150 fighters) forming up out there somewhere. We would fight in pairs when they hit. That was a basic article of faith in American fighter training. Our group of fifty-eight planes would break up into twenty-nine pairs (eight had aborted with problems); a leader, who was also the shooter, and a wingman to cover his tail and to back him up with another set of guns. After a year in combat, we did those things intuitively. We hadn't been in escort position more than thirty minutes when the enemy force was sighted pulling condensation trails and approaching from Brandenburg. They were coming at us from out of the sun at about 32,000 feet.

"Judson Red Leader, contrails at eleven o'clock high, about 100 of 'em." "Judson Red Leader here, roger. Dollar, Cement, and Greenhouse, drop your tanks."

That was understood to be the order for our three squadrons to attack, no need for any other chitchat. What was there to talk about? The moment of truth had arrived; this was where the propaganda stopped. It was time to "clothesline" the opposition and to put some numbers on the scoreboard for our team.

"Jeezus, look at 'em comin'" . . . "Shut up and drop your goddamned tanks!"

Switch to an internal tank, punch the red button on the top of the stick, and away they drop; 116 wing tanks streamed fuel out of broken connections into the stratosphere as a prelude to the clash. It was a reassuring sight to the crews and gunners in the Flying Fortresses below. They knew we were spring-loaded and ready to go. Flick on your gun and camera switches. It all took five seconds. The head-on rate of closure was fast. The opposing force was about sixty Me-109s at 32,000 feet flying as top cover for the sixty FW-190s at 28,000 feet, which was the main attack group. The Focke Wulf 190 group was spread out into the anticipated "company front," flying six or eight abreast and several lines deep.

Both fighter forces drove home the attack. We had not been pulling contrails at our altitude, so they had no idea what our actual strength was. The odds were 2:1, in favor of the Luftwaffe. My squadron and the one on the left flank met the FW-190s head-on. Colonel Dregne met the Me-109s with his high squadron. Our position and timing were perfect but we couldn't completely stop the first assault—nothing but a brick wall could have.

"Hot Shot Charlie" Duncan had kicked his Mustang about four wingspans out to my right, where he could see me in his peripheral vision and watch the 190s come in. He was waiting for my first move. We both fired as we met them and just a half second before the first wave passed. I hauled it around at full power in a steep, tight chandelle to reverse course and attack from the rear. At this point our three squadrons broke up into fighting pairs, a leader and a wingman.

The Focke Wulf 190 *Butcher Bird*

I closed to about two hundred yards on a Focke Wulf and fired a good burst, getting strikes all over the fuselage and then closed the range to about fifty yards. No long-range gunnery here. Just shove all six gun barrels up his butt, pull the trigger, and watch him fly apart. I hit him again, and he rolled to the right and peeled down and started a series of rolls that became more and more violent. He was smoking badly and the damaged ship was obviously out of control. I pulled up and watched him fall. The pilot did not get out. In fact, he didn't even release his canopy.

Duncan and I were pulling back up toward the bombers when we saw another formation of twenty or thirty Focke Wulfs to our rear. Another P-51 joined up so there were three of us. We turned 180 degrees into them; it was all that we could do. Pure chance had put us on the spot. We fired head-on but got no hits. I popped maneuvering flaps and again with full power, did the tightest chandelle with all the G-force I could stand (probably about five or six G's). I fired at about three hundred yards, getting strikes on the nearest 190 that was turning into me. He headed into me violently but evidently pulled too hard on the stick in the turn and did a couple of high-speed snap rolls and wound up on his back with his auxiliary fuselage tank perched upward against the horizon. While he was poised there, I hit him with another burst. Pieces came off of the ship and he began boiling smoke. He split-essed and headed for the deck. I followed until he hit the sod at a shallow angle, bounced in a shower of dirt, and crashed. Again, the pilot never left the ship.

I was by myself now; Duncan and the other Mustang having left to take care of their own fortunes. That's the way it was in a massive dogfight such as this; it quickly broke down into forty or fifty private battles. I learned later that Duncan was busily engaged in the destruction of two FW-190s in another corner of the sky.

I climbed back up to 14,000 feet when two Me-109s with barber pole stripes on the spinners came beneath me. The reason for the stripes was that we were up against Jagdgeschwader 300 of the Reich Defense Force located around Berlin. Neither one saw me as I dropped to their rear and fired at the closest one. They dropped partial flaps and broke violently away from my line of fire. I used my excess speed to haul back up and regain my altitude advantage. The two enemy ships pulled into a tight Luftberry circle but I stayed out of it. I made a fast head-on pass at their defensive circle but got no hits. The bore of the cannon mounted in the center of the 109 spinner looked as big as a laundry tub in the brief instant we met. The leader broke out of the circle and headed for the deck. I dropped down to engage "tail-end Charlie" as he too headed for the deck in a nearly vertical dive. All of a sudden, he pulled it up into a climb and chopped his power, losing nearly all of his speed. This was the old sucker-trap maneuver that would put me in front and him behind in firing position. I kept my excessive speed and fire-walled the Merlin and started firing, all the while closing the range down to forty or fifty yards. I was so close that the 109 virtually blocked my vision through the windshield. I was getting hits all over the fuselage, and as I pulled up vertically over him, a maneuver that he could not have followed at his low speed, his engine coolant blew. Over my left shoulder I could see that he went into a tumbling spiral, out of control. Again, undoubtedly, the pilot was hit.

**The Me-109 (Olmsted chafed at the term "Bf-109"
as does this author)**

So ended the engagement for me, two FW-190s and one Me-109 destroyed; 1050 rounds of ammunition fired. Our group destroyed 56.5 enemy aircraft [Author's note: the official tally is 55.5 enemy aircraft destroyed in the air and one destroyed on the ground], that's an Air Force record that still stands today. We lost three pilots as the price of the victory. Things were not all that great, however, in the Combat Wing of the Flying Fortresses. One entire squadron of B-17s of the 390th did not return. The 390th's C Squadron was attacked by Focke Wulfs and all eight Fortresses went down. The reason that the FW-190s hit the 390th Forts so hard is that they were lagging a few miles behind because of engine trouble and could not catch up. When the attack came, they lost the benefit of the fighter escort ahead of them and the collective defensive firepower of the Ninety-fifth and 100th Bomb Groups. The Luftwaffe singled them out as the obvious weak spot in the division column and chewed them up with cannon fire for half an hour. Cut off from the support, nine Fortresses and nearly a hundred men disappeared from the sky.

About five hours after takeoff, our squadron telephone reports on confirmed victories began trickling in to Group Ops. They couldn't believe it. There were so many claims; maybe the same planes were being reported twice? "What the hell, doncha think I can count?" "Well, check it again, goddammit. Somebody's gone ape down there." "OK, OK, quitcher bitchin'." Hang up, wait thirty minutes and reconfirm. No individual was making excessive claims but nearly everyone did something to help the total score.

The report went on to Eighth Air Force at High Wycombe. They didn't believe it either and wanted it rechecked, unusual to say the least. It broke the old record of thirty-eight destroyed in a single engagement by 19.5 (one gets half a victory by sharing it with another pilot who attacks the same enemy ship). Everyone finally became convinced that the reports were correct. However, it was two days later before General Doolittle, assured that he had the correct figures, reported the victories at a staff conference. This follow-up report is about thirty years late, General, but we owe it to you anyway. The real reason for our success comes in two parts. First, our position and timing were perfect. We had fifty-eight Mustangs exactly where they were supposed to be when the attack came. Secondly, of the fifty-eight Mustang pilots at that spot, twenty-three of them were aces. You had the first team on the line, General; fifty-eight Mustangs with twenty-three positions manned by aces was one hell of a potent force. Those twenty-three pilots accounted for forty-one of the 56.5 destroyed.

That's the report that should have been made but it wasn't, because the facts were buried in the statistics of the pilots' roster for that day and no one thought to look there, but it's true. The Luftwaffe never attacked in such force again; the war was over four months later. General Doolittle sent a message to the pilots of the 357th Fighter Group which reads: "You gave the Hun the most humiliating beating that he has ever taken in the air. Extend my personal admiration and congratulations to each member of your command, both ground and air, for a superb victory." Coming from the man that raided Tokyo in an Army Air Force B-25 from the deck of a carrier, the message had a special meaning that will never be forgotten.

The Revenge Killing of 362nd Fighter Squadron Pilot Captain William H. Mooney, Jr.

Of the scores of pilots of the 357th Fighter Group who died in the line of duty during WWII, the deaths of two pilots stand out from the others because of the needlessness of the circumstances under which they died. Captains Fletcher E. Adams and William H. Mooney, Jr. were both murdered by German civilians in 1944.

In this author's first book, *Bleeding Sky: The Story of Captain Fletcher E. Adams and the 357th Fighter Group*, published in 2009, Adams's murder was thoroughly investigated and documented. Then in 2010, during the dedication of the Captain Fletcher E. Adams 357th Fighter Group Museum in Ida, Louisiana, the author met Arch Mooney and his wife, Veronica. Mr. Mooney's brother, Captain William H. Mooney, Jr. was also murdered by German civilians in eerily similar circumstances on Christmas Eve 1944. We discussed Billy Mooney and I agreed to include his story in my next book about the 357th.

During the spring of 1944, after the Luftwaffe had suffered a serious thrashing at the hands of the Yoxford Boys and other Allied fighter groups, Heinrich Himmler issued secret orders to the rural police forces throughout Germany that instructed them to execute any captured Allied airman from that time forward during the war. Although some of the police who received this order were skeptical and refused to carry it out, there were many others who did. As early as August 11, 1943, Himmler had issued orders stating that it was NOT the duty of the police to interfere in conflicts between civilians and downed Allied airmen.

In an attempt to inflame the public sentiment toward Allied fliers shot down over Germany and captured, on May 26, 1944, Propaganda Minister Joseph Goebbels released a news article in the *National Observer* and other public newspapers throughout the Third Reich. In it Goebbels listed many of these *flieger lynch-morde* (flier revenge killings) and excused them as justified reactions by a German public enraged by the lawless actions of this "murdering trash." In his opinion, the military had better things to do than to waste its time interceding on behalf of these "air gangsters" and "child murderers" in an attempt to protect them from the German population.

On May 30, 1944, the very day that 362nd Fighter Squadron member and leading ace of the 357th Fighter Group Captain Fletcher E. Adams was shot down in his P-51B *The Southern Belle* [Author's note: *The Southern Belle* was the real name of Adams's plane and not *Southern Belle* as has been reported, and it was written that way by Fletcher himself in a letter to his wife, of which I have a copy] and murdered, Martin Bormann released a confidential newsletter that referred to English and American fliers' low-level attacks (strafing and bombing). In it he described the lynchings of captured Allied fliers by angry civilian mobs and stated that these actions should be expected and thereby excused by the German police and judiciary.

One of the gendarmes affected by this hateful propaganda was Police Chief Adolf Funke who used it as an excuse to viciously beat, abuse, and then murder Captain Fletcher Adams after he was captured near the small town of Tiddische, Germany, on May 30, 1944.

Another German, Emil Hoffman (a Nazi party stalwart and former SA member), was also convinced by this hateful propaganda that he must avenge the "murders" of his innocent countrymen and women by these "air terrorists" and he was awaiting the opportunity to do so on Christmas Eve 1944.

Christmas Eve 1944

(The Great Eighth Air Force Air Assault)

On Christmas Eve of 1944, the Battle of the Bulge was raging as the German Wehrmacht attempted to break through the Allied lines in the Ardennes Forest in a last-ditch effort to turn the tide of the war in their favor. Although half frozen, the American troops (including my great uncle, Buck Mixon) were struggling to contain Hitler's forces whose momentum had been building over the previous weeks. In support of the American Army, the Eighth Air Force launched the largest air assault in military aviation history in hopes of pounding the Germans into submission. On the morning of December 24 over 2,000 B-17 and B-24 heavy bombers rumbled down their runways at airfields throughout England and took off into the early morning sky heading for the Ardennes Forest and other targets.

[Author's note: One of these B-24s was piloted by Lt. Charles Giessen, Jr. (458th Bomb Group/755th Bomb Squadron), who grew up with Fletcher Adams in the small village of Ida, Louisiana. For months, Giessen had been worried about his chances of surviving his tour of duty, so much so that he had been placed in the base hospital while suffering from a "nervous" stomach. His constant fretting nearly drove navigator Jackson Grandholm, his roommate in the infirmary, crazy, so when Giessen whined for the hundredth time, "I know they're going to get me! I just know it!" the navigator snapped, "Well I hope they do get you! At least then I could get some sleep!"

Charles Giessen, Jr. and crew
(Giessen is standing third from left)

Weeks later, while flying the mission on Christmas Eve, Grandholm would regret that statement as he watched in horror through the bomb bay doors of his own bomber as Charles Giessen's B-24 suffered a direct hit from flak fired by a German Panzer tank below. Giessen and his copilot struggled furiously, stomping on the rudder pedals and yanking on the control yokes of their stricken aircraft but their efforts were all in vain as the tail of the bomber had been severed just behind the wings. The Liberator quickly snapped into a vicious spin and after plunging earthward over four miles it crashed into the Ardennes Forest in a huge fireball. Only three members of the nine-man crew survived, including John E. Thompson (co-pilot), Alphonse Wolak (waist gunner), and Edward Racek (tail gunner).]

Captain William H. Mooney, Jr.

(The Last Mission of the Libby-B)

William "Bill" Mooney, Jr.

Shortly before noon on December 24, 1944, sixty-six P-51s from the 357th Fighter Group took off, and after forming up over Leiston Field they proceeded out over the English Channel in search of the bombers they were to escort. In addition to the bomber trains, the Eighth Air Force had issued "maximum effort" orders the night before, and as a result 1,000 fighter planes, including those of the 357th would be accompanying the heavies to their targets and back. Assigned as "spares" on the mission that day were Bill Mooney and Jesse Frey, both of the 362nd Fighter Squadron, and although no other pilots aborted, they elected to continue on with the group as it proceeded toward the continent. Mooney was flying his P-51D Mustang *Libby-B* (named for his mother Libby and sister Beth), and Frey was at the controls of his ship, the P-51D *Ain't Misbehavin'* (named after the popular instrumental song of that title).

Bill Mooney (right) and his P-51 *Libby-B*

Jesse Frey's P-51 *Ain't Misbehavin'*

After the Yoxford Boys located their "Big Friends," they settled in at various locations around the bomber train and began scanning the sky for "Jerries." At the same time, from Dresden came the Me-109s and FW-190s of the J. G. 300, and as they all neared the vicinity of Fulda, Germany, the entire group of bombers and fighters clashed at 24,000 feet.

Almost immediately, at 1:57 p.m., two of the American heavy bombers collided over Merlau, Germany, less than four miles north of Freienseen, and one of the Flying Fortresses crashed with a full bomb load, killing all but one of the nine crewmen on board. A few minutes later one of the Yoxford Boys called in "bandits," referring to FW-190s that had been sighted flying under the group, and the 362nd Fighter Squadron went to work.

On the ground below the melee, in and around the little village of Freienseen, Germany, the Freienseeners all stopped what they were doing and watched the approaching bombers and fighters, which appeared as tiny specks in the sky, trailing long white contrails. Suddenly the organ drone of the aircraft engines was broken up by the whining of maneuvering fighters and the chattering of their machine guns and cannons. Skeleton fingers of smoke trailed from the sky as the bombers released their "smoke pot" target indicators, and from the ground below the witnesses saw some of the contrails form into circles, snake lines, and loops as the fighters jockeyed for position in order to attack their opponents. Once again another struggle for life and death had begun in the subzero thin air over central Germany.

Jesse Frey of the 357th Fighter Group, who was flying Captain Mooney's wing, watched as Billy split essed and tacked onto a group of 190s. Following his element leader, Frey was surprised by another FW-190 which appeared behind Captain Mooney and then broke into him. Jesse immediately broke into the enemy aircraft, which reversed its turn and went after another Mustang. By the time Frey had regained his composure, Billy Mooney and his P-51 were nowhere to be seen. Later during the dogfight Captain Mooney's luck ran out as his Mustang was hit by enemy fire and began to burn. In addition to this, he found that his ship had become uncontrollable, and consequently Mooney was forced to bail out of the *Libby-B* over Freienseen. The time was exactly 14:25 hours BST (2:25 p.m.).

Freienseen is a small hamlet about fifteen miles east of Giessen, Germany. It lies at the foot of the Galgenberg (Gallows Mountain) in the western foothills of the Vogelsberg. Its proud history dates back to the fourteenth century when the village first received political autonomy. But on this day the new chapter being written into Freienseen's history would not be one that the citizens would brag about. As Captain William Mooney, Jr. dangled helplessly from his parachute above the mountain forest at the edge of the town, one might be reminded of the local term "at the Galgenberg," which refers to the judgment over life and death.

Before the war, Freienseen, Germany, had been a rural community of several hundred residents whose main occupations were agriculture, wood working, fish breeding, and the mining and processing of iron. Then after the rise of National Socialism and the beginning of World War II, the small community began to serve a more sinister purpose after a slave labor/prisoner of war camp was built there. The inhabitants of this facility (and the adjoined "Frankfurt Heddernhiem" Labor Education Camp) worked many jobs around the village, but the main purpose of the slave labor camp was to provide "compulsion workers" for the secret V-1 "Retaliation Weapon" armament factory built into a recently started and then abandoned railroad tunnel project. The bombproof armament plant which became operational in 1941 was two stories high and the length of three football fields. And on this Christmas Eve in 1944, even as the slave laborers were beginning to trickle back into the camp in hopes of having some easement of their labors that evening, events were taking shape that would ensure that they would not soon forget this "not so silent" night.

Meanwhile, on the outskirts of town, fifty-five-year-old Otto Heene, a textile merchant from Frankfurt, was riding his bicycle on the road to Laubach. Heene, who had resided in Freienseen for the previous two years, was the local *landwachtfuhrer* (home guard leader). As the middle-aged man peddled his bicycle along the country road he had just gone maybe 200 yards when he was startled by the sound of the screaming Merlin engine of Captain Mooney's P-51 Mustang as it plunged down out of the sky above his head. Looking up, he saw the American fighter spinning toward the ground, heading for a forested hillside a half a kilometer away. As Heene continued to watch the Mustang, his eyes were distracted by a white spot in the sky overhead. It was Mooney's parachute, and as the old man continued to watch, the spot grew larger and larger until he could see the pilot dangling underneath the chute.

**The crater is still visible today at the crash
site of the P-51D Mustang *Libby-B***

Otto threw down his bicycle, and although unarmed, charged through the brush and into the woods in the direction of the area into which the American pilot was descending. Within minutes he had reached the spot where the pilot was going to land, and looking up, Heene saw Bill Mooney throw his service pistol down to the ground in an evident act of surrendering. The German retrieved the pistol as Captain Mooney hit the forest floor and recovered from his fall, and then Heene pointed the weapon at the pilot. Mooney lifted his arms up and put his hands in the air, then proceeded to roll his parachute up, which he then bundled into his arms before awaiting instructions from his captor. Mooney and Heene then proceeded back to the dirt road and walked toward the nearby cemetery on the edge of Freienseen.

As the two men approached the cemetery, a large crowd (what appeared to be almost the entire population of the town) made up of old men and women, teenagers, and children had gathered there to meet them. Everyone wanted to get a glimpse of the feared enemy "terror flier" and to "look him in the eye." As soon as they surrounded the young pilot, a flight of Mustangs screamed in from overhead and started to strafe the crowd and Mooney. Otto Heene grabbed the pilot and pulled him into a wooden shed across the street. Eventually, after the Mustang pilots had lost interest and disappeared, the crowd reappeared around the captive and things turned ugly. At one point, Captain Mooney asked for a cigarette and this enraged certain members of the group of onlookers. One of them, Kurt Hartmann, an engineer from Frankfurt, shouted, "Give him no cigarette! He is a pig and has killed women and children!" and another man screamed at Mooney, "If you smoke, I will punch you in the face!"

Before the crowd could make good on their threats, another Freienseener arrived on the scene. His name was Emil Hofmann, a longtime Nazi Party member and the local party director, and Hofmann immediately let it be known that he alone had authority over the prisoner and would take charge of him. Heene protested and told Hofmann that he was going to take the enemy pilot to the local POW camp in order to surrender him to the soldiers in charge there, but Hofmann refused and an argument ensued involving both men and other members of the mob. In the end, Hofmann prevailed and he ordered Otto Heene to take the pilot to Laubach and to turn him in to the police there. At that point, Otto Heene proceeded on foot with Captain Mooney toward Laubach while behind him a "rat tail" crowd of onlookers followed. Emil Hofmann returned to his residence where he changed into his Nazi Party uniform, retrieved his service revolver, and then set out to rejoin Heene and the prisoner on the road to Laubach.

Emil Hofmann, like Adolf Funke was a dedicated Nazi stalwart. Hofmann had joined the National Socialist Party in January of 1931, not too long after its inception and founding by Adolf Hitler and others. He was a member of Hitler's S. A. (Sturm-Abteiling) or Storm Detachment, which was politically important in the Nazi Party until 1937 when the *Brown Shirts'* top leaders were purged by the Fuhrer during the "Night of the Long Knives." Having been a member of the party since before it came to power in 1933, Hofmann and others like him considered themselves party "elites."

After changing and retrieving his weapon, Emil Hofmann rushed to catch up with Otto Heene and his prisoner, and in twenty minutes or so he was able to overtake them on the road leading to Laubach. Hofmann passed the straggling crowd of onlookers just after the group arrived in front of the barracks of the slave labor camp on the edge of Freienseen. Witnesses later recalled how the inmates, standing along the road inside the fence surrounding the camp, screamed and hooted "like animals" as the mob passed by escorting the American out of the town. The witnesses later admitted that the Russian prisoners and forced laborers had seen what was happening and were registering their disdain for the ill treatment of the young pilot in the only way they could. Their shouts faded as the procession moved on a few hundred meters down the road and it was at this time that Hofmann stepped in front of the crowd of onlookers and approached Otto Heene and Bill Mooney from behind.

As he got within a few meters of the pilot, who was walking on the right side of Heene, one of the witnesses saw Emil Hofmann fiddling with something in his coat, which turned out to be a pistol. Approaching from behind the American pilot, Hofmann pointed his service revolver at Mooney's back and fired. Before

Heene or Bill Mooney could react, Hofmann ran up to the captive, grabbed his right arm, stepped in front of him, and fired a second shot. Captain Mooney swooned and then fell down face up on the road. He did not die immediately, as witnesses later claimed that he was still moaning and making gestures as he lay in the dirt bleeding from the mouth.

As soon as this occurred, Emil Hofmann rushed back to his house and ordered a slave laborer who worked for him to retrieve his horse and wagon. Once he and the young Belgian arrived back at the scene of the shooting, the boy loaded the mortally wounded American into the back of the wagon, and then Heene and Hofmann climbed up onto it and proceeded on their way to Laubach. According to Otto Heene, Captain Mooney died shortly after the wagon had traveled 300 yards or so.

On December 26, 1944, Captain William H. "Billy" Mooney, Jr. was buried unceremoniously near the western wall of the cemetery in Laubach, Germany, in what witnesses would later recall as a "150 percent Nazi" funeral. His corpse was thrown into an unmarked grave, sans coffin.

William Mooney on the wing of one of his fighters

The Americans Arrive in Freienseen

On March 23, 1945, the Americans crossed the Rhine River at Oppenheim and advanced with little resistance toward Frankfurt. After some partially heavy fighting at Limburg, they reached Giessen and on March 28 that city was occupied. Meanwhile, in Freienseen, the citizens were busy cleansing their homes of every vestige of Nazism. Pictures of Hitler and swastikas were ripped from the walls and *Mein Kampf* was removed from the bookshelves. Military uniforms and medals joined these items as they were heaped onto bonfires and hastily destroyed. Deserting German soldiers could be seen darting about and racing down the roads on bicycles, horses, and other pilfered forms of transportation heading east in a vain attempt to avoid capture. Those deserting soldiers unlucky enough to be caught by the free ranging SS squads adorned the trees like rotting fruit along the roadsides, where they were hung by the neck and left there in order to serve as a reminder to other Wehrmacht troops who might decide to desert.

Then, at 3:00 p.m. on the afternoon of March 29 in the town of Laubach, the roar of tanks and trucks was heard as the American troops approached. Leading the procession was a vehicle upon which a "Liberty Bell" had been mounted and its tolling could be heard over the din of the motorized convoy as it was rung by a GI declaring the liberation of the town.

Just a few kilometers away, the citizens of the village of Freienseen awaited the arrival of the conquering American forces, and many of them were nervously recalling the incident on the previous Christmas Eve and wondered what the Americans would do when they found out about the fate of their Mustang pilot. Soon, Freienseen too was overrun by the gum chewing GIs, and more onerously, their MPs who darted about from house to house in their jeeps, asking questions about the missing American. Their first order of business was to liberate the inmates of the POW/slave labor camp, and the inhabitants of this squalid institution were overjoyed, as one might imagine, to see the American Army burst through the gates. The troops then set about formally occupying the town as the MPs continued their investigation into the killing of the 357th Fighter Group pilot.

As in the case of Fletcher Adams, the truth came out fairly quickly and soon arrests were made of the German citizens involved in the capture and murder of Captain William H. Mooney, Jr. (although his identity was still unknown to the investigators at the time and would remain so throughout the events leading up to and including the trial of the principle parties involved). In a matter of days, American investigators were shown the burial site of the murdered pilot, and on May 7, 1945, the body of Billy Mooney was exhumed. That evening, between 5:00 p.m. and 7:00 p.m., a graveside autopsy was conducted on the corpse by Laubach physicians Dr. Fisher and Dr. Philippi under the close supervision of the Americans. After digging down approximately five feet, they discovered a body lying face down with its left arm behind its back. The corpse was dressed only in an undershirt, underwear, and socks, and the men who uncovered the grave immediately noticed that attempts had been made by someone to speed up the putrefaction process. [Author's note: No mention was made as to how this was allegedly done, but the use of lime on bodies was a common practice. In the case of Fletcher Adams, it was recorded in the autopsy report that his head, hands, and feet were missing when his body was retrieved from his grave, and as I noted in my first book, it is highly likely that the person or persons responsible for Adams's death dug up the young pilot's body and removed those items in hopes of making his identification more difficult. As ghoulish as this sounds, it was not an isolated occurrence during the last months of the war.] In the autopsy report of Captain Mooney, it was noted that two gunshot wounds were found upon examination of the corpse. One bullet had traveled through the upper body of Mooney, piercing his lung and shattering several of his ribs. The other gunshot wound, undoubtedly the fatal one, had been to the head of the pilot.

The remains of Captain William Mooney, Jr. were then transferred to the American Cemetery in Margraten, Holland, where they remained until his relatives requested that he be returned to the family back in the United States. Finally, in January of 1949, Billy Mooney's body was transported back to Georgia and he was laid to rest in Riverside Cemetery in Columbus near his home town of Hawkinsville, Georgia.

The Dachau War Crimes Trial

May 8, 1945, marked the unconditional surrender of Germany and already the Allies had begun hunting down Nazi war criminals throughout the war-shattered country. A war crimes tribunal was established at Dachau, the site of one of the most notorious of Hitler's concentration camps, and the so-called Flier Trials began there.

Emil Hofmann was the first person arrested for the killing of Captain Mooney. Shortly before the liberation of Freienseen, Hofmann had fled the village and taken refuge in an abandoned stone quarry a mile and a half southeast of the town. He hid out there until a Belgian forced-laborer discovered him hiding and told the authorities of his where-abouts. The Americans quickly located and jailed Hofmann and the arrest of Otto Heene soon followed. Kurt Hartmann was arrested in Frankfurt on June 5, 1945, and released, but he was then rearrested on November 21 of the same year. All three suspects were then imprisoned until their trial began in Dachau on April 15, 1947.

As was the case with Gustaf Heidmann and Eriche Schnelle, the men tried and convicted in the Fletcher Adams murder trial, all three defendants in the Mooney murder case were tried together at Dachau. Kurt Hartmann, possibly the least guilty of the three, was indicted after a witness claimed that he had seen and heard Hartmann screaming and cursing at the American and most importantly "threatening to kill" Mooney. The witness, a certain Albert Weber, conveniently forgot to inform the court that he was a former Gestapo agent.

In the end, no other witnesses could be found who could corroborate Weber's accusations against Kurt Hartmann. Also, in his defense, it must be remembered that the fifty-one-year-old engineer traveled by rail quite often during the war and on several occasions the train he was on was attacked by low flying American fighters. As a result, he had witnessed quite a bit of destruction and death during these attacks, and it requires no stretch of the imagination to understand why he would have been upset upon confronting Captain Mooney that Christmas Eve. At the end of the trial, Hartmann's lawyer successfully argued that if his only crime had been to be enraged at, to curse, and to refuse the prisoner a cigarette, then Hartmann had certainly paid his debt to the court due to his having served over a year in prison awaiting trial. When his verdict was read on April 21, it was "Nicht schuldig!" (Not guilty!), and he was acquitted by the U. S. military court.

The case involving Heene and Hofmann was not so cut and dried though, as both men tried to pin the murder on each other. First, we will examine the testimony of Otto Heene.

According to Heene, in his testimony before the court, he had indeed been ordered by Emil Hofmann to march the prisoner to nearby Laubach and to turn him over to the local authorities there, and witnesses supported his statements to that effect. He went on to tell the court that after he and Captain Mooney had left Freienseen on foot and neared a dirt road that veered off of the main highway toward Laubach, he and the prisoner left the main thoroughfare and continued down the dirt road to the right. Otto and the witnesses who followed along behind him and his prisoner, all testified that Heene was walking on the left side of Mooney with the pilot marching along directly beside him on his right.

Suddenly, according to the defendant, Emil Hoffman raced up behind Mooney and fired a bullet into his back. The local party director then stepped forward, grabbed the American by the right arm, and while turning Mooney toward him, Hofmann fired another shot into him from the front. Heene was then questioned by the court as to what Emil Hofmann's demeanor was like at the time, to which the landwacht commander said, "Cold-blooded, rather calm."

When asked by the court whether he, himself, had been armed at the time, Otto Heene said that yes, indeed he had been, and admitted to have still been in possession of the prisoner's service pistol. Heene then added that the weapon was inoperable at the time but this is highly unlikely to have been true unless the gun had been damaged when Mooney dropped it to the ground while descending by parachute into the woods near Freienseen. Although many discrepancies were uncovered during the testimony of the accused, several other witnesses supported his story. By the end of the trial, the court agreed with Otto

Heene and his defense attorney and the verdict, as in Kurt Hartmann's case was again, "Nicht schuldig!" (Not guilty!), and fifty-eight-year-old Otto Heene was also acquitted.

Then came the time for the main suspect in the murder of Captain William H. Mooney, Jr. to testify and, immediately, Emil Hofmann attempted to divert attention from his own actions and to place the blame for the killing onto Otto Heene. Hofmann admitted to shooting the prisoner once from the back and a second time from the front, although he stated that he could not remember much about the second shot as he had been terribly excited and "trembling all over" at the time it happened. He claimed that he only fired at the pilot after he observed Mooney lunging to the left toward Otto Heene in an evident attempt to attack his captor and escape. His story was invalidated by not only the testimony of Heene but also by several other witnesses who had been in the crowd trailing behind Hoffman, Heene, and the prisoner at the time of the shooting.

As for the condition of the American after being shot, Hofmann claimed that he was still very much alive. He went on to say that he had ordered the Belgian forced-laborer that worked for him on his farm to retrieve his horse and wagon and that they had loaded Mooney into it. Then he and Heene had climbed in and proceeded toward Laubach with the American pilot in the back. On the way there, just as it was becoming dark, Hofmann told the court that he had stopped the wagon and climbed down to relieve himself (urinate) and upon completing this task he looked back from his position in front of the horses and saw Otto Heene pulling something from his coat. According to Hofmann, he was walking back around to climb up into the wagon, when he was startled by a gunshot and it was then that the accused said he was able to see that Heene had a pistol in his hand still pointed at the head of the American. According to Emil Hofmann, after he climbed back up onto the seat of the wagon, he glanced back and saw the prisoner's head roll to the side, and it was only then that he (Captain William "Bill" Mooney) expired.

The military court did not buy Hofmann's story and the preponderance of evidence was indeed against him. When it came time for the verdict in the case of the United States vs. Emil Hofmann, the verdict was, "Schuldig! (Guilty!)," and the sentence, "*Tod durch den strang*! (Death by hanging!)" So ended the trial of the three defendants in the murder of Captain William H. Mooney, Jr. of the 362nd Fighter Squadron (357th Fighter Group), the second Yoxford Boy murdered by German civilians during the Second World War.

Captain William Mooney, Jr.'s foot stone at his gravesite in Georgia

On October 22, 1948, Emil Hofmann took his final steps between his prison cell at Landau Prison (United States War Criminal Prison Number 1) and the gallows, where after speaking his last words to the crowd of witnesses over the prison loudspeaker, the trapdoor dropped and his life was extinguished at the end of a hemp rope. Of course, this was of little comfort to Billy Mooney's family back in Hawkinsville, Georgia, but justice had indeed been served.

Emil Hofmann speaks his last words moments before
his execution at Landau Prison on October 22, 1948

Tell Ma I'm Comin' Home!

(The Dittie Jenkins Story)

Otto "Dittie" Jenkins

Another 357th Fighter Group pilot that died a senseless death was Otto "Dittie" Jenkins of the 362nd Fighter Squadron. During the same museum dedication in Ida, Louisiana, in 2010 this author met members of Dittie's family and as with Arch and Veronica Mooney, they asked me to tell their own Yoxford Boy's story in my next book and I readily agreed.

The first question I asked them was, "Where in the world did Otto get the nickname 'Dittie' from?" and his niece told me that it came from one of his favorite songs. One line in the song mentioned a "ditty," which of course is another name for a song or tune and Otto was so enamored by it that he repeated it until the nickname stuck. [Author's note: I paraphrased this conversation with Otto's niece concerning the origin of Jenkins's nickname, and as I have been unsuccessful in my attempts to locate her again to verify the details, I apologize if I got the story about her uncle's moniker wrong. I included it here as I recalled it a year later.]

Otto Jenkins joined the 357th Fighter Group as a replacement pilot during the fall of 1944. Like Chuck Yeager, Jenkins was not a commissioned officer when he joined the group. Both he and Yeager had become fighter pilots through the "Flying Sergeants" program during the last few years of the war and instead of entering the Group as Second Lieutenants, they were ranked "Flight Officers." Despite the fact that they had begun their fighter pilot careers as lesser ranking officers, both Jenkins and Yeager soon proved themselves as true "tigers" by racking up many kills over the course of their combat tours. By the time Otto Jenkins had flown his last mission, he was almost a double ace with 8.5 victories to his credit. Yeager, of course, finished his last tour as a bonafide double ace with 12.5 victories.

[Author's note: Before Chuck Yeager enthusiasts begin howling, let me say that 11.5 of these kills were officially credited to Chuck and credit for the other victory, over a Ju-88 which he shot down against orders, was surreptitiously given to fellow Yoxford Boy Lt. Eddie Simpson. After Yeager had been shot down in March of 1944 and evaded, he refused to return to the Zone of the Interior, and while his case was being reviewed, the young fighter pilot was rat-racing in the vicinity of the base one day when he was diverted by Control to the Heligoland area to provide cover for a B-17 crew down in the water there. After spotting their dinghy, Yeager saw a Ju-88 approaching it and his instincts kicked in. Without considering his previous orders not to engage enemy aircraft (technically he *was* under orders from Control), Chuck splashed the German plane "and rolled it up on the beach" before it could attack the American bomber crew (or more likely, vector in another German fighter to do it). Luckily for Eddie Simpson, he received credit for shooting down an enemy aircraft he never saw, and his wingman, Hershel Pascoe, got Yeager's combat time that day!]

Dittie Jenkins's first P-51 was a B model named "Floogie" (code G4-P) which he had inherited from Robert Wallen who had flown the Mustang under the not-so-glamorous name "Joan" until his combat tour was up. In addition to the P-51, Dittie also got Wallen's crew chief (assistant?), Merle Olmsted, in the bargain. Olmsted later became the official historian of the 357th Fighter Group and spent the remainder of his life documenting the history of the Yoxford Boys.

On October 9, 1944, Flight Officer Jenkins had his first close call while escorting fellow pilot Lt. Herman Delager home from a mission after his Merlin engine had begun to run rough. Ironically, when the Mustangs arrived over Belgium, it was Dittie's engine that gave up the ghost and he was forced to make an emergency descent and landing from 20,000 feet.

**Jenkins was escorting Herman Delager (above)
home when his own engine failed**

Jenkins later filed the following report about the incident:

I spotted a large airfield and belly landed in it. I did not put down my wheels due to low airspeed and altitude. The field was a Spitfire base, with Norwegian pilots.

They had just moved in, causing all kinds of confusion for all, including myself. I tried to talk to the commanding officer, but he seemed to be angry because Lt. Delager had continued to circle to see if I was all right. I finally walked five miles to a town and engaged a civilian for 100 francs to take me to Brussels. Instead, he took me to Antwerp. Finding this out, I gave him another 200 francs to take me to Brussels. There I reported to Lt. Col. Foot, who got my statement about the condition of my plane and where it was. He sent me home on a C-47 the next day.

This was the end of the P-51B Mustang "Floogie" G4-P (tail number 42-106829) and it was later salvaged on November 30, 1944. Upon returning to Leiston Field (Station AAF-373), Jenkins was reassigned a P-51D (tail number 44-14245), again with the code G4-P, which he named "Floogie II." A few weeks later, two days before Christmas of 1944, Dittie suffered another mishap when the Merlin engine in this Mustang overheated and the coolant relief valve popped open while on a test flight. Once again, the young pilot bellied in and survived. This apparently did not affect Jenkins's fighting spirit though, because on the very next day (now) 2nd Lt. Jenkins borrowed another 362nd Fighter Squadron P-51 and used it to destroy four German fighters during a single mission (December 24, 1944), the same day that Captain Bill Mooney was shot down and subsequently murdered by German civilians. After the Floogie II had been repaired, Dittie continued to fly this aircraft until 13 January 1945, when it was destroyed in a crash near Leiston which killed 362nd Fighter Squadron pilot Robert Schlieker who had borrowed the aircraft that day.

After the crash of the *Floogie II* one can only speculate as to whether or not Dittie Jenkins had begun to see his planes, or at least the name "Floogie" as being jinxed, but we do know that he did change the name by the time he had received his last fighter, another P-51D Mustang (tail number 44-63199). This aircraft, which Dittie named "Toolin' Fools Revenge" also carried a different code, which was G4-X. It is likely that he got this plane from John Schlossberg and that it previously sported the name "Joker!" but this has never been historically proven. What has been documented is the fact that this was Lt. Otto "Dittie" Jenkins's last Mustang and that it was the one he died in on March 24, 1945. The original *Toolin' Fool*, a P-51K model, had been destroy during a bomber escort mission on December 23, 1944, after its wings had ripped off in a compressibility dive over Prum, Germany, killing 362nd Fighter Squadron pilot Walter Perry, Jr., who's story is also included in this book. It is certain that Jenkins named his last Mustang after this aircraft as Walt Perry was a good friend of his, and Walter Perry's sister, Anna Mae Perry Beachem confirmed this in 2011 during a phone call with the author.

Toolin' Fools Revenge

The Big Show

The facts surrounding the fate of Otto Jenkins on 24 March, 1945, have always been murky but during the researching for this book, the author thinks that he has finally solved the mystery of what happened the day Jenkins returned from his last mission and decided to put on the "big show" for his squadron mates at Station AAF-373.

In his book, *Yeager*, Brigadier General Charles "Chuck" Yeager tells of a 357th Fighter Group pilot who was killed after returning to base after his last mission. In the book, Yeager says that the pilot, whom he does not identify by name, radioed the base upon his approach to Leiston Field and said, "Tell Ma I'm comin' home!" and then attempted to roll his Mustang. Before the fighter completed the roll, it hit a tree and augured in killing the unlucky pilot. Although Chuck Yeager could have been describing the event that occurred to Dittie Jenkins on March 24, (Jenkins was the only 357th pilot killed on the base while returning from a last mission), we don't know. One thing is for certain though, Yeager was long gone from Leiston by the time this happened, having completed his last combat tour of WWII during the middle of January 1945. What *is* documented about the events of that day are as follows.

The official Army Air Force accident report filed after Otto Jenkins's crash states:

> *Otto Jenkins, 1st Lt. O-1998554, was dispatched on an operational mission on 24 March 1945, as White flight leader of the 362nd Squadron, flying P-51D-20 aircraft number 44-63199. This was to be the last mission of Lt. Jenkins's tour of combat. Upon return to the field, Lt. Jenkins proceeded to "buzz" the field at a low altitude. On several occasions he flew over the building area at such [a] low altitude that personnel in the vicinity were forced to lay flat on the ground to avoid being hit; trees and buildings were narrowly missed.*
>
> *After the third pass, Lt. Jenkins pulled up sharply and attempted to split-ess from approximately 1,500 feet. The aircraft was observed to mush at the bottom of the pull-out and one wing hit a tree. Wing was torn off, aircraft flipped over on its back, and hit the ground, catching fire and sliding over 100 yards before coming to a stop. Aircraft was demolished and Lt. Jenkins [was] killed instantly.*

As all fighter pilots will tell you, some official accident reports and even encounter reports can be misleading as in some cases they include inaccurate information. This might be the case with the AAF accident report about Otto Jenkins's demise or it might not. During the summer of 2010, this author sat down with 362nd Fighter Squadron pilot Lt. Col. Joseph "Joe" Shea, a squadron mate and friend of Jenkins. During the conversation we discussed Jenkins and what Yeager had said in his first book. After thinking for a moment, Shea turned to me and said, "Let me tell you what *really* happened to Dittie that day." The following is Joe Shea's account of the incident:

> *The morning of March 24, 1945, dawned as a very pretty day as I made my way to the 362nd Fighter Squadron pilots' ready room. I had gone there even though I was not scheduled to fly on that day's mission. My plans were to grab a bite to eat at the pilots' lounge. [Author's note: The 362nd Fighter Squadron's pilots' lounge was constructed by the original pilots of the squadron in early 1944 and they named it their "Westminster Abbey" after the famous church and tourist destination.] I also wanted to chat with the mission pilots when they arrived from the briefing, and later, after they had taken off, I planned to go out and polish my aircraft; that extra 2 or 3 miles an hour just might make a difference one day in combat.*
>
> *One of the mission pilots, Dittie Jenkins, was flying his last mission and he told us that when he returned he would "put on a show that we would never forget." So later that afternoon, when the mission was due to return, we all made sure we were in a good spot to witness the big show. As we all left the ready room, most of the pilots turned left when they walked out the door of the building and headed toward the runway. For some unknown reason, I took a right as I exited the Nissen hut and went out behind the pilots' ready room into an open field.*
>
> *When Dittie returned, he came screaming across the end of the runway and through the 362nd Fighter Squadron operations area and right in front of the pilots' ready room. He flashed past, no more than twenty feet from my position and pulled up into a loop. He completed the loop and came screaming by me a second time and completed another loop. On his third pull up, he horsed it in too abruptly which caused the aircraft to execute a momentary high speed stall. The high speed stall resulted in a quick loss of airspeed which, in turn, meant that the airplane was significantly lower at the top of his last loop.*
>
> *At this point, if Dittie had recognized the dire situation he was in and simply rolled the Mustang into an upright position, this story would have probably had a much different ending, but apparently, at this point Dittie did not fully realize his plight.*
>
> *I have been told by others who were on the runway side of the scene that Dittie really was sucking it in tight on the way down, so much so that he was in a constant high speed stall. The sad part of this story is that he was successful in leveling out a few feet above the ground, but because Dittie's ship was still in the stall, he did not have full control of his aircraft. Unfortunately, the result of this was that he was unable to*

steer clear of the one lone tree in the middle of a field that stood in his flight path. I was standing about fifty feet short of the tree and off to its right side. Toolin' Fools Revenge darted past me less than a second before its left wing struck the tree and was ripped off, leaving the plane's .50 caliber guns imbedded in the tree's trunk. The Mustang flipped upside down, skidded to a stop, and seconds later began to burn. I ran to the crash site but there was nothing I could do. Dittie perished in the fiery crash.

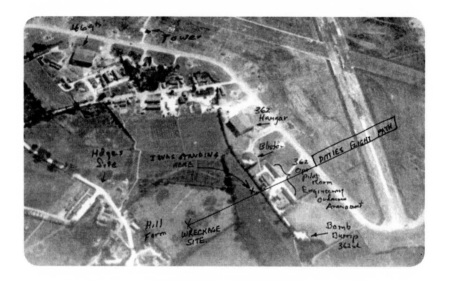

An aerial view of the 362nd Fighter Squadron area at Leiston with notations by pilot Joe Shea showing Jenkins's crash site

Later that day, after Shea had told me this story, we went into the 357th Fighter Group Museum in Ida and on the wall was a framed group of pictures I had been given by MSGT Merle Olmsted's son, Michael, in 2009. In the center of the frame was a scrap of silver canvas that at one time had been part the "skin" covering one of the control surfaces of First Lt. Otto Jenkins's *Toolin' Fools Revenge*. Surrounding the relic were photographs of Dittie and his Mustang and at the bottom was a picture of the burning wreckage taken moments after the fatal crash. Joe Shea leaned in close to the photograph and after scrutinizing it for a moment said, "There I am right there." Sure enough, at the bottom of the picture Shea could plainly be seen squatting down while holding a fire hose on the flaming wreckage.

Months later, in a phone call to the author, Joseph Shea told me something about Jenkins's accident which he claims he has never told anyone else before. Seconds after the crash, before the fire broke out, Shea said that he had run up to the Mustang which was cocked up on its side and looked into the plane's cockpit. He has never told anyone but this author what he saw in that cockpit and I cannot repeat it now, as I promised him I wouldn't, but suffice to say that Joe Shea is still haunted by that image to this day.

Dittie Jenkins, Johnny England, Alva Murphy, and Kit Carson prepare to throw one more "bomb"

Major Alva Murphy's Story

By Merle C. Olmsted

Murphy on the wing of his P-51 Mustang *Bite Me!*

Alva Murphy was not an original member of the Group, and it is not known when he joined the 357th. However, since he scored his first two victories on the twenty-seventh of November 1944 (and added two more on December 2), he had probably arrived in early fall. He was a captain at that time, and possibly came from a staff assignment or had been an instructor.

Assigned first to the 362nd Fighter Squadron, he was transferred in January, 1945, to the 364th as Operations Officer.

The second of March 1945,was a very bad day for the 357th as five pilots failed to return from a long mission to Ruhland. Captain Don McKee led the mission that day with take-off at 0806 hours, and a "down" time of 1320-well over five hours. The Group pilots claimed 13 enemy aircraft shot down and another 25 destroyed on the ground. Two of the victories were Me-109s shot down by Murphy. Bank, Crawford, Lepore, and Murphy were shot down by ground fire, and Patrick Mallione was probably the victim of an enemy fighter. Ray Bank and Rocco Lepore became POWs and the other three were KIA.

**Alva Murphy (with right hand on drop tank) points
to the .50 caliber guns on *Bite Me!***

Murphy was leading the 364th Red flight with Howard Wesling on his wing. In a recent letter to the author [Merle Olmsted], Wesling says he recalls the incident well. "We were strafing an airfield with quite a number of planes on it. Murphy was hit in the coolant [system]. We pulled up to about 3,000 feet and after a few minutes his engine quit. He rolled over and bailed out. His chute did open, but I did not follow him down."

Wesling's statement in Murphy's Missing Air Crew Report (MACR) confirms two 109s shot down, and relates his bailout, as above, but adds that he saw him land in a field.

The picture clouds up at this point as the records I received from the Army do not tell us what happened to him except that he was killed in action. This is in sharp contrast to the extensive investigation into the Browning/Simpson cases and also with William Mooney.

The group records for March tell us that there would be no more airfield strafing unless ordered and adds, "At this late stage, results do not justify the cost."

Many documents in Murphy's MACR contain translations of Luftwaffe records pertaining to that particular case. One of these German documents, "Report of Captured Aircraft," under "Fate of Crew" says, "One dead officer, Murphy, Alva C., 0-441009, name ascertained by 1st Lt. Oertel, Airbase Headquarters, Koethen, buried in Grosbzig Cemetery." The document also says, "probably shot down by a FW-190," which would appear to be in error.

Murphy was listed as MIA until September of 1945, when enough evidence had been gathered to change his status to KIA.

His father, Joseph Murphy, of Knoxville, Tennessee, apparently made the decision for his son's body to remain permanently in Europe, and he is in the American Military Cemetery in Hamm, Luxemburg.

The question of what happened to Major Alva Murphy must remain open since we know that he bailed out successfully and apparently landed unhurt. What happened after that is still unknown. [Author's note: Merle Olmsted painted a portrait of Murphy using the picture above. That portrait of Alva Murphy hung for years over his desk and it is now in the Captain Fletcher E. Adams 357th Fighter Group Museum.]

My First Christmas in England

By William "Obie" O'Brien

William "Obie" O'Brien in his P-51 *Billy's Bitch*

This story begins at Raydon Wood Air Base, which was located about 15 miles west of Colchester, England, where our enemy was *tons* of mud. The 357th Fighter Group arrived during November of 1943. Weeks later, a Christmas party had gotten underway at Raydon Wood on Christmas Eve.

Plenty of local maidens joined us in dancing, eating, drinking, etc., and generally celebrating the festive occasion. The 363rd Fighter Squadron had a new commanding officer named Joe Giltner and I told Joe that this was too good of a party to shut down just because it was time to close up the Officers Club. I had a jug of "hooch" in my quarters, so we should, I told Giltner, transfer the party to our pilots' shack on the flight line. Joe, being a fine Christian, thought this was a *splendid* idea, and he agreed to meet on the flight line, but said, "Don't take my jeep!" So I went right out the door, got into the first jeep that would start, and, along with some blond, set course for my quarters.

A problem arose when I didn't make the first turn, scattering jeep and blond all over the place! Well, I got the babe to the trucks going to Colchester, and thanked her for a pleasant evening. About then, I scrubbed the late party and hit the sack in my quarters.

The next morning, I felt kinda achy, and someone said, "Do you know what happened to Giltner's jeep, because they found the jeep with Eddie Simpson beside it." I didn't respond and decided to wait until I talked to Simpson. Ed said that he was walking home from the Officers Club party and found the jeep with no one in it. As near as I can tell, Simpson decided to take a nap, which he did. That is how he got tangled up in the jeep accident. When I got to feeling a little better, I decided that I had better tell Joe Giltner the truth. I did. Joe let Simpson off the hook for the jeep wreck and restricted me to the base. Later, Joe Giltner managed to get himself shot down over Germany, and Simpson and I got off free. So you see, honesty pays!

The Bernard Seitzinger Story

By Curt Brown

Bernard Karl Seitzinger, also known as "Seitz" or "Ben," was born on November 5, 1914, in Belgrade, Minnesota. He was commissioned in the Air Reserve in 1939 and went through Army Air Force flight training at Randolph Field during 1940. While serving as a flight instructor at Foster Field, Ben earned the reputation as being a "tough, fair, and excellent instructor."

In 1943, Captain Seitzinger joined the Sixty-fifth Fighter Squadron of the Fifty-seventh Fighter Group in North Africa. During that summer, Ben was on a strafing mission near the base of Mount Etna, where he took some ground fire and was wounded. Seitz radioed for assistance, but none of the other pilots were able to locate him. He managed to belly-land his aircraft, but was captured by enemy troops. He later was able to escape and evade the enemy, and made his way back to friendly lines.

Ben joined the 364th Fighter Squadron of the famous 357th Fighter Group in early September of 1944. Later that month, he was flying his P-51B Mustang *Almost* in the Arnhem Affair. Ben was shot down over Belgium that day, shortly after scoring an aerial victory. He spent the rest of the war in Stalag Luft I.

After World War II, he arrived at the K-2 Air Base in Taegu, Korea around the beginning of November 1951, and was soon assigned as the commander of the Seventh Fighter-Bomber Squadron. Seitz was a veteran aviator with hundreds of hours of actual combat flight. This highly experienced combat pilot referred to his duty in Korea as being, "rugged."

On Tuesday, November 27, 1951, Ben Seitzinger was killed while strafing boxcars in his F-84E near Chinnampo. As the area was firmly under the control of the North Koreans, no attempt was made to recover his remains. Bernard was a courageous man who volunteered for combat duty in Korea, and who gave his life in the service of his country. Though he may lie in an unmarked grave in some forgotten, nameless field in Korea, he is still remembered.

This portrait, entitled "The Bailout," was hidden by Ben Seitzinger while he was a POW at Stalag Luft I, and he later brought it out with him after the camp was liberated in 1945

Another painting kept by Seitzinger during his internment in Stalag Luft I and later "liberated" along with him when the POWs were freed

The Norwegian Odyssey of Bill Dunlop

By Merle C. Olmsted and William Dunlop

Bill Dunlop

As the 357th Fighter Group Historian, the name of William Dunlop was familiar to me because of a brief note in the Group records for September 1944. An added paragraph to the mission report for 15 September has this to say: "Lt. W. R. Dunlop, spare on mission separated from Group over West

Frisian Islands. With gyro out, Lt. Dunlop got lost in the clouds and when he finally found his bearings. He was over Christiansand Harbor in Norway. He strafed three sea planes anchored in the harbor at 10:45 a.m., and damaged a DO-24. He then took a heading for the nearest land and landed at Crail, Scotland, at 4:30 p.m."

I had often wished I could ask him about that adventure but Dunlop was listed as a lost sheep. In mid 1972, by a stroke of luck, I found him, now a psychiatrist living nearby in the San Francisco Bay area. Subsequently, he and his sons, and later he and his wife, came by to visit us and they also attended the Long Beach 357th Fighter Group reunion. During these visits, I asked Bill about the long ride to Norway and asked him to write it up for the [357th's] newsletter. The following is the story of Bill Dunlop's Scandinavian adventure on the fifteenth of September 1944:

I did preplan going to Norway. For the trip, I could only procure maps of the nearest Norwegian coast. The night before, I asked to be put on spare. The next morning we were briefed for a mission to the Stettin area via the Frisian [Island] Chain and Denmark. We took off as low squadron; I was with a second spare on my wing. After a non-eventful takeoff and assembly, we began the long climb to the enemy coast. Five to ten minutes from the first of the Frisians, we suddenly ran into a solid front. After trying to get through it, the entire Squadron split up. Just before entering the soup, I told my wingman to return to base. He had lost one of his drop tanks and had insufficient fuel to make the long trip ahead. Once in and split up, I was alone, and spotting one of the islands through a temporary break, I felt my responsibilities to the mission were over. A spare is only required to accompany the Squadron to the coast.

I began a tight spiral in an attempt to stay in the hole. At 3,000 feet, I had built up 300-350 mph airspeed and couldn't keep it tight enough with a full gas load. Entering the stuff half-ready to spin, I barely gained straight and level at 500 feet still on instruments before edging down to 200 feet. I broke out into a driving rain storm and over a high running sea. After turning to my heading, setting the airspeed and mentally noting the time so as to make a bend into the Skatterak, I snuggled down to fifty feet over the North Sea. I switched my radio to channel B, which was Air Sea Rescue, and hoped I was low enough and far enough away from the Danish coast to elude the enemy radar sweep.

I computed a one hour on a steady course prior to the turn into the Skatterak. As the first hour passed, it was only with great concentration that I kept from hitting the wave tops. The water had a disillusioning effect on my depth perception and it seemed to draw me down like a magnet. Somewhere in route I passed over a drifting German mine. From my low altitude, it seemed huge and its protrusions looked very deadly. I contemplated exploding it with the fifties, but thought better of it and left the mine alone.

After approximately one and three quarter hours of this "mist flying," I had the surprise of my life. The mist and rain ended suddenly in a wall just as it had begun. Bathed in sunlight and framed by pearl-like clouds, the mountains of Norway rose before me straight out of the sea. For a moment, it took my breath away, and I almost went into the water again!

There was no doubt that I had overshot my planned destination and had come upon the south coast somewhere in the vicinity of Lister. I decided to parallel the coastline hoping to pick up a plane or a transport a few minutes after climbing up over the mountains from the sea. This country is wild and rugged, and the terrain is almost beyond imagination. The mountain ridges and ranges run into the North Sea and make contact perpendicularly. The mountains, with their dividing valleys, contained rushing rivers which hurdled cliffs to form waterfalls of great violence. The only agriculture seemed to lie along the narrow space between the riverbanks and the valley walls. There was, however, an abundance of lumbering apparently going on there, as the streams were choked with logs and great floats lined the edges of the fiords.

Still attempting to elude German radar, I would dive down into the valleys and zoom up the other side flat on the deck in a porpoising motion. Perhaps due to the kick I was getting out of this experience, or because I lacked the proper maps, I never did locate my exact position. Off the coast several miles, there was a considerable amount of shipping. In each of the large fiords, there seemed to be at least one fair-sized town usually with one half of it on the mountainside. The houses were all wooden and generally painted white, but some of them were red and others were unpainted. Everything seemed extremely neat, and the towns gave the impression that a hardy civilization lived below me.

At first, I contented myself by staying away from built-up areas, but eventually, my attention was attracted to a wooden church, beautifully and massively built, and since I was receiving no flak fire, I flew over everything from then on. I never tired of flipping over a ridge and diving down into the next valley. Each time I did it, there was a new and awesome sight in store for me. Finally, I came upon a fiord which dwarfed the others with a lush green, well planned countryside, extending five to ten miles along either side of it. I later learned this was Oslo. It was in a cavity in the fiord with bordering hills and an island in the harbor making it an ideal spot to defend, and it provided a smooth patch of water for the takeoffs and landings of seaplanes. On the island, which was a "half-moon" affair, stood a powerhouse, and I was soon to learn that the power station also contained several 20mm or 40mm flak guns. In the town of Horten due south of my position, several ocean going vessels were docked, perhaps transporting aircraft parts that a factory nearby produced, to Germany. What particularly interested me and had me excited were a HE-115 and two large Dornier flying boats floating serenely in the center of the bay.

I remember popping over hills on the west side of the small harbor and firing at the Dorniers with most of my fire missing. I tried kicking the rudder in order to bring my gunfire back on the target, but I only succeeded in getting a few hits on one wing of one of the flying boats. Later, I found out that all the guns on the left side of my Mustang had not fired. I could not let the fat target go though, so I circled low and made another pass from the west. Suddenly, all hell broke loose from AAA guns located in a number of locations around the harbor. I can't remember if I fired again, but I do remember the AAA was heavy, so I took off south down the fiord at full throttle, all the while watching little balls of fire floating by on all sides of my ship. After I had managed to escape the flak guns, I remember being amazed that nothing had hit me.

Out of range, I briefly considered going to Sweden, which was in plain few to my left. I knew I had used up too much gas and could not get back to England, so I decided that I might be able to make it to Scotland. I remember thinning the mixture, lowering the RPMs, and climbing back into the clouds to approximately 10,000 feet. I set my course for what I thought was the nearest part of Scotland. Now that radar could pick me up, I wondered if the Germans would send up fighters. I flew on instruments all the way west. I tried to make some kind of radio contact but couldn't.

As the gas gauge registered near empty, I descended gradually wondering if I could make it to the coast. I had it in my mind that the Scottish coastal range was 1,000 to 2,000 feet high. As I got down to that altitude, the visibility outside my canopy was still zero. I thought about bailing out when I ran out of gas, but that was an unattractive option at best. Finally, I decided to inch down hoping to come out over the sea near land. I broke out at no more than 100 feet, not over the sea, but miraculously over an airfield. I dumped it in without ground contact; I couldn't wait and taxied up to an apron. A British officer, probably the commanding officer, met me in a jeep. He seemed irritated by my unexpected arrival. I don't think he believed my story, that I had been lost in Norway, and probably thought that I was just another crazy Yank.

Finally, he became a little friendlier and promised to put me up and service my plane. We did have a momentary run-in when he told me to give him my gun camera film. I refused saying that it was U. S. property, and later, I hid it under the cockpit seat. The airfield was the British Naval Airbase at Crail, Scotland. I was shown to the mess hall and later to the Officers Club. It was a scene hard to believe. Not a sober citizen could be found, as everyone was smashed and they were all singing and shouting. It seemed they had sunk the German pocket battleship *Tirpitz* earlier that day, of all places in a Norwegian fiord. I remember talking to a flying officer from Ceylon. The pilots were from countries all over the world.

The next day I checked out my airplane, and it had been serviced, as promised. The line mechanic told me I had landed with four gallons of gasoline left in my tanks. I made a hot takeoff wanting to show the British what a P-51 could do, pulling it off quickly and as straight up as it would go. At something like 500 feet over the end of the runway, it started to fall off into a stall, but I was able to get the nose down and steady it with the rudder, and I soon regained flying speed. I remember thinking how foolish I was, but also happy that the British could see what our planes could do. The trip south was uneventful except for some Spits and Hurricanes that wanted to dogfight me, but I quickly left them behind. As I made my way back to Leiston, the hills in southern Scotland and northern England were rose colored and quite beautiful, as they tend to be at that time of year." [Author's note: Bill Dunlop was shot down on "The Big Day" (January 14, 1945) and spent the rest of the war in a stalag luft (POW camp).]

A Speech Worth Dying For

By C. V. Glines

Colonel Henry "Russ" Spicer

Those who served with him remember that big, mischievous grin under the wide, thick mustache, the close haircut, and the ever-present pipe. Equipped with a fabulous memory for names, Major General Henry Russell Spicer was known as "Hank," "Russ," or "Pappy," depending on when and where you served with him.

For those who were prisoners of war with him in Stalag Luft 1 at Barth, Germany, in World War II, he is remembered as the senior officer in the North No. 2 Compound, the one who went to great lengths to antagonize his German captors and make them adhere to the Geneva Convention in their treatment of POWs. Spicer, then a colonel, once was accused of inciting the camp to riot with a speech he gave to the 1,800-man compound. He received a German death sentence for that speech and thus became an enduring part of the lore of the Air Force.

Spicer graduated from the Army Air Corps advanced flying school in 1934 but had to remain a Flying Cadet for another year because the service was short of funds to commission new flying officers. He was later assigned to fighter units at March Field, California, and Wheeler Field, Hawaii, before becoming an instructor at Randolph Field, Texas, in 1941.

Spicer's fighter background was evident to those of us who were flying cadets at Randolph in the summer of 1941. As our flight commander, he gave us the all-important forty-hour flight checks in the BT-14 basic trainer. You knew you passed if, after demonstrating your skills, he would say, "OK, mister, I've got it," and then put on a demonstration of aerobatics stretching the BT-14 to its limits. You knew you flunked if he merely took over and returned to the field.

Spicer's skills made it inevitable that he would get into combat in fighters. He was assigned to the Eighth Air Force as executive officer to the Sixty-sixth Fighter Wing and then took command of the 357th Fighter Group in February 1944. He was in England only a short time and had led only fourteen missions, with three enemy aircraft destroyed, when his Mustang was damaged by flak.

Colonel Spicer on the wing of his P-51B Mustang "Tony Boy" (named for his son) in which he was shot down by flak soon after taking command of the 357th Fighter Group in 1944

Spicer bailed out into near-freezing waters of the English Channel and drifted two days in a one-man dinghy. Rescue boats and aircraft couldn't find him. His feet and hands were badly frostbitten when he finally drifted ashore near Cherbourg, France. Unable to walk and near collapse, he was found lying on the beach by some German soldiers. He was taken to Oberursel, near Frankfurt, for interrogation and medical treatment before being sent to Stalag Luft 1.

Unintimidated

The Germans didn't know what a strong-willed person they had on their hands. He was not about to be intimidated or give any information of value, especially names of who might later become a POW. He was questioned by Hanns Scharff, a master Luftwaffe interrogator who spoke excellent English and later became a U. S. citizen. [Author's note: Scharff also became a world-class mosaic artist and even did huge mosaics in Snow White's castle at Walt Disney World in Florida. A book was written about Hanns Scharff's interrogation techniques which emphasized fair treatment and conversation rather than threats and abuse. That book is required reading for all U. S. intelligence officers.] Scharff admitted that Spicer was expert at dodging questions and made a fool of him.

Spicer was still suffering from frostbitten feet and hands when he arrived at Stalag Luft 1. Lt. John J. Fisher, a fellow POW, recalls him lying on his back for long periods, rubbing his legs to restore circulation. Lt. Richard McDonald, who walked the perimeter of the compound with him, recalls how Spicer had set himself a rigorous rehabilitation program, determined to regain full use of his legs and the ability to walk normally.

Gerald W. Johnson, then a major and one of the top aces in the European Theater of Operations, was a fellow POW. He recalls spending many hours with Spicer playing chess. Sometimes a game would go into a second day, the two not exchanging a word. Henry Spicer also played Parcheesi by the hour, umpired softball games, and was said to have taken up knitting to keep his mind off of the pain in his feet.

Even before his feet healed, however, Colonel Spicer began to give his captors trouble. New POWs gave him news of the war and told him about the atrocities that had been documented. Greatly affected by this, he organized a program of resistance and took every opportunity to harass the guards and cause as much trouble for them as he and his fellow prisoners could get away with. They paid for it with frequent "appell" (roll call) turnouts in the middle of the day when they would have to stand in formation while the "goons" and "ferrets" went through their barracks looking for anything they said was illegal to possess.

Captain Mozart Kaufman, who wrote a book about his experience as a German POW, said, "We felt it was a small price to pay." He added that he regarded Spicer as a good example of a commander—one who kept morale high by challenging the Germans every chance he got. This helped the whole compound maintain a feeling of solidarity against the enemy.

The Speech

On the very cold morning of November 1, 1944, the entire prison camp population had been rousted out of the barracks for a required daily roll call, usually a fifteen minute procedure. "The Germans kept us there shivering for an unusually long time," recalled one POW, Lt. Phillip Robertson, "claiming they weren't getting the correct count."

Robertson went on, "After about two hours, Colonel Spicer dismissed us, over the loud protestations of the German guards. He then called us over to his barracks, and we gathered around him, standing on the ground, as he stood on the steps about three feet above us and began to talk loud enough for the guards to hear."

In his postwar book, *Fighter Pilot*, Captain Kaufman recalled what Henry Spicer said:

"Yesterday an officer was put in the 'cooler' for two weeks. He had two counts against him. The first was failure to obey an order of a German officer. That is beside the point. The second was failure to salute a German officer of a lower rank."

Then he got really to the point, saying, "I have noticed that many of you are becoming too 'buddy-buddy' with the Germans. Remember we are still at war with the Germans. They are still our enemies and are doing everything they can to win this war. Don't let them fool you around this camp, because they are dirty, lying sneaks and can't be trusted."

"As an example of the type of enemy you have to deal with, the British were forced to retreat in the Arnhem area. They had to leave the wounded in the hospital. The Germans took the hospital and machine-gunned all those British in their beds. In Holland, behind the German lines, a woman with a baby in her arms was walking along the road, evacuating the battle zone. Some British prisoners were passing her. She gave them the V sign. A German soldier saw her and without hesitation swung his gun around and shot her on the spot."

"They are a bunch of murderous, no-good liars, and if we have to stay here for fifteen years to see all the Germans killed, then it will be worth it."

Loud cheers arose from all of the men. The German major in charge of the guards was furious! Within a short time, Henry Spicer was put in solitary confinement in the "cooler," a small cell that measured about six by eight feet. Meanwhile, Kaufman, sensing that Spicer had just made a speech that should be remembered, returned to his barracks and began, with the help of his roommates, to reconstruct Colonel Spicer's words. He recorded them in a logbook, which he then buried under the barracks in a tin can.

The Sentence

Colonel Henry Russell Spicer was hauled away for a court-martial, charged with inciting prisoners to riot. Later, his fellow prisoners learned that he had been convicted and sentenced to serve six months in solitary confinement and then be executed by a firing squad. Spicer was returned to the cooler to serve his sentence while awaiting the execution order.

Occasionally, some of his men would be led by the guards past the building in which he was incarcerated, and they would shout out words of encouragement. Robertson recalled, "Then we would hear Colonel Spicer shout back, 'Keep fighting! Don't give in to the bastards!' When asked if he needed anything, he always replied, 'Yeah, send me machine guns!'"

In the end, Henry Spicer managed to evade the firing squad—by a single day—and the death sentence was never carried out. Shortly before Stalag Luft 1 was overrun by Soviet troops on the night of April 30, 1945, the German guards fled and left the camp unattended. When a fellow prisoner awakened Spicer and told him they had been freed, Henry wouldn't leave. "I have one more night to make it an even six months," he explained. "I'm staying here tonight!"

When Colonel Spicer finally did come out, according to Robertson, "Every prisoner, to the man, gathered at the entrance to greet him, while cheering and trying to pat him on the back. He gave a short speech and said that seeing us and hearing our shouts made the whole experience in solitary confinement worth it."

In the next few days, Spicer was evacuated with the 6,250 other former "kriegies" and flown from Barth to Camp Lucky Strike in France for processing before going home. Colonel Spicer, who later became an Air Force major general, retired in 1964 and passed away in 1967, but he will always be remembered for the speech that not only brought him a death sentence, but also brought strength and fortitude to his fellow prisoners.

The Short War of Don Rice

By Merle C. Olmsted

It is the twenty-fourth of February, 1944. The 357th Fighter Group has been operational for fourteen days. It has flown six missions; three of them French coastal sweeps and three to German targets. The latter three brought contact with the enemy fighters and resulted in the group's first victories, eleven of them. Six pilots were already gone—Giltner, Hubbard, Ross, Lichter, Boyle, and Carroll. Two of them were dead, the others would return in fifteen months or so.

The target on the twenty-fourth was Gotha, a short mission, only four hours. Two 190s, a 109, a 110, and a rocket carrying JU-88 were shot down, and two pilots, Chuck McKee and Don Rice did not return. At the end of the day, 362nd pilot Kenneth Hagan reported, "My wingman Lt. Don Rice and I were flying together near Coblenz at an altitude of 24,000 feet, to the left and rear and above a box of B-24s. Suddenly Lt. Rice called me and said that there were two bogies under us at one o'clock at about 10,000 feet. I made a turn to the left so that I could come down on them from the sun, Don remained during the turn. Immediately after the turn, I called Rice and told him that I couldn't see the bogies anymore, that I was low on oxygen and that we'd better head home. I heard him say excitedly, 'They are 190s!' I call him again and asked, 'Are you with me, Don?' There was only a garbled reply. Hagan did not see or hear Rice again, so tagged on to a couple of P-51s and went home."

362nd Fighter Squadron pilot Ken Hagan

Fifteen years later, Don Rice carried on the story in his encounter report in which he claimed the destruction of a FW-190. "I started down in a split-ess and Hagan turned as though he was following me from the right. Getting close to the enemy plane, I noticed it had a yellow nose. In my dive, I had developed too much speed and although I retarded the throttle, I overshot him, but managed to get under him and when about a hundred feet away, I opened fire with a five- or ten-degree deflection. I observed strikes on his right wing root and all over the cockpit. I must have killed or wounded the pilot for the 190 suddenly nosed down and went straight into the ground. The pilot had not bailed out. Climbing back upstairs, I called Lt. Hagan, but just then I was shot down by another 190. I was able to bail out but broke my leg in trying to extricate myself from a tree in which I had landed. The Germans found me and I have been a POW until recently."

The aerial battles that swirled above them were of great interest to a generation of German boys, just as they had been to a similar group across the English Channel during the Battle of Britain. Many of the youngsters on both sides were lucky enough to be just young enough to avoid getting caught up in a savage war as participants.

Erich Pfarr was one of those on the ground that day and he remembers. He said it was his last year in school, having been born in 1929. It was a sunny cold day, with a cloudless sky and eight to ten inches of snow on the ground. They had expected an air raid which came at about 11:30 a.m. but the alarm came too late because the bombers were already above them on their way home. There was an intense air battle above them and then everything happened very fast. Parachutes flew above him in a westerly direction. Suddenly, there were increasing motor noises, a big bang, a smoke plume and one pilot in a parachute. It was the crash of Jaeger (fighter) north of Unterbreizbach. The German pilot landed near the Ulster Bridge, badly injured. A four-motored bomber flew lower and lower, in a line from the south toward the Ulsterberg, and crashed in the woods.

Almost fifty years later, another German, Heinz Jerousek, who had been about four years old in 1944, now an avid researcher of the vicious battles, located the wreckage of Rice's plane. He also managed to track down Erich Pfarr and other witnesses and to identify the German pilot involved. The following was sent to both Don Rice and Merle Olmsted and it is recorded hear courtesy of Mr. Jerousek. "What a day today," Peter Gottbehut recalls, "the whole morning the bomber streams were going eastward. Now at 13:40 hours (1:40 p.m.), they came back just over our little village of Rott. Everybody was standing outside counting the little shining points with contrails; one hundred, two hundred, and more. A deep roar was in the air, and you could feel it in your stomach. Suddenly, from the east, just over the top of a hill, a four-engine bomber showed up, very low and aflame. Everybody was running for cover, like chickens hunted by a hawk. The bomber, a B-17, crashed only a few miles from us into a hillside. A parachute was seen floating down. Everybody started to run to the scene of the crash."

As Rice indicated in his narrative, he broke his leg getting out of a tree. He was then carried from the woods to the road by workers from an iron mine and he was then picked up by a German farmer named Seul and taken to his farm. That same evening, a car from Neuwied took him to the Garrison Hospital in that town.

The German pilot who shot Don Rice down was Oberleutnant (1st Lt.) Waldi Radener, the commander of the Seventh Staffel of JG 26. By the end of the war, he had thirty-six victories, of which seventeen were four-engine bombers. After the war, he joined the new German Air Force, only to be the first air victim of the new Luftwaffe. He was killed in a crash on January 8, 1957.

Waldi Radener, Don Rice, and Gerhard Loschinski

Heinz Jerousek has concluded that the FW-190 shot down by Donald Rice was flown by Unteroffizier (NCO) Gerhard Loschinski, also of JG 26, and that he was killed. At the time, Loschinski had flown ten missions and had one victory to his credit.

Don Rice's missing air crew report (MACR) contains translations of several German documents including the following: "The American Air Corps member, Lt. Don Rice, reported by letter of 24 February 1944, has escaped through the barred window of an especially fit room for the purpose on March 24, 1944, about three o'clock. Endeavors to recapture the prisoner have been started already by the local commander at Neuwied." Rice was indeed soon recaptured and spent the rest of the war in Stalag Luft 1, at Barth in Northern Germany. Heinz Jerousek has invited Rice to visit him in Germany, and plans were made to do so early in 1994. On the twenty-fourth of February Don planned to be standing on the spot on which he landed fifty years before to the day after his "Short War."

Don Rice did go to Germany during the last two weeks of February and the first two weeks of March 1994. There Don met Mr. Heinz Jerousek and two of his friends who are also very interested in tracing various airplane crashes that occurred during World War II. Mr. Jerousek arranged to have Don picked up at his hotel in Frankfurt and driven to his (Jerousek's) home. From his home, he took Don to another friend's house who had a large collection of souvenirs from various crashes. Jerousek's friend had a 20mm cannon from a German plane, a .50 caliber machine gun from an American plane, plus several propeller blades of all kinds; it was like a small museum. After having lunch at his friend's home, they all (five) drove to the vicinity of the crash site of Don Rice's P-51. When they got there, they met four local citizens who had heard about Don's coming and they joined the others for a walk through the woods to the crash site itself. Don had several pictures taken. One of the locals said that he remembers seeing and hearing Rice's plane before it crashed, but he did not see Don's parachute.

Every German at the scene was extremely friendly and made Don Rice feel more like a lost buddy rather than a former enemy. One of the locals produced small bottles of "schnapps" and they toasted friendship and no more war. They all agreed that America *saved* Germany and they were very grateful for our help.

Heinz Jerousek gave Don the name of the German pilot who shot him down. His name was Oberleutnant Woldermar Radener. He was killed in an AT-6 during a training flight January 8, 1957. He was the first casualty of the post war Luftwaffe. He had thirty-seven victories to his credit.

The name of the pilot Don Rice shot down during this same encounter was Unteroffizier Gerhard Loschinski who had ten missions and one victory. His plane dove straight into the ground and his remains were recovered

1989 and Loschinski was interred in a military cemetery. Gerhard had been buried with the wreckage of his FW-190 for forty-five years before he was located and exhumed.

**Don Rice stands on the spot in Germany where
his Mustang crashed in 1944**

Heinz told Don that he had recovered and identified the pilot of a P-47 shortly before Rice's arrival. He turned the remains over to the U. S. Armed Forces. The pilot had been carried MIA all these past years. Heinz gave Don a great memento of his Mustang consisting of the tip of the horizontal stabilizer along with a Mfg. plate from the oil filter, plus one of the actual .50 caliber bullets he had recovered from the crash site.

Kit Carson's Narrow Escape

By Jim McLane

Jim McLane

No doubt about it, the Great War was winding down. I'd been busting my butt for two years, ten months, and seventeen days trying to get into action, and there had been nothing but frustration and delay at almost every turn. But at long last I'd arrived at the Air Corps Replacement Center at Stone, England, and my goal seemed to be in easy reach. A week later, after becoming fully acclimated to the miserable late winter British weather, I joined forty-four other replacement pilots that reported to the Leiston encampment of the 357th Fighter Group. It was March 24, 1945, the day that the Army Airborne crossed the Rhine River. No one could foresee the future, of course, but the 357th was celebrating its last really big day, having shot down 16 enemy aircraft and destroying four more on the ground while on patrol. This was a clear and present sign to the newcomers that opportunity was still knocking. I fully expected to be heading across the Channel in just a few more days to meet the enemy above his home turf. What a letdown it was to learn that several more weeks of training in Captain Bochkay's "Clobber College" were necessary before I'd be trusted to confront the Boche! Along with Johnny Metcalf and G. A. Robinson's little brother Joe, I'd be assigned to the 362nd Fighter Squadron. The day finally came when Captain Chuck Weaver, the Ops officer, gave me the choice of flying the next day's mission or taking a three-day pass to London. That was the easiest decision I'd ever made!

Donald Bochkay

Thus, I joined sixty-three fellow birdmen of the 357th and the crews of perhaps 950 other Eighth Air Force bomber and fighter planes on Tuesday, April 17, 1945, intent on doing away with the Aussig Chemical Works somewhere in Germany. (Or maybe it was Czechoslovakia? During my four forays into the heart of the Evil Empire, I never knew for sure where we were; after all, wingmen weren't issued maps!) It was a classic 1,000 plane daylight raid in near-perfect weather, just as we'd seen in the Pathe Movie newsreels, only in living color and better focus. All of the expected elements of high drama were there; strings of bomber formations stretching box after box across the sky, swarms of fighter planes maneuvering over the bombers as if daring the Luftwaffe to approach, black puffs of exploding enemy flak, each containing a surprising momentary bright, red flash that hadn't been captured in the black and white newsreel pictures, more bright, red flashes far below as the bombs exploded, excited voices in the earphones of my British flight helmet tolling the count of parachutes from a B-17 which was headed for the ground some 4 miles below at an angle of descent never intended for that majestic flying machine. From the three bombers that exploded in front of my wide eyes, I saw only 3 open chutes, and one of them caught fire. There were German fighters, too. In sharp, clipped transmissions on the VHF radio, my fellow warriors reported spotting them and even giving chase, but all I saw were a few jet contrails that looked to be higher than an airplane could possibly fly.

Jim McLane's P-51 *Dainty Dotty*

So why wasn't I bursting with joy to find myself at long last in the midst of this Grand Spectacle? The answer came as if I'd never thought of it before; people are being *killed* here! I'd been witness to the demise of a number of friends in training accidents back home, but this was different. It was all so on purpose! Looking around at all there was to see, my thoughts drifted to the single-minded efforts I'd made to arrive at this particular place at this instant in time. Then, as now, it didn't seem cowardly to wonder whether I had been right in fighting against assignments that would have kept me in the U. S. A. near my pregnant wife, and far from this newly observed carnage.

But of course, it was a little late for that. There were also a couple of petty annoyances during the 5 hour, forty-five-minute mission that took the edge off of my elation. First, the extra equipment like the shoulder holstered .45 caliber automatic pistol and the inflatable G-suit worn for the first time felt strange and uncomfortable. [Author's note: Lt. Fletcher Adams of Ida, Louisiana, was one of the first pilots to wear a G-suit having been assigned to test the brand-new and "Top Secret" device while he flew his P-51B Mustang *The Southern Belle* in the spring of 1944.] But mainly, there was a matter of a loosened rubber trim tab control rod. We'd flown nothing but B and C model P-51s in the twenty-hour Clobber College transition period. This was my first go at a fully equipped "D" model carrying two full 108-gallon paper drop tanks. Not knowing what to expect in the way of different flying characteristics, it took a while to conclude that something must be wrong to have caused the rudder trim tab control knob to have no effect on the rudder trim. I'd have a hard time preventing the plane from veering sharply left during the takeoff roll. By the time we reached cruising altitude, my right leg was bordering on a muscle cramp from holding right rudder. Finally, I rolled in enough aileron trim to counteract the offset rudder so the plane would fly straight ahead on its own (actually, sideways ahead on a steady course with its right wing down). I thought about the difficulty in aligning the platform if there were cause to fire the six .50 caliber machine guns which, after all, was the excuse for me being there. Well, that just didn't happen. The long flight came to an inglorious end when I misjudged spacing from Lt. Cheever, my flight leader, in the pattern and had to go around for a second try at landing. To top off the emotional binge of that first day, upon return to the Squadron Operations building for debriefing, I was caught unawares and royally chewed out by the conscientious sergeant in charge of personal flying equipment. He noticed that I was wearing a pair of Gaucho boots instead of regulation GI high-top shoes. My father had sent the boots to me from Brazil where he was a constructing air fields and I prized them greatly. Having been caught flat-footed, I suffered through a ten minute lecture in which it was pointed out that the loosely bound boots would probably fly off instantly if I had to bail out, and in any case, would not serve as well as GI shoes for walking out from behind enemy lines. Given all the food for thought, it was surprising that a few hours of sleep were all it took to reset everything for a fresh new start the next day.

A close-up of the nose art on McLane's "Dainty Dottie"

It's amazing what one day of experience on a new job can do to build confidence! After a good breakfast we were briefed for a new kind of mission that caused me to put aside all thought of the downers of the previous day. The enemy had been scrambling their Me-262 jet fighters just in advance of the stream of invading American heavy bombers. They could climb quickly to an altitude of 30,000 to 40,000 feet, well above the effective fighting ceiling of our P-51s. Then, when the bombers arrived, each Me-262 would make a very fast diving pass through a box of bombers, seldom failing to knock down one or more of the heavies. Because of the limited fuel capacity of the German jets, there was usually no second pass and a good many were destroyed as they sought to land with low fuel remaining. Some strategist reasoned that our P-51s might be able to cover the airdromes at the right time. The selected airfields for this raid were near Prague, and each unit of the 357th was assigned responsibility to watch over activity at a particular field. Major Kit Carson, our Squadron Commander, was to lead the group and I was to be his wingman. I carefully laced and double-tied my high topped GI shoes before riding out to the hardstand for the quick walk-around inspection of the airplane. My main concern, of course, was with checking the safety-wired locknut on the rudder trim tab control rod. In due course it was time to start engines, and to fall in behind Kit Carson's legendary *Nooky Booky* leading the pack to takeoff position.

At times, when the weather borders on perfection, the exhilaration of flying has become almost a religious experience for me. I had that feeling at midday on Wednesday, April 18, 1945, as the fields of East Germany some 13,000 feet below spread their greenery in panoramic spring splendor before me and my wonderful machine. Of course, I didn't know exactly where we were, but according to the notes from the morning briefing on the small clipboard strapped to my knee, it was about time for us to reach our destination. Major Carson, who was not noted for long-winded speeches on the radio, had not broadcast a word since we started engines at Leiston. Suddenly, to my surprise and still without saying anything, he pitched directly over, sort of a quarter outside loop, until he was in a vertical dive. Miraculously I was looking right at him when he started this maneuver and somehow managed to stay with him, albeit trailing a bit behind. Had I been looking away for a few seconds, I probably would never have caught up with him. As it was, the second half of Dollar Red flight, led by G. A. Robinson, had missed the initial pushover, and was already far behind. Again, without announcement, Carson's two drop tanks flew off (it was a clean miss, slightly off my left wing), so I figured that I'd better drop mine too. Even though I still didn't know what we were doing, it was obvious that he was on to something, and I will admit to letting the excitement build within me. I reached for the switch that armed the bomb shackle circuits so that the little button on top of the control stick could be used to drop the tanks, and then squeezed the button *hard*. The Mustang shuddered, and a faraway staccato sound reached my ears. The voice of G. A. Robinson, now watching from a good way back, came through to me five by five, "Go get 'em, Mac!" Suddenly, it all made sense. The airframe shudder, the staccato sound, G. A.'s exhortation, and the realization that my fist was rigidly encircling not only the small button at the top of the control stick, but the gun trigger on its front as well, could only mean that I had loosed the armor-piercing outpour of six .50 caliber machine guns on a piece of airspace *very* close to the Squadron Commander! It seemed apparent that I missed him, and thank goodness the use of tracers had been abandoned some time back, so he didn't get to see all of the lead go by. My main worry now was what would appear on the gun camera footage, but that would have to wait until later. Apparently, in the excitement and haste to arm the bomb shackles, I flipped on the adjacent gun arming switch as well, permitting the guns to fire when the trigger was accidentally squeezed. G. A. had seen something that I couldn't-the smoke from the six firing guns.

Now that it seemed that Major Carson had survived my attack, it was time to turn attention to other things like trying to figure out what we were doing. Still going straight down, full throttle and matching RPMs were required for me to stay up with him. The airspeed quickly built up and passed the redline mark on the dial. I resolved not to worry about that; instead, when his wings flew off, I would throttle back. About this time, I noticed that we were diving on an airfield,

in all likelihood the one we'd been assigned to. Eventually, I was even able to
spot the Me-262 in its takeoff roll that had attracted Carson's attention from on
high. We swooped in behind soon after it cleared the aerodrome boundary. At
about 1,000 feet in altitude, we were traveling about as fast as the P-51s could,
but the Me-262 was clearly pulling away. Carson fired on him from marginal gun
range, and got a couple of hits but soon the German jet was gone.

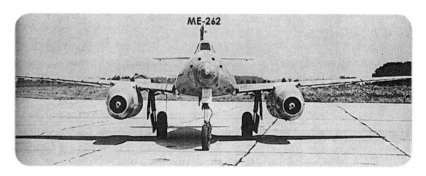

We climbed back up to about 5,000 feet and circled near the airfield, hoping
another "blow job" would venture out. Since now there were only the two of us,
I spread out to the side enough to turn into my companion if a Jerry showed
the bad judgment to approach us from behind. Soon we spotted another jet
and gave chase at about 700 feet. Kit fired on him without visible effect as he
was still a bit out of our range. I concluded that it would do no harm for me to
lob a few .50 caliber slugs in his direction, so I did, being careful to allow for the
extreme range. There weren't any bright flashes, and in fact, he was so far away
that his tail-on image is missing from the gun camera film, one of life's great
disappointments for me. The surprising thing was that while we weren't gaining
on the jet, neither did we seem to be losing ground. Shortly, the German began
a wide turn to the left that made my heart pound, for now I knew we had him.
All we had to do was cut him off in the turn to get into firing range. Strangely, my
leader adopted the exact opposite tactic, and pulled wide to the outside of the
turn. Using logic that is available only to the pathologically obsessed, I quickly
deduced the reason for this unusual maneuver. Major Carson was going to let
me have this one. After all, he'd been credited with over twenty victories, surely
enough for one pilot, and he knew that the war was about to end on me without
me having fired a shot at even one. So he was giving me my big chance! What
a guy! I pushed again on the fire walled throttle and started lining things up in
the gun sight as my adversary came out of his wide turn and resumed straight
flight, still a bit out of range. Suddenly, a virtual blanket of small white puffs
of smoke appeared to form just above my flight path, and it became obvious
that the "crafty kraut" had led me directly over the light flak batteries situated
around his airfield. Of course, Major Carson had seen the airfield and was not

fooled into following the jet as I was. The German advanced his throttle and was gone to parts unknown as soon as the flak started.

Given the apparent density of the "golf ball" canopy of flak shells I'd penetrated, I concluded that the airplane must have been hit in several places, even though everything appeared to be working properly. Since the P-51 was particularly vulnerable to breaks in the oil and coolant lines that extended from the engine to the radiators, I maintained a close vigil on the instruments that would disclose such a problem. I also made up my mind to belly in rather than bail out if the engine failed, and kept picking out satisfactory fields ahead to do this in. For the last 18 months I'd had a recurring dream about ditching, and felt that this was practice enough to belly in with confidence. Finally, I noticed that my fuel remaining was down to the minimum value to return home and I called Major Carson to tell him so. This unnecessary and ridiculous call spurred him to break radio silence for the first time that day to tell me that we had been on our way home for twenty minutes.

Back at Leiston, the crew chief was happy to see that the guns had been fired; I didn't bother mentioning that the red muzzle tapes were broken when I almost shot the Squadron Commander. I apologized for all of the flak holes he would surely find in his airplane, but a careful inspection showed the apology to be unnecessary. I viewed the blank gun camera film with mixed emotions and great relief when *Nooky Booky* turned out to be completely out of the camera's field of view, but lifelong disappointment when the Me-262 I'd shot at could not be seen. I flew two more missions before being ordered to take a pass to London which marked the end of the Great War for me. But it is this day that lives most vividly in my memory forty-eight years later; the day I first fired my guns in combat—at the Squadron Commander. Was it worth the many months of preparation? You bet it was!

The Trials and Tribulations of Joe Shea and *My Bonnie*

By Lt. Col. Joe Shea

Pilot Joe Shea flew the second P-51 named *My Bonnie* in the 357th Fighter Group. Shea, a late comer to the war, joined the 362nd Fighter Squadron as a replacement pilot in January of 1945. Joe named his P-51D Mustang *My Bonnie* after his fiancée, and only found out after the war, when he returned to the United States to marry her, that his "Bonnie" was *already* married! The following are just a few of Lt. Col. Joseph Shea's stories about his adventures with the 357th Fighter Group.

Yoxford Boy Lt. Joseph "Joe" Shea in the cockpit
of the P-51D Mustang he named *My Bonnie*

The 357th Fighter Group
Traps German

"Blow Jobs"

"I am combining the stories about the following two missions because there is a definite link between the two of them. Although I didn't fly the mission to Prague-Pilsen, Czechoslovakia, on April 17, 1945, I did fly both missions on the eighteenth and nineteenth of that month.

On these missions we picked up the bombers deep inside Germany because most of the country was occupied by our forces at this time. As we approached Prague-Pilsen we observed German Me-262 fighter jets taking off from a field near the target area. We were totally amazed at how fast they were flying at the bombers' altitude before and after decimating several of the heavies. We were able to shoot down two of the Me-262s but the *kill* ratio that day proved to be unacceptable. The Luftwaffe had, by this time in the war, abandoned the head on attack and its pilots were now using another tactic. The "blow jobs," as we called the 262s, would form up at an altitude of 40,000 feet or more which was higher than we could effectively operate. Then, on a signal from their flight leaders, the German jets would zoom down through the bombers, slashing at them as they sliced through the boxes. After each attack, they would quickly climb right back up to 40,000 feet and reform before making their next aerial assault. Because of the Me-262's superior speed advantage over our Mustangs, we could do very little, if anything, to stop them.

When the 357th received orders the following day (19 April 1945) to return to Prague-Pilsen, our leaders came up with a plan to even up the odds. One of our fighter squadrons, the 362nd, would go high and join up with the bombers. The other two squadrons would fly into the target area at tree top level below the German radar. We pilots in the top squadron would then direct our sister squadrons to a point off the north end of the airfield near Prague and have them poised there waiting for the German Me-262s to taxi out and start their take off roll, during which time they would be most vulnerable to attack. Once the jets began taking off and forming up, we directed the pilots from our other two squadrons to attack them and the 363rd and 364th Fighter Squadrons were able to ambush and destroy eight of the jets shortly after they left the ground. As a result of this strategy, our bombers fared much better that day."

Circling Dan Myers over the
North Sea off the Frisian Islands

Dan Myers

"We were on our way back home after a mission to Hamburg. Since we were so far north in Germany, it was logical to go out over the North Sea and fly back over the water rather than take a chance flying over German held territory.

One of our planes developed engine trouble, and the pilot had to bail out. After parachuting down into the North Sea and getting into his dingy, he found that he had landed just a mile off shore from one of the Frisian Islands (Borkum) which was occupied by the Germans.

We had called ASR (Air Sea Rescue), and they were dispatched to pick the pilot up, but since our P-51s were low on fuel, most of our squadron had to return to base. Our commander called around to get a 'fuel remaining' reading, and it turned out that I had the most fuel. So I was elected to stay behind and circle Dan Myers in his dingy until the Air Sea Rescue flying boat arrived.

While circling Dan, I would approach the shore of the island, and on each pass the Germans would shoot at me. As I was sufficiently out of range, they never really posed a threat, but that did not stop the Germans from taking a crack at me each time I flew by. After a while the ASR plane called to say that they had me in sight and that I could return to my home base. By this time I was really running low on fuel, so I quickly began high-tailing it toward Leiston.

The sea plane landed to pick Dan up, and at about that time, two Me-262 jets came streaking in and shot up the flying boat while it sat in the water. Now we had Dan Myers *and* the crew of the flying boat all floating in the North Sea.

It was getting very close to sundown, and that made it impossible for any further rescue attempts that day. During the night, Dan Myers's dingy drifted ashore, and he was captured by the Germans. Dan was sent to Oberursel for interrogation by Luftwaffe Intelligence officers before being transported to Stalag Luft 1. Fortunately for Myers, he only spent a short time as a POW and was liberated after the Americans overran the prison camp several weeks later.

The crew of the flying boat was much luckier as the ASR personnel were rescued by the British before they too fell into the hands of the Nazis and had to spend the rest of the war in a stalag luft compound."

The Lucky German
Motorcycle Courier

"This was undoubtedly the most humorous incident of the war for me. We had completed our escort mission, took the bombers back out to friendly territory, and then went back into Germany to search out targets of opportunity. Frequently we would run up and down the Autobahn searching for military vehicles which, of course, were legitimate targets during these 'search and destroy' forays. On this occasion we spotted a German military courier on a motorcycle. This looked like shooting fish in a barrel to us, but that dude had one thing in his favor. He had just crossed under a couple of overpasses where two highways intersected. As soon as he saw us in the distance, he immediately came to a screeching halt and scooted back under the concrete overpasses. When we would approach from the south he would scoot up to the north side of the pair of overpasses. When we would turn around and come back from the other direction, he would dash to the other side and hide there.

We made several passes and wasted a bunch of ammo but never did ruffle a feather on him. I guess the only thing hurt during that foray was our ego!"

Tony Schoepke Takes a
20mm Cannon Hit

"By very late in the war, the German Luftwaffe had retreated into Czechoslovakia, and the few remaining targets worth bombing were also there. So on the seventeenth, eighteenth, and nineteenth of April 1945, we escorted bombers to the Prague-Pilsen area of Czechoslovakia.

On the mission of the seventeenth of April a close friend of mine, Tony Schoepke, took a hit from a 20mm cannon shell fired at him from the airdrome near Pilsen. Tony was really indignant as his family had migrated from Pilsen to New York State!"

357th Fighter Group pilot Tony Schoepke holds the damaged panel from his P-51D after it was punctured by a German 20mm cannon round over Pilsen, Czechoslovakia April 17, 1945

Barrage Balloons in the Valley Ahead

"The 357th Fighter Group had taken the bombers back out to friendly territory and, as always, we wanted to go back into enemy territory and kick a few butts. We were flying up a river valley that day and the ceiling was quite low, so it was kind of like flying up through a tunnel. All of the sudden we saw barrage balloons up ahead of us.

Now, that's a serious situation. Each barrage balloon had a steel cable running from the ground up to the balloon. Hit that cable with your wing and goodbye wing. As a result we had to abruptly pull up into the clouds. Not a good situation with several planes in close proximity to each other in the clouds, and to make matters worse, our gyros had tumbled because of the violent pull ups.

When you lose your gyros it is a very bad situation. You are in a steep climb, your airspeed is dropping like a rock, and you have to nose down (to avoid a stall). But how much? You have no idea where the horizon is because you've lost your gyro. Also, you are in the mountains!

It took some really good flying that day and lots of luck, but we all got through it with no losses."

Anton Schoepke, Joe Shea, and Hank Gruber in front of the P-51
Skin-n-Bones

The Day the Germans Blasted the 362nd over the Hague

"On many of the missions I flew, we would enter the Continent over the Hague and always at about 18,000 feet. This had become more or less a routine, and we never expected the Germans to shoot at us. In fact, I recall being told in Clobber College (the 357th Fighter Group's informal school for training new replacement pilots) just that.

One morning though, the Germans had apparently been observing our pattern, our air speed, etc., and had polished the barrels of their 88mm antiaircraft guns one last time before we flew over. There were probably twenty-four planes in the formation, four ship flights in trail and all tucked in nice and close. I guess we wanted to show the Germans what pretty formations we could fly.

Suddenly, about a dozen rounds of 88s exploded right at our altitude and right in the middle of our formation. I happened to be 'tail-end Charlie' and as I peeled off to the right sharply, I looked back and I have never seen a bomb burst of planes the likes of which I observed!

The old saying goes, 'If you can see the flash and hear the noise, you're dead!' Well, that's not true. I was at the rear of the formation and saw the flash and heard the noise and I am sure the rest of the pilots saw and heard the same thing, but we all formed back up and continued on the mission. I guess the only casualties were the crew chiefs that had to patch up all of the holes in our aircraft.

The moral of this story is to never get too cocky and let your guard down."

The Thoughtless Train Engineer

"On one occasion, we had gone back into Germany to search for targets of opportunity when we ran across a train carrying a load of gasoline. The train was in a small German town and the engineer disconnected the engine from the rest of the train and high-tailed it to the south. Our leader dispatched a couple of 51s to take out the engine and the rest of us stayed behind to work over the tank cars.

There was a huge lumber yard right next to the train tracks on the west side. Our leader instructed us to drop our external fuel tanks, which still had a small amount of fuel in them, into the lumberyard on our first pass and then fire into the lumber on the second pass. The armor piercing incendiary bullets did a great job of setting the lumberyard ablaze.

We then started working over the twenty-two cars of gasoline and the two cabooses. On my first pass at the train, the tank car I was shooting at exploded in a beautiful fireball perhaps a couple hundred feet high and I had to fly right through it. My gun camera captured a beautiful shot of the top of the conning tower on the tank car spiraling up right in front of my plane. Very fortunately I missed all the pieces and broke out into the clear in a second or so. On my second pass I was relegated the two cabooses which I managed to splinter quite well with the six .50 caliber machine guns we had on the P-51s. We destroyed all the cars of gasoline and made a proverbial mess of that small town in the process.

There was also another interesting part of this whole episode. About a block beyond the railroad, a road paralleled the tracks. All the time we were beating up the place there was a little old German woman walking north on that road with a cloth satchel over her left arm. I presume she was on the way home from the grocery store with food for that night's meal. Every time I made a pass I could see the little old lady walking along, looking up sheepishly at us. When we left and headed for home the little old lady was still walking along the road. It must have been a terrifying experience for her and the ricocheting bullets must have been extremely frightening."

Thirty-Eight Germans Sighted Coming Up

"We were on a bomber escort mission deep inside southern Germany when someone in the group spotted thirty-eight German planes coming up to intercept the heavies. Our entire Group of probably 60 P-51s went into a steep dive to intercept the German aircraft. Since we were so far into Germany, the Group leader instructed us to keep our external tanks [attached], as the fuel remaining in them would be needed to finish the escort and get back to England.

As we were screaming down, suddenly both of my external fuel tanks came unglued and were gone. They simply disappeared! I immediately called in that I had to abort because at this point it was problematic as I might not have been able to get back to England with the fuel I had remaining. I immediately took up a heading for home base and ventured out across Germany on my own. I also went into emergency lean mode which would consume the least amount of fuel per hour. The emergency lean mode called for reducing the prop speed to 1,900rpm, and I recall as I droned across Germany, it seemed as if the front end of the plane was gyrating in a slow circle.

That day was probably the most stressful day of my tour in Europe. Not only did I have to worry that perhaps I did not have enough fuel to make it home, but also, I was all alone crossing several hundred miles of enemy territory. As a result, I constantly had to be on the watch for any German plane that might see me as an easy kill. On one occasion the [rear directed] radar alarm went off in my cockpit and I nearly unscrewed my head looking to see if someone was behind me. Fortunately, the alarm was probably set off by a piece of chaff that the bombers had dropped on the way in.

I did make it back to our base that day, but when the rear of my plane dropped onto the tail wheel, my engine cut out. What little gas I had left drained to the back of the tank! The crew chief drained all the tanks and I had less than five gallons of fuel remaining in the Mustang. When you consider that the 51 guzzled forty-two gallons per hour on emergency lean, I could not have gone much farther."

The Urge to Kill

"During the spring of 1945 it was quite common for us to perform our escort duties, and after shepherding the bombers back to the safety of friendly territory, we'd turn around and go back into Germany to strafe targets of opportunity.

On one such occasion, probably somewhere south of Hanover, we encountered an unusual cloud pattern. The clouds were in rows separated by perhaps a half mile of clear space and then another row of clouds and so on and so on in the same pattern. We would fly up one clear area and if we found nothing of interest we would dive down under the clouds and come up in the next clear area. This went on for a while with no success.

During one pass, when we dove down to go to the next clear area, we very unfortunately flew directly over a German airfield, and believe me, these fields were heavily defended with 2omm antiaircraft guns. I recall looking back and seeing a solid red stream of tracer bullets just a foot or so behind my tail. I proceeded to slam the throttle full forward and was able to stay ahead of the bullets.

End of story? No, not quite. I have never been able to erase the memory of an almost overpowering urge to flip my plane upside down and split-ess in order to shoot up that gun emplacement. To have done so at my low altitude would have been sure suicide. I simply could not have completed the maneuver before hitting the ground.

It is the only time in my days of flying combat over Germany that I experienced any degree of hatred. Later, I rationalized that those Germans had every right to be shooting at me; after all I was invading their land. But at that moment all I could think of was, 'How dare you!' I guess you might say I took it personally."

Going My Way?

"My mind is really sketchy so far as names of individuals, the date, and the exact location involved are concerned, but the details of this incident are burned in my memory, so I am certain about the main facts. If asked, I could draw a picture of the country road with the field on the east side, etc., where this took place. The general location was probably away from any large city but north of Frankfurt if my internal 'GPS' unit is correct.

One of the pilots from the 357th Fighter Group experienced mechanical problems or had taken a hit, and for whatever reason was forced to belly the plane into Germany. It was decided that he would land in a large field that had a straight paved road along its west side and that another of our pilots would land on the road and pick him up. That would entail dumping the parachutes and one pilot sitting on the other pilot's lap on the flight back to England. Also it would be impossible to close the canopy.

The pilot in the crippled plane made a beautiful belly landing perhaps 100 yards from the road and our other pilot successfully landed on the road. However there developed one 'fly in the ointment.' A group of farmers were working in the field to the north and started running toward the downed pilot with pitch forks. This called for remedial action so the rest of us flying around set up a pattern flying from west to east and sprayed bullets in front of the German farmers. It did not take much to convince them to retreat.

The downed pilot was picked up and returned to home base unharmed." [Author's note: In his book, *Pursue and Destroy*, author Leonard "Kit" Carson quoted the pilot sitting in his squadron mate's lap as quipping, "Don't get an erection or you'll push me right out of here!"]

From 30,000 Feet to the Deck

"We were on our way home from a mission somewhere in the Brunswick area of Germany. It was quite late in the evening, perhaps 8:30 p.m. but in late spring it stays light there till nearly 10:00 p.m. We were flying at somewhere in the vicinity of 33,000 feet when we came across a couple of planes at the same altitude, heading in the same direction. There was some discussion about the identity of the planes, but since they were a goodly distance in front of us, we could not tell for sure.

That question was soon answered when the pilots apparently saw us and split-essed, heading straight down at full throttle. We could now plainly see that they were Me-109s and gave chase plummeting down from that height at full throttle. My P-51 soon reached its critical mach [speed] and due to the build up and breaking away of air molecules on the leading edge of the wing, the plane was undulating up and down like a bucking bronco only not so severe. Unfortunately, it was severe enough that I could not get my gun sight on the German planes.

Soon, however, the Germans leveled out right down among the trees with us in hot pursuit, still screaming along at probably close to 600mph. With the 'Krauts' swinging from side to side and darting around trees, it was virtually impossible to get in a shot.

That all soon came to a screeching halt when we observed a German airfield straight ahead and opted out of flying through their murderous 20mm cannon fire. The pilots of the two Me-109s thus lived to fight another day!"

The Last Mission to Berchtesgaden

(The Eagle's Nest)

"The Allied troops of America, Great Britain, and Russia were rapidly closing the noose on the Third Reich. We had been told previously that we had flown our last mission but the 'powers that be' decided upon one last mission to bomb the SS barracks at Hitler's hideout in the Bavarian Alps, the Eagle's Nest. That was really stretching the range of the P-51, as the target was some 600 miles from our base in England.

But it was a beautiful spring day and there was a feeling in the air that we would not see any German fighters. So for all practical purposes it was like a sight-seeing tour and the Alps *are* such a beautiful sight. I can still remember the feeling that day; there was no more of the tension we had experienced before while flying over Germany as had been the case during every other mission.

It was so nice [that day] to be able to casually look around and observe the beauty of the countryside. We had no idea whatsoever that we would be returning to Munich in a couple of short months to take up our duties as the Army of Occupation!"

The Radio Relay Mission

"The radio equipment we carried on the P-51 Mustang was what we called a 'line of sight' radio. When our missions carried us 500 or 600 miles from our base in Leiston, England, the curvature of the earth prevented this type of radio from being capable of contacting the base (once our mission had taken us beyond the North Sea). To solve this problem we had one P51 assigned as a 'radio relay' ship on every deep penetration mission.

On one such mission, I was as the radio relay aircraft and since the mission was to Big 'B,' I took up a position at 30,000 feet, half way between the base and Berlin. All I did for hours and hours was sit up there at that altitude and circle around and around. For a diversion, I might fly a figure 8 for a while or a square, or perhaps do a few rolls, etc., but it was an extremely boring experience. The only thought that broke the monotony was the possibility that a German plane might come up and challenge your right to be there. However, I don't think that ever happened." (Author's note: It did happen on occasion with other pilots. Sometimes, these radio ships even attracted the attention of other Allied pilots and when this happened, the end result could be fatal if the ships did not properly identify each other in time.)

The One that Got Away

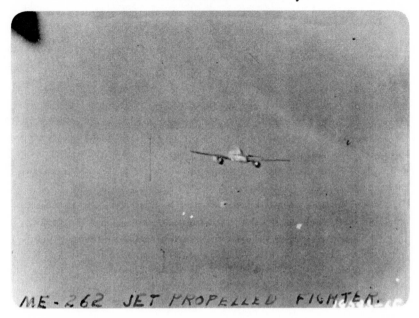

ME-262 JET PROPELLED FIGHTER.

Pilot Joe Shea's Me-262 as it appears in his gun camera film

"It was near the end of the war when while on the return home from a mission someone shouted, 'Break!' One of our pilots made a fast break, his guns accidentally fired, and one of our P-51s went down. That evening a TWX came down, advising us to turn our guns off after we left the target area.

The next day or so we went to the Brunswick area, and after we left the target, I turned my guns off as directed. We were in a four-ship formation heading home. I was on the flight leader's left wing and the other two-ship element was off a hundred yards to the right.

I had just checked my tail, swept my eyes around past the leader to check the element's tails and saw nothing, so I started to return sweep. As my sight went past the leader, I saw a small cloud-like affair forming out ahead of us. I knew instantly that what I had seen was a string of 20mm shells exploding. My eyes darted to my tail, and sure enough, there was an Me-262 firing at me. In a split second I observed that he was closing very fast and could not continue to fire much longer. I also rationalized that he was missing me, and I made the decision to not make any movement which might result in me flying into his stream of bullets. I was correct because he stopped firing and started fish tailing in an effort to slow down and stay behind me. He was unsuccessful and slid up past me ever so slowly. It was an odd feeling to be sitting there staring into the eyes of a German pilot not more than twenty-five feet away from me.

I should have backed off and let the leader have him, but I never thought of that. All I could think about was, you had your turn. Now it's mine. I slid in on his tail but since I was probably less than two feet behind him I realized that I could not fire because I would end up flying through pieces of his plane. I waited until he was out there a couple hundred yards in front of me and pressed the trigger. NOTHING HAPPENED! Oh my god, I thought. My guns are turned off! I dove for the gun switch and in the process banged my head on the gun sight and knocked myself out. I came to with the sound of spent casings from my flight leader's guns rattling as they bounced off of my plane. He knocked some pieces off of the 262, but it got away. I did get some gun camera images since the camera works even when the guns are turned off. (See the picture above.)

Ever since the war ended I have wanted in the worst way to find out the name of that German pilot so I could make his acquaintance. I think it would be fun to hash over the story of that day over northern Germany with him."

The *Buzz Buggy* Incident

By Will Foard

William Foard

Pilot William Foard of the 364th Fighter Squadron wrote the following account of this mission to Munich, Germany, in his war diary dated April 16, 1945:

"Six-hour plus mission to rail yards southeast of Munich. I was flying *Buzz Buggy* and the engine was running rough. I kept running up the RPMs to clean it out and smooth it but it was using extra fuel at the higher RPMs. I left the group with three other P-51s and headed home. When we got to the North Sea we were at 10,000 feet when my engine quit (Wow, I never heard such quiet!). I turned back looking for some solid ground but could see only trees sticking out of the water in flooded areas. After going through all of the procedures I could think of the engine started running halfheartedly. I headed south, mushing along nose high into a thick haze, just barely holding altitude. At the briefing that morning we were told with much emphasis NOT TO LAND ON ANY NINTH AIR FORCE BASES AND MUCK UP THEIR RUNWAYS-PUT IT DOWN IN THE DIRT!

I got a steer for a repair base in Belgium but started running into the bomber stream returning home. I could not see very well in the haze and with the nose high I was seeing bombers go by above, below, and on both sides. After dropping down below all that hardware I lost contact with the repair base. After watching each fuel tank go dry, the engine quit. Then I saw an airfield off each side of the plane. I rolled into a glide to the nearest airfield and hit the runway just right. *Buzz Buggy* rolled to the middle and I climbed out feeling proud, when all of a sudden red lights were flashing and a jeep with a bunch of guys hanging all over it with horn blowing was bouncing across the field toward me [and they were] hollering as a squadron of A-26s came roaring across the field, peeling off on the runway where I was feeling 'fat, dumb, and happy.' We pushed *Buzz Buggy* off the runway just as the first A-26 touched down.

I spent a couple of days at Lyon, France, getting in the way of two mechanics trying to fix my engine. Having no experience with the Merlin, they never did get it to run right. A B-24 stopped at the base, so I bummed a ride back to England and I got a ride back to Leiston in a truck. I was assigned a new P-51 and got to name it *Swamp Fox* for the revolutionary general Francis Marion, whom the British called 'the Swamp Fox' due to his ability to disappear into the swamps of the Pee Dee River country.

I flew *Swamp Fox* for the remaining short period of the war."

Will Foard's P-51 Mustang *Swamp Fox*

Night Raid on the Stalag Luft

By Bill Dunlop

William Dunlop

Pilot William R. Dunlop of the 363rd Fighter Squadron was shot down during the mission on January 14, 1945, or "the Big Day" as it is called by the Yoxford Boys. The following is his account of an air raid he survived while incarcerated as a POW:

The first indication that there was a raid coming was in the 8pm report from Ashman (one of our officers who spoke German and acted as a liaison

111

to the camp command): Word from the German or from whatever source was routinely spread through the camp by runners. The report said a large formation of heavy bombers was on a direct course for Nuremburg. A German "voralarm" was sounded, followed by a shelter call to get into the slit trenches outside the barracks. I stayed in the block by the window just in from the trenches, so I could go through if the bombs came too close. "Goon" searchlights in all directions were hurriedly rallying the night fighters, telling us that a "big show" was near. Suddenly the searchlights went off and the BLAM of the flak guns which surrounded the camp was heard (we had heard that there were something like ninety guns on the camp periphery). Their fire seemed directed at pathfinder planes, target selecting for the bombers following and marking our camp. The area around us became like the Fourth of July.

A line of parachute flares in clusters of red and green separated our camp from Nuremburg across the railroad tracks to the north of us. Then, at about the same time, we all had a scare as one of our men yelled, "Falling flak!" followed by a piece crunching into the roof next door. To the din of the flak guns was added the deep rumble of RAF "cookies." (We always removed our dishes from the walls because concussion from the cookies, even miles away, shook the barracks and on one occasion blew out windows.) Slowly a stream of bombers made an appearance. (Someone said there were 200-300 "Lanes" and "Rallies" [Lancasters and Halifaxes].)

From the slit trench where I had just taken refuge I watched as the city became a deep red glow. Over the glow there was an occasional streak of white flame racing across the sky in a backdrop of numerous star-like flashes. This was apparently burning gasoline as flak found its mark. Then the streak would tragically turn red as the plane burned. As it came closer, it seemed to be floating earthward, a twisted burning mass of wings and parts. I watched one such streak in an area where there were no flak flashes.

A split second after the white streak, what must have been a night fighter "lit up" and spun in. The bomber came down in 3 pieces, trailing skirts of red and emitting a terrible death whine. I also saw a bomber hit but then the fire went out and the plane seemed to continue on its way. Most often it was the other way around. The destruction in the sky seemed part of the destruction on the ground. The fires in the city reflected from scattered high cirrus and the flak barrage smoke at something like 20,000 feet could not be seen clearly. For fifteen to twenty minutes it was nearly [an] unbelievable scene and then a last bomb, the flak stopped and the planes drone home. The searchlights came on again and several low-flying Jerry fighters were seen headed in the direction of the retreating bomber stream. Cold and wet from crouching in the trench, I hit the sack. Twenty-four hours later there were still explosions, probably delayed action bombs.

I Had a Lot of Help

By William "Obie" O'Brien

William "Obie" O'Brien almost didn't make it into combat during his tenure with the 357th Fighter Group's 363rd Fighter Squadron. Obie told this story about how he almost missed his chance to fight the "Huns":

"When stationed at Oroville, California during 1943, Al Boyle, my assistant flight leader, shot me by accident with a .45 caliber service pistol. The bullet went through my upper right bicep without causing bone damage. The injury was to nerves and muscle. After hospitalization and being grounded, I walked around with my arm in a sling for about a month. My right hand was inoperative. The medical decision was to let nature take its course-if the nerve endings rejuvenated themselves to restore feeling then I had a chance to be of use to the Group. John Bricker Meyers the 363rd Squadron intelligence officer and a lawyer, had a briefcase full of court martial papers that remained unfilled. Boyle's charges were among the many. No one said a word to me about the future. Thanks to John Bricker Meyers!

Don Graham was my Squadron Commanding officer. I bled all over his pants, ruined them as I was being taken to the Oroville field dispensary. I owe him not only for the slacks but I'm sure he knew what Meyers was doing. Thanks to General Graham!

While recovering, I did a little work at Group Operations, till the Group moved to Casper, Wyoming and on to Shanks (POE), the staging area for shipment to England. At Camp Shanks, Lt. Colonel Edwin Chickering, Group Commander, called me to his office and said, 'Obee, you know you don't have to go with us.' I replied, 'Sir, I've come too far to turn back. I want to go if only to hold someone's hat.' He replied, 'You are dismissed.' Thanks to Colonel Chickering!

I made it on and off the *Queen Elizabeth* without assistance to prove to myself that I was not helpless and could do well using one arm. At Raydon Wood, our first base in England, I could shovel mud with the rest of the guys. My fingers were just numb but my arm motion was returning. Now the problem was what to do with me. During my recovery period there was little flying, (and) I was in the position that if I didn't soon log some flying time I would lose flight pay and the group needed pilots, not cripples. Soon the Group would receive new airplanes and combat would not be long in coming. There was only an L-4 (Cub) liaison aircraft on the flight line at Raydon.

Major John Barker, MD, and the Group flight surgeon, drove with me to the closest general hospital for a medical evaluation by a neurologist. After demonstrating to this captain that my freedom of motion was acceptable and being made uncomfortable while undergoing his sensitivity testing for two hours, I was asked to leave the room. I did, but kept the door ajar and heard the specialist tell Major Barker that I should be sent to the zone of the interior for discharge as I was unfit for duty.

I left the hospital with Major Barker and when getting in the jeep I asked him 'what are we going to do?' He asked me, 'Obee, can you fly an airplane?' When I said yes, he said, 'Go and fly.' I asked what about the specialist, (and) John Barker said, 'He doesn't fill out the forms, I do.' May God bless John Barker as I owe him a big bunch. That had to be the finest decision demonstrating wonderful medical judgment. I was flying the L-4 that afternoon at Raydon.

Physically, I may have encountered trouble pulling the emergency canopy release and the parachute D-ring, but no emergency occurred. Early in 1944 the first two fingers of the right (hand) were still numb; I had to use my left hand to fire the guns but later in the year all fingers had some feeling. Remember, it does not take great physical strength to fly an airplane. The RAF had several pilots missing one or more limbs.

So with the help of these fine people, I was able to continue with and complete my tour with the group."

Don't Give Me a P-39!

By Bill Overstreet

William "Bill" Overstreet

Don't give me a P-39
with an engine that's mounted behind.
It'll tumble and roll
and dig a big hole.
Don't give me a P-39!

(*This little ditty was sung by the 357th pilots.*)

Bill Overstreet was an original member of the 363rd Fighter Squadron and he remembers training in the P-39 Airacobra while in Tonopah, Nevada, and elsewhere. Here is his description of his fellow pilots, his hair-raising experiences flying the P-39, and close calls during combat:

I was the studious one in the group. Instead of doing the bars, I'd read books. (Author's note: After the passing of 357th Fighter Group Official Historian

Merle Olmsted, Mrs. Olmsted informed me that her husband had left his 357th collection to me. The day before Merle Olmsted's memorial, I met with his widow and son and they gave me this collection. In it was Bill Overstreet's Pilot's Information File and a letter from Bill to a friend or family member. On the back of this letter was a hand scribbled study guide written by Overstreet which he used to study for one of his early military aviation exams. The Pilot's Information File and the letter/study guide are now on display in the Captain Fletcher E. Adams 357th Fighter Group Museum in Ida, Louisiana.) There was no "pilot" type. Eddie Simpson and Jim Browning were the gentlemanly type, just like Anderson. Ellis Rogers had a master's degree in mathematics. At Tonopah, I remember (William) O'Brien taking off in the morning with two hours' fuel and not coming home until dark. He'd landed on the road by some bar. We all idolized (Lloyd) Hubbard. We were flying loops around the Golden Gate Bridge when his engine quit and he put the P-39 down in the surf, steering into the shore and didn't even scratch it or even get wet. And Irving Smith was a concert pianist. Imagine that, with tuxedo and tails!

I'm not making any claims to be a hot pilot, but I had a feel for engines and probably saved a couple of airplanes, nursing them home, but the P-39s were temperamental and tricky to fly. You'd move the stick on a P-39 an eighth of an inch and you could throw it into a spin before you knew what was happening.

357th Fighter Squadron P-39 Airacobras

An example of the P-39 Airacobra's unpredictable flight performance happened to Overstreet while in training in Santa Rosa, California on June 28, 1943. While dog fighting with Lloyd Hubbard, Herschel Pascoe, and Charles Peters, Overstreet suddenly lost control of his P-39.

"At some point in the rat race, I lost control of the airplane, possibly due to an over-control. The P-39 snap rolled to the left and then tumbled tail over nose, ending up in an inverted spin. At that moment it was obviously time to part company with the airplane. I pulled the release handle on the doors but they did not separate, possibly due to the air pressure on the doors. By getting my shoulder against one door and knees against the other, I was able to push enough to get the door off. I got out immediately and pulled the rip cord. When the chute opened, it slowed my fall at the same instant my feet hit the ground. I landed standing up, didn't even bend my knees. I landed amidst the wreckage of the P-39, right beside one of the prop blades and among the 37mm ammunition. Since the chute opened below the trees, the rest of the flight went back to base and reported my demise."

"I had a couple of close calls (later in the war). We dove into a wave of Germans and one put a 20mm cannon shell through my canopy. [It] took my helmet right off of my head but only gave me a burn. On a dive bombing mission, the release failed and I had to land with live bombs, ver-ry softly! And there was the time that I dove on a Messerschmitt and my sinuses swelled so badly that my eyes closed up. 'Daddy Rabbit' (Charles Peters) talked me back to base and through the landing."

Charles "Daddy Rabbit" Peters of New Orleans, Louisiana

Drop Tank Blues

By Frank Gailer

Brigadier General Frank Gailer, who also attended the Captain Fletcher E. Adams 357th Fighter Group Museum dedication, tells the story of learning a lesson about dropping tanks while flying missions with the 357th.

"I was a brand-new pilot in September, 1944, and was flying Chuck Yeager's wing during the first Arnhem mission. The call came over the radio 'bandits, drop tanks.' As Chuck's tanks fell off, I jettisoned mine. Everything went strangely quiet. It was just like the movie *Hell's Angels*-airplanes going around in a great melee and no sound. Chuck's plane was pulling away rapidly and then I realized I had not switched to internal fuel. I quickly switched tanks, the engine caught and I caught up with Chuck. Talk about lucky.

The next day, again at Arnhem, I was again on Chuck's wing and the same thing occurred! 'Bandits, drop tanks.' I dropped the tanks and again Chuck pulled away. I reacted a bit quicker this time, switched tanks and caught up with Chuck. I shared my first kill with Chuck on this mission. It shows how green I was and how lucky. Chuck never chewed me out-just smiled both times." [Author's note: Gailer and Yeager both went on to retire from the United States Air Force as Brigadier Generals and both pilots attended the official dedication of the Captain Fletcher E. Adams 357th Fighter Group Museum in Ida, Louisiana, in 2010.]

Chuck Yeager (center) with the ground crew of one of his famous Mustangs

The Price of War

(Operation Market Garden)
By Ted Conlin

It was late in the afternoon of a very weird day, weather wise. The 357th Fighter Group was prowling around northwestern Europe and my squadron, the 362nd was split into two halves with Captain Lowell Williams leading one flight. I was his element leader and had Jim Blanchard as my wingman. Williams took us north toward the Zuider Zee, the huge inland waterway in northern Holland. The weather to the east of us was clear and bright. To the west, a large front had rolled in off of the North Sea. It had many angry, multicolored storm clouds in it and they cast a gray pallor on the afternoon sky.

As we neared the Zee, we began to pick up a considerable amount of radio traffic, indicating a fight was beginning somewhere to the south of us. Williams ordered a course change to due south. When we altered our direction, the radio activity picked up almost at once. It was apparent to us that elements of our Group had gotten into action. We could hear guys cussing and shouting as they engaged the Germans. Most pilots, in the excitement of combat, would inadvertently hold down their mike buttons. This gave us a good picture of what was happening.

Williams gave the order to "drop tanks" and just as he did, the "fit hit the shan!" It was standard operating procedure, in a dogfight, to break down into the smallest unit. Williams and his wingman banked over and onto an Me-109. At that moment, three aircraft crossed my nose; an Me-109, a P-51, and another Me-109, all headed straight down. I rolled over and down to attack, chasing the "tail end Charley" 109. My closure was rapid and my new, high-tech gun sight was on. Just as I drew into firing range, I saw a cluster of 20mm shells arcing over my left wing. I broke off at once to handle my problem, climbing straight up to 10,000 feet. I knew I was able to gain altitude on my adversary. At this height, I went into a tight turn but saw nothing. I called for my wingman, Blanchard, and for my flight leader, Williams, but received no reply. Now I was mad and scared and wanted to shoot something. So I nosed over and dove down to the battle area. At 2,000 feet, I leveled off and circled. I saw nothing, zero, zilch! Nothing, except nine burning wrecks over an area of several square miles.

I amazes me that the sky can be filled with airplanes one minute, and totally empty the next. After milling around for several more minutes, I turned west, climbed up to altitude, and headed on a course for home base.

Years later, while attending a 357th Fighter Group reunion at Dayton, Ohio in 1987, I was discussing this battle with fellow pilot Colonel Robie Roberson and Master Sergeant Merle Olmsted, crew chief and official historian of our group. At that time, I told them that I was almost dead certain that the P-51 in the middle of the chase was our group leader that day, Major Ed Hiro, who was on his last mission. Both Hiro and my wingman, Blanchard, failed to return that day and both were later classified as killed in action.

A combat report was filed that day by a certain Lt. Wroblewski of the Luftwaffe and he claimed the destruction of Blanchard's Mustang. This report was filed after the war with the newly created German Air Force. The German officer stated that, after destroying Blanchard's P-51, he was immediately shot down himself, and later became a prisoner of the Canadians for the next two years. He was released in 1946.

Among the many ironies of the war, Wroblewski later became the German air attaché in Washington, D.C., and I believe that he became Chief of Staff of the German Air Force and retired as a general officer.

The aircraft of Lt. Blanchard was recovered in 1946, imbedded in a canal. Jim was found, still strapped into his seat in the Mustang, and a positive identification of his body was made.

Operation Market Garden was not a 100 percent success for the Allies. My personal opinion is that too many people knew when it was going to happen, where it was to happen, and who the major players were to be. The enemy were well prepared and waiting for us. They hit the British hard at Arnhem and our Eighty-second Airborne found them waiting at the Nijmegen Bridgehead.

Our 357th Fighter Group played an important role in this battle which took place over four days, for us, and we paid the price by losing key men and aircraft. Thus is extracted the "price of war."

Mistaken Identity

By Harvey Mace

Harvey Mace

Pilot Harvey Mace of the 362nd Fighter Squadron tells this story of the B-17 that was mistaken for a V-1 buzz bomb:

I had just gotten up one morning when I heard a buzz bomb approaching the coast (of England). I went outside in time to see the second or third round fired by the nearby triple A gun hit the bomb which exploded in a big orange and yellow flash. It was a quick kill.

Not long after I heard a very familiar sound of a B-17 returning from what must have (been) an abort from the morning mission. It was quickly followed by the sound of the gun going off again. I rushed outside to see the B-17 falling out of the clouds in flames, followed by several chutes and I later heard that all ten men got out. The B-17 had the misfortune of coming in at about the same altitude and track of the buzz bombs, and (the) gunners could not recognize the sound of the 150 mph B-17.

Many years later I became good friends with a Brit who was selling cars in California. One day we were sitting around shooting the breeze and I decided to needle him a bit with the B-17 story. He came back with, "You want to know something strange? I was the captain of that crew that shot the B-17 down."

I did not press a vindictive attack in view of the two Mosquitoes that we shot down. [Author's note: While researching my book *Bleeding Sky*, I found a passage in Fletcher Adams's war diary that mentioned one of these mistaken Mosquito shoot downs. Pilots R. D. Brown and Rodney Starkey of the 362nd Fighter Squadron attacked the British aircraft after mistaking it for an Me-110. I did include this story in my first book and as there were two "Browns" in the 362nd Fighter Squadron at that time and Adams mentioned no first names or initials in his diary. I later concluded it was R. D. Brown after finding proof that the other pilot named Brown was in the hospital at the time of the destruction of the Mosquito having suffered two broken legs after bailing out of his Mustang weeks earlier over the English Channel. After the incident, the other 357th pilots nicknamed Rod Starkey "Mosquito Mauler"!]

The Normandy Invasion

By Mark Stepelton

Captain Mark Stepelton on the wing of his P-51 *Lady Julie*

I was a young fighter pilot flying with the famed 357th Fighter Group stationed at Leiston, England. Our main mission was to escort the Eighth Air Force bombers on missions deep into Germany. We flew the greatest fighter plane of World War II, the P-51 Mustang. Our performance was outstanding.

We had flown many combat missions prior to June 6, 1944, during which time we had saved thousands of lives of bomber crews on long combat missions over enemy territory. Our fighter crew losses were serious and we all wondered when the Invasion would take place. Upon returning from a combat mission on June 4, 1944, we were told that our P-51s would be in a grounded condition temporarily. Little did we realize the magnitude of the upcoming events.

Our ground crews began painting white stripes on the wings of our Mustangs and even then we didn't realize those stripes would soon be recognized as

"D-Day" stripes. The purpose was for our ground troops to easily recognize our aircraft as friendly planes.

When not flying, our favorite meeting place was the Officers Club, so it was there, about 9:00pm or 2100 hours military time on June 5, 1944, that an announcement was made that all combat flight officers would report to the Group Briefing Room immediately. Of course, the excitement was tremendous. No previous combat briefing had created this much attention, even our first mission over Berlin, Germany.

Identification was required at the Group Briefing Room and one could feel that something tremendously vital to us was about to take place. We were seasoned combat pilots by now and had seen many fine friends lost in combat. We felt confident in our abilities as fighter pilots to succeed in any mission assigned to us.

We were called to "attention" as our Fighter Group Commander, Colonel Donald Graham, entered the briefing room. He immediately requested the Intelligence Officer to brief us first about the "Top Secret" aspects of the mission we were about to hear.

We were sworn to secrecy. We were not to tell our ground crews or talk to anyone. Phone calls were "off limits." Our group commander then made a very terse announcement that we had been assigned to fly cover for the greatest of all combat missions, the "Invasion of Europe" by our combat ground forces en route by sea. This mission would be called "D-Day" and was to begin during the early hours of June 6, 1944.

CAPT. STEPELTON - 364 F.G. E.T.O. 1944

I well remember a feeling of supreme excitement, similar to the feeling I'm now experiencing as my mind races back to those indescribable events. We were all young men who a few years before had never dreamed of being given such a huge responsibility. Our assigned mission was to protect the Normandy Beachhead from attack by German fighters. The U. S. ground combat troops would be asked to invade France while heading right into the teeth of the seasoned German Wehrmacht forces entrenched there. Only a few of our troops had combat experience and needed to be reassured that the only aircraft above them would be friendly.

The Group Commander, Don Graham, ended the briefing by stating that we should retire as soon as possible because a specific mission briefing would be held at our Squadron Briefing Room at 2:00 a.m. How could we possibly sleep with such a tremendous mission about to be dropped into our laps? The responsibility seemed awesome. Needless to say, I couldn't sleep. I laid down on my cot, fully dressed in my flight suit and sought the help of our Lord Jesus Christ. I prayed for the safety of the thousands of young men in those ships, waiting for the signal to board their Higgins boats. I had no thoughts or concerns for my own safety, as I already had 38 combat missions under my belt.

I didn't look at my watch when an officer entered our Nissen hut and quietly told us to report to the Squadron Briefing Room immediately. Now the excitement was beyond description. Only combat pilots were allowed at this briefing. The world's best squadron commander, Lt. Col. John Storch of Long Beach, California, gave us individual assignments in specific areas along the Normandy Invasion areas. We noted that a light rain was falling and the sky was very black; however, all of England was "blacked out." Due to weather conditions, we would fly to our assigned area in pairs. My great buddy, Captain Leroy Ruder from Nekoosa, Wisconsin, would be my partner. Of course, you realize that a P-51 Mustang holds only one person, so we would take off in pairs and be on our own from the moment of our departure.

John Storch

After synchronization of our watches, we received our assigned "start engine" time. We raced to our revetments where our planes were parked and sporting a new set of white stripes on the wings. I carefully checked my plane which I had named *Lady Julie*. She was no lady. My crew chief and armorer knew that something important was about to happen because we had never taken off at this time of the night. No questions were asked and the only comment made to me by my crew chief as I strapped into my Mustang was, "Take care of yourself" as he patted me on the back.

Waiting for "start engine" time always allowed time for reflection about your lost buddies, and fond memories of times back home. I was never afraid of being shot down. Previous dogfights had given me self-confidence. The sound of the Rolls Royce Merlin engines of our Mustangs barking as they were energized jolted me back to the realization of the job ahead. Captain Ruder began taxiing to the takeoff runway ahead of me. The nose of the P-51 is so long that it is necessary to S turn the aircraft in order to observe the airplane ahead of you.

We finally reached the area of the active runway, turned the Mustang so as to avoid damaging the plane following you and went through the "takeoff" check. My engine roared to a high pitch; the sweet sound found only in the Merlin engine.

The rain now was rather severe. No turning back due to bad weather on this mission though. Captain Ruder taxied out to his takeoff position and I joined him on his right side. He motioned to me with a forward motion of his hand and with the throttle firewalled we raced down the runway and zoomed upward into the black night. Leroy turned out over the North Sea and headed southwest toward the greatest event in our history, the D-Day Normandy Invasion.

Captain Leroy Ruder was an "ace" and a very fine fighter pilot. He was one of those pilots who was extremely confident of his capabilities and was not afraid of anything. We timed our approach to arrive over Normandy before dawn. As we approached the coast, we dropped down from our approach altitude to a very low altitude and began our patrol. *No German fighter pilot would approach the Invasion landing area that Leroy and I were responsible for!*

As dawn slowly arrived, we could see the vast armada of ships heading toward Normandy; a sight that is etched into my memory for all the days of my life. I prayed hard for the safety of our landing troops. I cannot begin to describe the panorama unfolding before my eyes, so vast and powerful looking. As I watched, the large battleships began firing toward the shore.

After about four hours of patrolling, Captain Ruder called me over the radio to state that he had been hit by ground fire and was going down. We were not in close formation. He crashed and died soon thereafter. The loss of my friend, Leroy, was so shocking to me because it happened so fast and it was beyond his ability to avoid. Now, I found myself patrolling alone with a very heavy heart.

Captain Leroy Ruder, a very brave and experienced pilot, always extremely aggressive against the German fighter pilots, now lost his life during the early phase of D-Day. He was the only pilot in our Fighter Group and the entire Eighth Air Force Fighter Command to lose his life on June 6, 1944.

Finally, as my fuel became dangerously low, I returned to our base at Leiston, England. I had logged the longest combat flying time of the Group on this mission and as a result, I could barely climb out of my Mustang.

The cockpit of the P-51 is very confining and not a place for anyone who is claustrophobic. I was the last Yoxford Boy to arrive back at Station 373 after that momentous first mission.

After debriefing, I went directly to my barracks and slept for two hours. I was awakened by an announcement that we should assemble at the Squadron Briefing Room again in forty-five minutes. I had not undressed and was still in my flight suit. Even though I was extremely tired, the excitement of this great day kept all of us young pilots thriving on adrenaline. At the Squadron Briefing, we learned that we would patrol the back of the German lines behind the "beachhead" and we were ordered to destroy anything moving toward the front. About an hour later, we were back in our P-51s for another "area support" mission on this great day.

We located a train moving in the direction of the Invasion area. We circled the train at a very low altitude, knowing that if it was moving, it was the enemy. The engineer had pulled the engine into a tunnel, leaving the passenger cars exposed. While making a circle, our engine noises alerted the German troops who then flooded out of the cars into the area next to the tunnel. We knew what we had to do in order to ensure that these German combat troops never reached the Invasion site.

After several hours of patrolling at low altitudes, we returned to Leiston. I was totally exhausted as my crew chief helped me to, once again, climb out of my cockpit. Now it was dark and raining again. After debriefing, all I could think about was getting some sleep. I had logged this combat mission a 5.25 hours, somewhat less than my first mission of the day. I considered myself lucky. The combat troops invading Normandy had no place to sleep.

357th Fighter Group

Random Shots
(A Photographic Retrospective)

The photographs on the following pages come from many sources. I have included them here because many of them are extremely rare and have never been published in books about the 357th Fighter Group before. The montage is in no particular order and all of the pictures were taken at different times during World War II and shortly after it ended.

An unknown officer at Raydon Wood, England

The control tower at Raydon Wood

An exterior shot of the Raydon Wood control tower

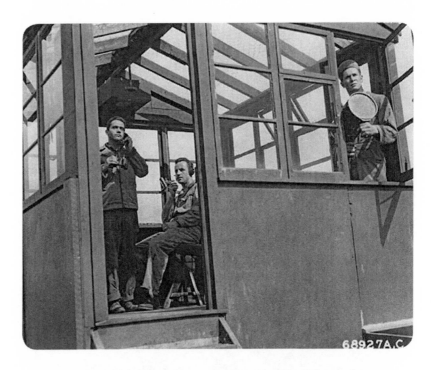

The observation shack above the Raydon Wood control tower

Sightseeing in Raydon Wood

A group shot of 357th pilots in front of a B-17

Bud Nowlin (right) and crew on his P-51 Mustang which may have been named *Hells Bells* or *Vicious Viv*

A very popular stop for many of the 357th pilots after missions

The 357th Fighter Group Command site at Leiston, England

The B-24 Liberator *Crow's Nest* at Leiston Field

A group shot of the 362nd Fighter Squadron's *Rat Patrol*

Cleaning up after a fire at the armament shack

A typical line shack at Leiston built from drop tank crates and tar paper

**Myron Becraft (left) and Jim Gasser (right) inspect remnants
of the defeated Luftwaffe**

B-17s seek refuge at Station 373 (Leiston Field)

Typical Nissen huts at Leiston, England

357th pilot John C. Howell and "Yippie"

**Paul Hatala's *Nellie Jean* after it was bellied into Czechoslovakia by
James Monahan**

Roland Wright stands on a P-38 Lightning with German markings

A 354th Fighter Group Mustang which crashed at Leiston Field

A 364th Fighter Squadron blister hangar at Leiston

**The long and the short of it, Howard Egeland and "Big Jim" Dendy
during early flight training**

Carson, England, Hill, and Kerr

Belated birthday greetings to der Fuhrer

Tom Martinek, George Roepke, and Roger Stops with the P-51 _Morning Star_

Parmer and Morrisey loading the .50 caliber guns of a 362nd Mustang

A forlorn Me-262 at Neubiberg, Germany, after the war

Memorial service for FDR held at Leiston

R. D. Brown, the consummate "Ladies' Man" meets his match

Jim Gasser touches down in G4-K *Muddy*, named for his mother

Franklin and crew with the P-51 *Cherokee Kid*

Shoo Shoo Baby **escorts the Big Friends**

Queuing up for chow at the 357th enlisted men's mess hall

The 357th Fighter Group photography lab

The 357th Fighter Group control tower with line shack in the foreground

Hurry Home Honey **escorts B-17s over Europe**

Glen Zarnke and his P-51 Mustang *Junior Miss II*

Glendon Davis and Thomas "Little Red" Harris

**Willie Williams, Robie Roberson, Tom Beemer, and
Johnny England examine underwear sent to the
362nd Fighter Squadron by Hollywood starlets**

Only fighter pilots could get away with this and still maintain their manhood!
Three of them model the skivvies sent to them by Hollywood's biggest female
stars, including Rita Hayworth,

The 357th Fighter Group's bomb dump at Leiston, England

Jim Sehl and the crew of *Naughty Auty!*

Jesse Frey and the crew of his P-51 Mustang *Ain't Misbehavin'*, including crew chief Pasquale Buzzeo on the far right

A Yoxford Boy "toasts" a recent victory

Kit Carson directs runway traffic during a typical winter day at
Station 373 as the 357th Fighter Group takes off on another mission

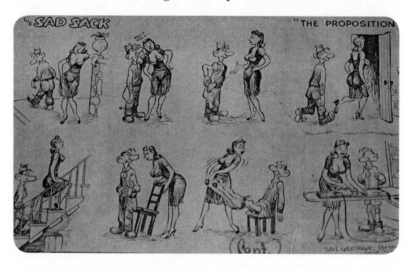

This comic strip must have amused Fletcher Adams as he clipped it out of
Stars and Stripes and sent it to his wife Aline in Ida, Louisiana, sometime
during the winter or spring of 1944

**357th pilots sightseeing in Italy while returning
from the Russian Shuttle mission**

**Fletcher Adams and his wife Aline (third and fourth from left)
party with other members of the 362nd Fighter Squadron and their
better halves in Pocatello, Idaho shortly before disembarking for the war**

There is no doubt as to what was on the minds of the crew of this
458th Bomb Group B-24 Liberator

Skara, Sehl, and Powers tempt fate while taking a break at the Leiston Field
bomb dump area

Tom Norris's P-51 Mustang *Miss Satan* with her ground crew

**Joe Jenkins's C5-M *CheeChee Gal* had seen much
better days before this picture was taken after it crashed
on takeoff with Ray Sparks at the controls**

Glen Zarnke's AAF pilot's license

Jim Roughgarten of the 362nd Fighter Squadron flew the P-51 Mustang *Jersey Bounce* and regaled the author with stories about Fletcher Adams at the 357th Fighter Group reunion in Columbus, Ohio in 2007

Colonel C. E. "Bud" Anderson, the 363rd Fighter Squadron's "Biggest Gun" at his induction into the Aviation Hall of Fame in 2008 (note that his picture appears on the wall above his head alongside *Apollo* astronauts Bill Anders and Neil Armstrong)

Herschel Hill and his P-51 Mustang *Texas Ranger*

DRYDEN

SE: 0928 09/0 TO: 0920 0934 TH: SO: 0954

N. HAGUE	120	28	104°	10
R/V.E.NORDHAUSEN	290	64	102°	11.
TARGET	40	19	145°	11
S. TARGET	35	04	164°	11
S, FULDA	110	36	272°	12
S, MARSBURG	45	14	316°	12
S, DUMMERLAKE	120	38	354°	13
N, W. DUMMER W.	20	05	317	13
L/B EGMOND	140	46	277°	14
BASE	130	36	264°	14

MIN. GAS. 150/220   SUN - 175°

CRSE HOME - 270° - 58 MIN - 307° 58 MIN

S - DUMMER L.   F - NORNBERG
H - HANNOVER   T - MEININGEN
O - NORDHAUSEN   E - STUTTGART
P - WEIMAR   R - WURZBURG
L - PLAUEN   W: 330° - 35 MPH
I - COBURG

BOMBERS:

FIGHTERS: 23 FEB. 1945

RECALL: WEIMAR AREA

AVERAGE COURSE HOME:

SUN FROM TARGET:

Joe Shea's mission notes for February 23, 1945

**Burret, Layman, Austin, Barber (standing left to right),
and Fletcher Adams (kneeling)**

**Postcard from Fletcher Adams to his mother while in New York before
departure on the *Queen Elizabeth***

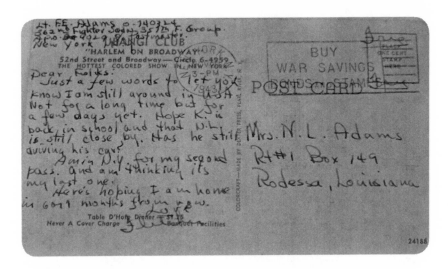

The back of the Ubangi Club postcard

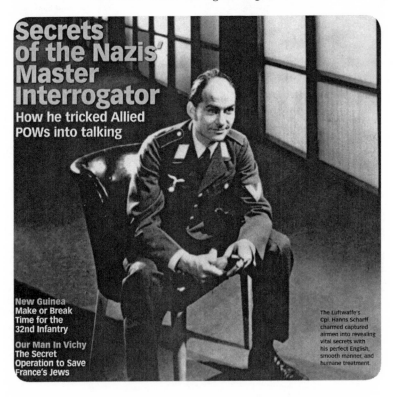

The cover of World War II magazine featuring Hanns Scharff, the "master interrogator" of the Luftwaffe at Oberursel

**A collection of patches from the Eighth Air Force,
the 357th Fighter Group, and the three squadrons**

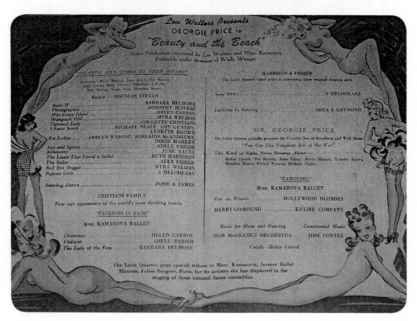

A nightclub program from New York in 1943 sent home by Fletcher Adams

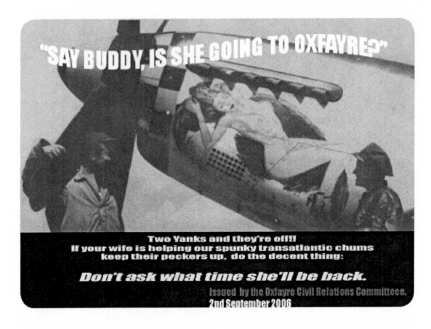

A rather racy commemorative poster from Oxfayre in 2006

Don Bochkay, Chuck Yeager, Jim Browning, and Bud Anderson

**Franklin Mint reproduction of Bill Overstreet's *Berlin Express*
on display at the Captain Fletcher E. Adams 357th Fighter Group
Museum in Ida, Louisiana**

Colonel Arval "Robie" Roberson of the 362nd Fighter Squadron

The *Stars and Stripes* headline says it all

Memories of a Wingman

By Ted Conlin

Jim Sehl, Ted Conlin, and Howard Egeland

The date was July 25, 1944, the time was around 11:30 a.m. and the 357th Fighter Group was on the prowl. Dollar Blue flight and Green flight were enjoying one of those rare *"Frei Jagd"* missions (in English, a free hunt or fighter sweep) as our enemies would call it. We had made landfall near the invasion beaches of France in the Northern Normandy Peninsula and were ranging south down near Kennes.

Captain Becker was leading Blue flight and Captain Carson, Green flight. Carson maintained about 600 yards between the two flights to give us all maneuvering room. After about fifteen minutes, Captain Becker began a sweeping left turn to head back north. Kit then executed his easy left bank to follow in trail. As I recall Green flight was slightly higher than Blue as we approached the famous City of Lights, Paris, the most glamorous city in Europe.

The two flights arrived on the western edge of the city; in this area were the large railroad marshalling yards. It was noon when one of our guys called in that P-38s were bombing and strafing below. We all looked down, and at that moment a gaggle of Focke Wulf 190s and Messerschmitt 109s appeared dead ahead of us and at our altitude. I do not think that they could have seen us because they rolled over and started an attack on the P-38s below. I was flying as number two on Captain Kit Carson's wing. He rolled over, and I followed him down as he tacked onto the rear of a FW-190. The element leader and the number three man in Green flight, Captain John Pugh, broke away and jumped on the tail of an Me-109 that was heading down.

A rare photograph of John Pugh's P-51 Mustang *Geronimo* sporting large red and yellow diamonds on its nose (this was an early experiment by the 362nd Fighter Squadron's painter at the end of the "White Nose" era)

The game was on, and I was in a wild ride earthward trying to stay in position behind Carson. At the time, it seemed that we were almost vertical chasing the 190 and the pilot was doing big barrel rolls as he headed downward, trying to keep us off of his tail, but we stayed right with him. As Captain Carson closed into range, he started to get strikes on the enemy's ship. This and the ground coming up rather rapidly caused the German pilot to flare out and level off.

We were now at approximately 300 feet and Kit was getting hits all over the FW-190 when the Hun's engine failed! We were heading east just above the Grand Armee-Champs Elysees Boulevard. It looked like the Focke Wulf was going to crash into the Arch de Triumph; the pilot must have been dead because he did not try to bail out.

Captain Carson broke away and I was fascinated watching the propeller windmilling as the FW-190 headed toward its fatal end, when all of the sudden, I realized that Carson was gone and there I was at 300 feet with every enemy soldier with a weapon firing at me. The Germans also had antiaircraft guns on the roofs of the buildings and in the parks and they were all concentrating on me. I saw the River Seine off to my right so I swung over and down into it as low as I could without becoming a boat, while hugging the North Bank which is about fifty feet high.

Computer graphics artist Len Krenzler spent months recreating the scene described by Ted Conlin in this story. Note the German soldier (bottom left) firing his service pistol at Carson and Conlin.

The guns could not be lowered down enough to get at me there, so I flew about two miles along the river until it looked safe for me to break out and head home. I came up from the river and started a gradual climb for the French coast and then on to Leiston. When I arrived back at home Base, I found that Captain Carson had taken the same route out.

In summing up this story, I had a new appreciation of the daring and flying skills of the man who would become the leading ace of the 357th Fighter Group.

Nowotny's Revenge

By Richard "Pete" Peterson

On January 20, 1945, I was Red flight leader and my wingman was Ernest Tiede. Lt. Ed "Buddy" Haydon was my element leader and his wingman was Lt. Roland Wright and White flight was being led by Lt. Dale Karger. I have forgotten what the original mission was, but about the time that we were to return home, we engaged two Me-262s near Brunswick, Germany. It appeared that one 262 pilot was checking the other one out in the jet. They did not run away, but seemed to want to engage in a fight. We were at about 20,000 feet and the 262's split; one went down to about 18,000 feet and the other stayed at 22,000 feet. Both flew in a large, lazy circle, one opposite the other, with me and the flight in the middle. It looked to me that the upper jet was waiting for me to attack the lower one. I called Lt. Karger and told him to turn back as if he were going home and to climb back up to attack the high jet while we circled. Lt. Karger and his flight did just that and the upper 262 never saw them return. They shot him down without any trouble and then Karger's flight headed for home. When the upper Me-262 was eliminated, the remaining jet headed down for home in a hurry.

I rolled over, split-essed, and went to full power. In no time, I hit compressibility with the loss of all control at speeds in excess of 650mph. After finally getting control, I pulled out in a wide sweeping arc and pulled up behind the jet for a perfect shot at six o'clock. Unfortunately I was out of trim and my tracers went right over the top of his canopy. He hit the throttle and left me in a cloud of kerosene exhaust as if I were standing still. My flight had caught up with me so we headed for Lechfeld Airbase. This, we thought, would be where he was heading and maybe we could catch him landing.

We flew over Lechfeld at about 6,000 feet and there were about 100 Messerschmitt 262s parked nose to tail on the inactive side of the field. This meant they were out of fuel, pilots, or both. We were not sure which way the jet would approach the runway, so Lt. Tiede and myself cruised toward the south end. Lt. Haydon and Lt. Wright spotted him coming in from the north, so Edward "Buddy" Haydon went for the jet, but he was too high and made an easy target for the gunners. Lt. Haydon was hit and on the R/T he said he was on fire. He pulled up to 400 feet, bailed out and landed on the airfield.

Edward "Buddy" Haydon

Later he was captured and became a POW. Lt. Roland Wright, following Haydon, was at a very low altitude and the flak missed him, but he did not miss the Me-262. He shot it down on its approach to the field. [Author's note: Shortly before this incident, on November 8, 1944, Lt. Buddy Haydon was involved in a dogfight involving him, a P-51 pilot named Ernest Fiebelkorn of the Twentieth Fighter Group, and the famous Luftwaffe ace Walter Nowotny. Nowotny was Germany's third greatest ace with hundreds of kills to his credit, and was the world's first commander of a jet fighter group.

Walter Nowotny

After Fiebelkorn fired into Nowotny's Me-262, Haydon took over and began to jockey for firing position behind the jet as both he and Nowotny flew through the low cloud deck. Before Buddy Haydon could fire a single shot, Walter Nowotny flew the Me-262 into the ground. The jet burst into flames and Nowotny burned to death. According to German Luftwaffe personnel who were monitoring the radio at the time, Walter Nowotny's last words were, "I'm on fire. Mein Gott! I'm burning up!" followed by a garbled scream. Walter Nowotny was twenty-three years old when he died.

Walter Nowotny's Grave

Later when Haydon was shot down and placed in a German stalag luft camp, he hid the pilot's wings and other military paraphernalia that he had been wearing during the Nowotny encounter until the camp was liberated. These items were later given to this author, and as of today these personal effects of Lt. Buddy Haydon are on display in the Captain Fletcher E. Adams 357th Fighter Group Museum in Ida, Louisiana.]

The remaining three of us reassembled south of Lechfeld and I called for them to check their fuel. We would need approximately 135 gallons to get us back to Leiston. I had enough but Lt. Wright, who had been "tail-end Charlie" only had eighty-five gallons or less. It was pretty obvious that we were not going to make it home, so we needed to find a friendly airport as soon as possible.

Flying at about 8,000 feet, deep inside Germany, in really nasty weather, we headed west through the weather front on instruments only. By now, I was getting concerned about Lt. Wright as by now, his fuel was getting really low. Flying my wing, on instruments, he would not have a chance if his engine cut out. We finally broke out of the overcast and spotted a large town near a river and we turned toward it. Lo and behold, there was an airfield covered with snow but no tracks from aircraft traffic, and there appeared to be an Me-109 parked near a hangar.

I told Roland Wright to land tail first because I didn't know the depth of the snow, and to wave his arms if the airport was friendly. If it was not, I told him to get clear as I planned to shoot up his airplane. After Wright landed, out came a vehicle full of people to the Mustang, and as we continued circling, Roland eventually began waving his arms. After seeing his signal, Tiede and I both landed.

We were southeast of Paris at Auxerre, France, and the front line was sixty kilometers down the road at Dijon. Auxerre had a small company of MPs as the town had recently been liberated. We asked them to help get fuel. The gasoline was ordered and was supposed to come up from General Patton's tank corps but we didn't know how long it would take.

Finally, five days later, a truck arrived with five-gallon "Jerry" cans, so we filled up the planes and, in lovely weather, we flew off for England. By the time we got to the middle of the English Channel, the weather had turned against us. It was a solid wall of fog from 1,500 feet all the way down to the water. It looked like a wall of concrete along a straight vertical line. We radioed Leiston Field for information and heard quite a roar from them, as the last they heard was that we were in combat with the Me-262s. Major Gates got on the radio and said there was no way we would be able to land at Station 373 (Leiston) as the base was fogged in solid. He thought that we might have to bail out near the base. Can you imagine that after what we had been through to get us and our planes back? I decide to give an instrument approach a try!

At mid-channel, we were flying in a "V" formation with both wingmen stacked above me as I started a letdown in an attempt to get below the fog. I got down to where the altimeter read "0" and suddenly one of the guys said "Pete, you better get up here . . . . a wave has just gone by!!" At this point it was decided to climb above the fog to about 2,000 feet. We arrived in the approximate area of Leiston field and asked the tower to fire a rocket so we could get a fix, the rocket appeared above the fog so I told Lt Wright and Lt Tiede to circle that point whilst I tried an instrument approach.

Since the longest runway at Leiston had a bearing of 240 degrees, it gave me a clue that maybe I could apply my high school geometry to an instrument letdown and we could then make it in. So I headed out a little way toward the channel and turned straight North at 0 degrees. As I kept talking on the radio for bearings, they fed me bearings to the field back to me, First 300 degrees, then 290, then 280. When they called 270 degrees (making a 90 degree angle with my heading true North), I clocked the time that it took for the bearing to change to 240. Twice that time was the time it would take me to reach the field on a heading of 240 degrees which was the alignment with the runway. The runway 240 heading and a heading of 270 makes a 30/60 right triangle as I flew North. In a 30/60 right triangle, the side opposite the 30 is half the length of the hypotenuse. In this case, the "Hypotenuse" would be my line of approach toward the 240 bearing. As I descended toward the field I got down to about 50 feet above the ground, I could see straight down and spotted the end of the runway! I knew then that we could make it by repeating what I had done. I climbed back up on instruments and picked up Lt Roland Wright who flew off my right wing and we went through the same routine, we started the approach, I put down my landing gear; Lt Wright lowered his and stayed back just far enough to still keep me in sight and follow me down. I dropped flaps; he did the same. As we got to about 50 feet I saw the runway and called it out to him, he picked up the sight of the runway and landed, I then did the same with Lt Tiede and he landed. I was last and did a tight 360 degree turn at about 50 feet off the ground and landed.

The people in the tower could hear us; could hear the tyres squeal on landing; but could not see us. At no time did the tower see us until we taxied by. The tower and DF guys did a great job without them we would not have made it. Without an automatic pilot, instrument landing system, or GCA to assist us, we managed to get down safely without losing airplanes or pilots. It was the best flying that I had ever done . . . . or ever since!

A Day to Remember

By Leonard "Kit" Carson

Another shot of Kit Carson and his P-51K Mustang *Nooky Booky IV*

I was leading Blue flight of Dollar Squadron (362nd) providing escort for the 353rd Fighter Group en route to strafe the oil reserve stores at Leipzig. We were in the vicinity of Magdeburg, Germany, when two large formations of bandits were reported. One of the formations, still unidentified, made a complete turn from a head on position and made an initial attack on us from our eight o'clock. We dropped tanks, turned, and met them head on. We wheeled again and tacked onto the rear of the formation which consisted of fifty to seventy-five Focke Wulf 190's (Butcher Birds). I closed to about 300 yards behind the nearest one and fired a medium burst with no lead, getting numerous strikes. He started to burn and went into a turning dive to the left. I believe the pilot must have been dead as he never recovered from the dive. The 190 crashed and exploded. I returned to the main part of the fight again closing on the Focke Wulf nearest to me. I opened fire once again at about 300 yards, firing two short bursts resulting in .50 caliber strikes all over the cockpit and engine. He started to smoke and dropped out of the formation, then rolled to the right until he was in a split-ess position, never recovering from this attitude. I saw the 190 crash and burn, and the pilot did not survive.

Returning again to the scrap, I pulled into the nearest enemy aircraft at about 400 yards and fired a short burst, noticing a few hits. The German broke violently to the left and I broke with him. I pulled a lead on him and fired a long burst, getting strikes on his engine and cockpit. The FW-190 started to smoke and burn badly; the pilot jettisoned his cockpit canopy and bailed out. I watched him fall for some distance but did not see his chute open. The Focke Wulf crashed about fifty yards from a house in a small town. I could still see the main battle about two miles ahead of me and as I started to get near the fray, I saw a straggler on the deck. I dropped down to engage him but he saw me coming and turned left away from me. I gave chase for about five minutes before I caught him. I opened fire at 400 yards getting hits on the right side of his fuselage. The pilot turned sharply to the right and I picked up a few degrees of lead on him, firing two more bursts and getting more strikes on the fuselage. The German jettisoned his canopy and bailed out. As I was chasing this enemy aircraft, another formation of about thirty to forty FW-190s passed about 500 feet above me and 1,500 feet in front of my mustang, but they made no attempt to engage me or to help their fellow Hun. They continued on a heading of twenty or thirty degrees.

I pulled up and set course for home base when another 190 made an attack from seven o'clock high. My wingman and I broke into him and he wheeled around into a zooming climb. I chased him, gaining slowly. Suddenly, he dropped his nose and headed for the deck. I gave chase and caught him in about five minutes. I opened fire at 400-450 yards but missed. Moments later, I closed further and fired another short burst getting strikes on his fuselage. After his plane began to smoke, I fired again as he made a hard turn to the right and again I observed more hits on the fuselage. The pilot then jettisoned his canopy and I broke off my attack to the right, expecting him to bail out of the stricken aircraft. I waited for the pilot to jump, but he didn't, so I turned back in to engage him again. I was still about 700 yards away when the German pulled the nose of his Focke Wulf up sharply and left his ship. His parachute opened a couple of seconds later. During the whole encounter, my wingman, Flight Officer O. T. Ridley, remained with me. His performance as a wingman could not have been surpassed. I claim five Focke Wulf 190s destroyed in the air.

Komets and Crippled Forts

By Harvey Mace

**Harvey Mace heads out on another mission to
Berlin (Mace still has the map in his left hand)**

For the bulk of my combat missions while based at Leiston England,
I flew a P-51 that I had named *Sweet Helen* after my wife. I was in the 362nd
Fighter Squadron and my Mustang's code was G4-B. [Author's note: Mace was
an original member of the 362nd having arrived (along with the entire 357th
Fighter Group) in Scotland aboard the *Queen Elizabeth* on November 29, 1943.]
I had a really great ground crew that looked after *Sweet Helen* for me. My crew

chief was Ray Smith from Arkansas. He was a very quiet and reserved man and never really showed any emotion.

I recall one particular mission that had started early one morning. My P-51 was running sweet and we were headed into the "Land of the Hun" once again. I was leading my flight to a target deep inside Germany this day and we had started running into some anti-aircraft fire when my element leader and his wingman got separated from us, leaving me with only my wingman to continue on with. We carried on and when the bombers had finished their jobs, they and the rest of our fighters headed for home.

Normally, I would have been very happy to have stuck with them, but I was on the far side of the target at the time and had just spotted the unmistakable smoke trail of a climbing Me-163 "Komet" which was flying a little deeper into Germany. The Me-163 was no threat to anyone, but I was young and thought it would make a good trophy if I could spot it on its glide back down to its airfield. I rushed to the spot I estimated to be the area where it would be, but I think it was wishful thinking on my part as I searched for some time and found nothing. So I turned back and headed for home.

Very shortly, I must have passed over the most experienced flak battery in the whole of Germany. The noise of the explosions rang loudly in my ears and all of the twisting, turning, and climbing maneuvers I could muster just could not shake them off. I was in a bad position that seemed to go on for a long time, but eventually, I was able to escape their grasp. I was so lucky not to have been hit, that from then on, I carefully changed course every few seconds in order to avoid another similar experience. The rest of the Group had long since disappeared into the distant sky and there was no chance of me catching up with them.

It was not very long until I came upon a badly damaged B-17 limping home on considerably less than four engines. The pilot of the Flying Fortress reported that he had injured crewmen on board and that his instrument panel had been shot up. Consequently, he and his co-pilot were unable to tell if they were heading in the right direction. I got them on the correct heading and also gave the Fort a close escort until we were both over friendly territory, but then I had to get myself back to Leiston Field with the remaining fuel I had left.

All of the extra activity of avoiding the heavy flak and helping the crippled B-17 had really used up a whole lot of my fuel reserves. As a result of all of this, I landed back at Leiston some forty-five minutes after everyone else. For a ground crew, that is a very worrying time, as on many occasions it would mean that your pilot and his Mustang had been lost. As I was taxiing to my hardstand, I could see my crew chief, Ray Smith, sitting with his head in his hands. As I rolled up into my spot on the hardstand, Ray looked up and broke into the biggest smile I have ever seen. The smile and the relief on his face has stayed in my memory ever since!

The Hard Way Home

By George A. Behling, Jr.

George A. Behling, Jr.

It is ancient history. Specific dates, places, and names are forgotten, but the personal experiences and thoughts remain as vivid in my memory as if they had occurred only yesterday.

The Prologue

I was leading an element with the 362nd Fighter Squadron, 357th Fighter Group, on January 14, 1945. This was my forty-second combat mission over Germany. Later, after the war was over for me, I found out what a memorable day this had been for the Yoxford Boys when I had a chance to read the newspaper clippings that my dad had saved for me.

When I climbed into my P-51 Mustang *Chi-Lassie* that morning, my crew chief remarked that the spark plugs in the fighter's Merlin engine were "leaded," but he believed that they *were good for one more mission.*

All that morning as the other pilots and I dressed, ate breakfast, and prepared for takeoff, we heard the constant drone of the B-17 heavy bombers overhead. A good idea of their plight is fairly accurately portrayed in the postwar film, *Twelve O'clock High,* starring Gregory Peck and Dean Jagger. Because the bombers flew slower than our fighters, we took off later and caught up. When we arrived at our escort position over the North Sea, the B-17s stretched in a continuous line as far as I could see forward and backward, all headed for Berlin. In order not to pass the bombers, we flew above them and zigzagged.

The Preflight

Before getting into the details of the attack, a little "background music." I arrived in England during August of 1944. I should have been dead several times. Once, on takeoff when I couldn't correct for torque, I drifted to the left and almost tore my element leader's tail off. Needless to say, I was severely reprimanded.

Another time, we came down through overcast over the North Sea so close to the water that it was an absolute miracle that I was able to pull up in time. Once, we went through overcast so thick that I lost sight of my flight leader, had to go on instruments, and get through it myself. My wingman wasn't so fortunate. *He spun in.* I've lived with this, blaming myself, but rationalizing that it was *war* and these things will happen.

Coming back from another mission, the spark plugs in my Merlin engine were so loaded with lead that it sounded as if I was flying a "Tin Lizzie" instead of a P-51 Mustang. I decided to chance going across the North Sea and barely made it back to the field. My crew chief was aghast and stunned that the plane could be brought back in that condition!

Then, there was the time we came in to land with a low ceiling and a group of B-17 Flying Fortresses flying at about 200 feet crossed our path just as we were about to set down. It is a wonder that there weren't more midair collisions. Today, the FAA would have conniptions!

Not all of my memories of that time were bad though, such as the day I made my first kill. It was December 24, 1944, and on that Christmas Eve I shot down a Focke Wulf 190. I dove on him and almost outsmarted myself. My speed was so excessive that only a completely closed throttle and full flaps kept me from passing him and becoming the hunted instead of the hunter. My speed equaled his just as I came abreast. We looked each other over briefly, and then my plane rapidly lost speed. I kicked right rudder, slid over behind him and pressed the trigger. The German plane began to disintegrate; the pilot bailed out and somersaulted over me just barely missing my prop and canopy.

After the kill came the *real* test. I realized that I would have to *roll* during my approach to the runway (something I had never done), signifying my first victory. I found a convenient cloud, dove at it as if it were the runway, pulled up and jammed the stick to the left. To my amazement, the Mustang rolled, came around upright and I was still above the cloud! I tried it several more times-all were successful.

I proceeded home, dove at the runway, pulled up, pushed the stick to the left, held my breath, rolled, came out upright, banked to the left, lowered my gear and flaps, circled and landed. Eureka! This tryst is recorded on 16mm film so brittle that I'm almost afraid to touch it. It's probably the greatest record of a kill ever made. No one, not even *Chuck Yeager* would ever do it on purpose. But it did astound the personnel reviewing the film and raised me to hero level. Of course, I did not reveal the sorted details that I have just disclosed. Besides, the glory was erased several days later when I fired at a British Spitfire, mistaking it for a Messerschmitt. For that, I got my second reprimand and four weeks of aircraft recognition classes.

One last anecdote. In late December 1944, on a very cold night, I made my way from my Nissen hut to the outdoor toilet. As I stood relieving myself, my squadron leader stepped up to the next urinal and said, "Behling, I'm putting you in for first lieutenant." I claim the record for being the only officer in the 357th or possibly World War II to get promoted in the *latrine*!

This shot of the latrine is another rare photograph. It is only "rare" because no one has found it important enough to include in a book until this author found an excuse to use it here!

The Attack

Well, back to January 14. Several hours have passed since we rendezvoused with the bombers and we're approaching the target at about 30,000 feet. Berlin is easily discernible by the heavy flak smoke at our altitude. Suddenly, a maze of German pursuit planes comes screaming down on us from above. The sky is full of airplanes. B-17s begin bursting into flames, trail smoke, and spin like toys as parachutes begin popping open. I jettison my wing tanks and take a bead on an enemy fighter. Another P-51 drifts across my bow at a 30 degree angle in slow motion, so close I still don't know why I didn't tear its tail off with my propeller. I'm completely distracted and lose sight of my quarry.

I bank left and look behind me. Sure enough, there's a plane behind me and it isn't my wingman. It has a large radial engine and is easily identifiable as a Focke Wulf 190. What happened to my wingman who was supposed to cover my tail? To this day I have no idea.

Now I turned to the left. Left rudder, left stick, more throttle. I've got to outrun him. I see his cannon bursts but he can't pull enough lead on me. I wonder what I'm doing here; a person could get killed! Why did I ever want to be a pilot? I'm only twenty years old and should be home, going to school, and returning in the evening to my parents' comfortable home.

I pull into a tighter turn, feeling so many Gs that I can hardly turn my head. Then the stick goes limp in my hand. I'm spinning—but you never, *never* spin a Mustang because it might not come out. My primary training instinct takes over. I kick the right rudder hard. The plane stops spinning and I pop the stick forward. I'm flying again at 20,000 feet.

This time, I turn to the right and look behind. That son of a bitch is still there! He followed me through a spin and 10,000 feet! It can't be! These Germans are supposed to be undertrained, wet behind the ears, just kids!

Same scenario. Tighter and tighter to the right. More cannon bursts. Another spin, coming out at 10,000 feet. And he's *still there*! Well, if I can't out-turn him, I can surely out-run him. I shudder at the thought of one of those cannon shells tearing through my Mustang. In fact, I'm nearly paralyzed with fear.

I point the plane downward at an approximate ten-degree angle toward the ground and open the throttle. It's working; he's falling behind, out of range. Now I'm at treetop level just west of Berlin, passing over the Elbe River. My engine sputters, intermittently spewing white clouds. I cut back the throttle and lean the mixture, but the sputtering gets worse. Suddenly, the engine goes dead, streaming two contrail-like bands from each side. Hurriedly, I try the starting procedure several times, to no avail.

I'm directly over a dense forest and I can find no place to belly the Mustang in. Pull up and bail out! But I'm now going less than 200mph. Not enough speed to pull up to an altitude that will give my chute time to open. Look for someplace to put this baby down dead stick. *Dead stick!* It was my worst thing in basic training. Without power, I would have killed myself every time.

There, twenty degrees to the left is an open field running parallel to a railroad track. I'm barely flying, so don't turn too sharply. The stick feels mushy. Easy, easy! I'm lined up, fifty feet above the ground, wheels up. Then, right in front of me are high tension wires. I close my eyes and pull back on the stick. Somehow *Chi-Lassie* bounces over the wires and hits the ground with a thud. It's a frozen plowed field and my Mustang skids along like a sled. Up ahead is a line of trees and I'm zooming toward them with no way to stop. But I *do stop* fifty feet short. I slid back the canopy—nobody around. I hear the clickety-clack of a diesel engine. There's that FW-190 coming right at me. Get out of this plane and get behind those trees! I get tangled in the straps so I crouch down behind the armor plate in back of my seat. The German pilot in the 190 doesn't strafe me and passes overhead. Now, with him in full sight, I disentangle myself and head away. Up ahead is a bridge. But two figures are on the embankment coming toward me from the other direction. I stop and wait.

Captured!

I'd been well coached about Nazi Germany through newspapers, newsreels and service orientation. Here I was, first hand, right smack dab in the middle, miles from the border. I felt devastated, crushed, and hopeless. The best that could be said for my situation was that I was temporarily alive and able-bodied. Up until this point, I really hadn't had much time to think. Every decision I had been forced to make had been minutes apart and instinctive with no room for error. The fact that I was here, with both feet on the ground was incomprehensible to me.

I've thought many times about how this could have been avoided, but it's like any other accident. It happens quickly and cannot be avoided. Up until now, all of my errors had been educational and correctable, but this one was *final.*

Four Germans approached me and I put my hands into the air. They were all old men carrying rifles and I later learned that they were part of the *landwacht* (home guard) that had been organized just for this purpose. [Author's note: Each Landwacht or home guard unit was under the command of a Landwachtfuhrer or home guard leader. This Landwachtfuhrer was subordinate to the local police chief in each town. Their main purpose for being was to round up surviving Allied airmen who managed to survive a crash or parachute to the ground in Germany. In addition to the Landwacht, the local Hitler Youth were expected to participate in this job also.]

One of the four elderly men frisked me and began babbling in German. I couldn't understand him but perceived from his gestures that he wanted my gun. We pilots were issued .45s but I never carried mine while on a mission. What was I going to do, shoot my way out of Germany? I figured that I might do something foolish. I had a real time, by gesturing, convincing them that I didn't have a gun and that I had not dumped it.

The four men then marched me back to my plane. To my amazement, it was swarming with people from the local village, including children who were climbing all over and into the cockpit. *Chi-Lassie* was a sad sight. That beautiful P-51 that had been my faithful companion for so long, just sitting there with its torn undercarriage and twisted propeller, as helpless and forlorn as I was. The "Little Friend" (the term used by bomber crews of the "Big Friends" to describe the American fighters) was down and out. Then a horrible thought crossed my mind. I had not turned off the gun switches! If one of those children pressed that trigger on the stick, it would cut at least ten Germans in half.

An officer approached me. He was a colonel home on leave from the Russian Front, and he spoke English. He said, "For you, the war is over. I bet when you took off this morning you didn't think you would be here this afternoon." I don't think I've ever heard truer words spoken. I replied with true survival instinct, "Don't let those children in the cockpit. The guns are live." He simply shrugged and began marching me across a field, toward a ditch. "OK," I thought, "they'll just shoot me and lay me in that ditch. How long could my luck hold out?" But we went through the ditch and to a farmhouse where the colonel left me in the charge of a farmer, his wife, and their teenage daughter.

The people were friendly as the roar of the bombers continued overhead. Apparently, they had not experienced the devastating bombing directly. They produced an atlas and asked me to indicate where I was from. They were amazed that I was so young, but why wouldn't I be? Otherwise I would have known better than to volunteer as a pilot.

All the time, I was disinterested, worried about myself and what my family back home would think when they received the crushing news that I was missing in action. Several hours later, the frau gave me a sandwich but when I was about half way through eating it, a Luftwaffe officer came through the door. Thank goodness it wasn't the Gestapo! The officer grabbed the unfinished sandwich out of my hands and began screaming at the woman. I knew from his gestures and tone that he was berating her for feeding me and making me comfortable.

The Inquiry

It's dusk and I'm led to a half track and told to sit in it with five German soldiers. They're glum and don't speak to each other or to me. An hour or so later, we arrive in the dark at an airfield outside of Berlin where I'm placed in a stone walled cell for the night.

The next morning, I'm assigned a guard at least sixty-five years old and shorter than my five foot six inches. He slings a rifle over his shoulder, the butt just barely missing the ground. We proceed to a railroad station. It's loaded with civilians waiting for the train to Berlin. I stand out like a sore thumb in my American flying suit and I'm very uneasy and fearful for my safety. We board the train and are jammed in. One passenger shows me the front page of a newspaper with a picture of a huge German tank. He points to it and babbles but I don't understand his point. Another passenger gestures toward the bombed-out buildings and points to me. Him, I understand. Berlin is a rubble. I don't see one inhabitable structure.

Finally, we arrive at our destination and transfer to another train. Here, I meet my first fellow Americans. They're a sorry lot, foot soldiers and B-17 crewmen. We're all going to Frankfurt for interrogation. I'm glad to see some of my own, and I smile and perk up. They want to know what I'm so happy about. They're depressed, tired, and hungry. Some of them are injured, including several with badly burned faces. A B-17 pilot and copilot tell me that their plane was hit amid ship by flak and they managed to escape through a small window in the cockpit which they had been told never to try because the window wasn't big enough. They can't explain how they did it.

We're jammed into boxcars, about forty men per car. Twenty-five percent of the boxcar is reserved for our three guards. There's a pressed-coal burning stove in the middle of the car. Its sides glow, too hot to get near, but the inside walls of the boxcar are frosty and the floor is ice cold. We lay down, huddled, try to sleep and intermittently must stand up to get some warmth. The train stops occasionally for relief, and between stops, in an emergency, the guards slide the door open just enough for a man to hang his rear end out of the moving car. Breakfast is a cup of ersatz tea; lunch, two slices of black bread and a pad of margarine; and supper is boiled potatoes and rutabaga leaf soup. We're constantly hungry and always cold. I had never experienced being constantly chilled with no prospect of getting warm. It was a sorry state of affairs for Americans who were used to plenty of hot, cooked food and warm quarters even under adverse field conditions. I would never again underestimate the human survival instinct.

In Frankfurt, [Author's note: Behling was probably in Oberursel, Germany, the intelligence gathering camp where Allied fliers were interrogated by Hanns Scharff, Canadian Bill, and others for the Luftwaffe before being sent on to stalag lufts around the country.] we're put into solitary confinement. My cell is about eight feet high by eight feet long and four feet wide. It is bare except for a cot and a small electric heater at one end. The heater goes on for ten minutes every two hours, but I'm still cold. When I see the filament in the heater glow, I drape myself around it to absorb all of the heat that I can while it's on.

I'm fed the same food as before, through a small swinging door at the bottom of my cell door. There is no communication between me and the guards. Solitary really softens you up so that you crave conversation.

Unfortunately for the Germans, the place isn't well insulated. I can hear footsteps and the talking of the guards as well as the clanging of the doors. After hearing a tap on my wall, I carry on a conversation with the prisoner in the cell next to me by placing my lips close to the wall. One of the things he tells me is that he's worried because he is of Russian descent. Our voices reverberate throughout the entire complex. Now I hear clanging doors, shouts, and my door swings open. An irate guard gestures to me that talking is "verboten!" He knew someone was carrying on a conversation but couldn't pinpoint my cell or the one adjoining it. This scene was repeated a half dozen times during my three days in isolation.

Finally, my door opens and I'm taken in for questioning. My interrogator is a typical good-looking Aryan in his late twenties. It turns out that he was a flier who was shot down over London, imprisoned, and later repatriated. Because of his physical disabilities and the Geneva Convention rules of war, he is forbidden from participating in active combat.

To my amazement, he starts talking about women. "How are the women in the United States?" he asks. Women! I hadn't thought about them since before the air battle. I never knew it before, but women run a bad third behind a full belly and warmth. The German officer shows me a picture of a buxom girl in a bathing suit. "This is the way we like them, but I know you Americans like them a little skinnier." he comments. I agree. He tells me how the German people are on food rationing and how he and his fellow officers romance the girls, go to their homes, and then eat up their rations.

Now he starts asking me questions about where I came from, my squadron, and my fellow fliers. I say, "You know I can't tell you those things." He answers that it makes no difference because he already knows. I snicker cautiously. He said, "You landed your plane, it's sitting in a field and has numbers on it, right?" I answer, "Yes, so what?"

He pulls out a huge book about the size of a Sears catalog and proceeds to tell me about my fellow fliers, my field, and my group. I'm dumbstruck at the efficiency and thoroughness of German intelligence. He asks me the name of my group commander. Now I have him because we just recently changed. I reply that I can't tell him, and he says, "No matter; we already know." The German tells me that he will bet me. I tell him that I am a POW and have nothing to bet with. He says we're both officers and he'll bet me a bottle of wine payable after the war. I say OK, but if he isn't correct I won't tell who it is. I still owe him that bottle of wine.

Now I ask him what is the point of all of this solitary confinement and interrogation when the Germans know more than I do. He tells me that it is routine, and that once in a while they do pick up an unknown tidbit of information.

The Camp

The next day, we're put back into boxcars for the trip to our permanent POW camp, Stalag Luft III, near Potsdam, just outside of Berlin. The journey is the same as coming except for one divergence. About halfway back, we stop in a rail yard at night to refuel. Suddenly, air raid sirens start to shriek. The guards jump out of the car, secure the door and disappear. We have one small window about four inches high by eight inches long, just big enough for one man to peer out of. He gives us a running account. "I see the flares; they're way off in the distance," he says. We are absolutely sitting ducks and huddle, petrified, in silent, abject fear. We hear the bombs exploding several miles off. Then one explodes, sounding much closer, and the boxcar shakes violently. This is repeated several times. No one speaks, but I suspect that a lot of praying was going on. After about an hour, the all-clear sounds, the guards return and we continue on our sojourn. None of us ever speaks among ourselves or to others about the bombing.

Our camp at Potsdam is made up of various compounds: American, British, Norwegian, and Russian. Many of the prisoners have made forced marches from eastern camps overrun by the Russians. I meet Englishmen who had been captured at Dunkirk nearly five years earlier. We anticipate the war's end in several weeks; they say it will take years.

The sections of the camp are separated by wire fences. We have a view of the English and Norwegians but not the Russians. During my stay, the Norwegians gave us fish soup passed through the fence which they poured into our canteens. The English are amazingly bold such as during morning roll call when they mingled around and irritated the Germans by making it difficult to get an accurate count. They also strip wood from the latrines and use it for heating fuel. The Germans warn them that it is destruction of German property and could be punishable by death. The Brits also mimic the Germans by doing the "goose step" immediately behind the guards. I don't know what would have happened if one of those guards had suddenly turned around. We Americans are ordered by our superiors to obey the rules and to avoid making things more uncomfortable than they already are.

Our barracks are in two sections, each one housing about 100 men, with a sink in between that has cold running water. In the center of each unit is a huge brick furnace. Each day we get one bucket of pressed coal dust bricks. It's barely enough to warm the bricks of the furnace. The bunks are two-tiered with straw mattresses and a blanket. We spend most of our time lying in our bunks wrapped in blankets, trying to keep warm. The mattresses and blankets are full of lice and after several days, I look as though I have a case of the measles. The various postwar movies and especially the TV serial *Hogan's Heroes* are pretty accurate portrayals of the makeup and condition of the camp. Ours just wasn't so lighthearted.

Some of the men were burned and they lay quietly waiting to heal without medical attention. One man developed appendicitis and was taken away, presumably to a hospital. We never saw or heard of him again. An infantry officer gets up every morning and takes a bath in ice cold water. He's very quiet and stays to himself.

Our diet is as described before: ersatz tea in the morning, bread and margarine for lunch, and boiled potatoes for supper. After the potatoes are distributed, some of the men grovel around in the barrels for scraps. I prepare for possible harder times by saving half a slice of bread every day. I keep it fresh as possible by rotating the older bread for the new. Some of the men have a few cigarettes and others make their own by scouring small, discarded butts. Sometimes a cigarette is passed around to as many as six men, the ash never stops glowing red.

As bad as it was, we were never physically mistreated and I believe the Germans did the best they could by us, considering their condition and the state of war.

Finally, after about a month, several things happened that ameliorated our condition considerably. First we received Red Cross parcels. Never underestimate the Red Cross. They not only furnished the parcels, but actually get them distributed to us. Each package contained Spam, cheese, crackers, jam, coffee, five packs of cigarettes, and other things. We got a parcel every week and it did help. Some of the bigger men lost weight. I was lucky, only losing ten pounds.

The Red Cross parcels induced bartering. One of the men actually built up a store where you could trade for whatever you wanted. He built his inventory by requiring a premium for every item, a true entrepreneur.

Some men made bets that they could finish an entire parcel in twenty-four hours. None of them won, always being stopped by the cigarettes and coffee. One man had a quarter of a jar of powdered coffee left with half an hour to go and had to give up. His throat was so sore that he couldn't swallow.

There was no shortage of cigarettes. To pass the time and alleviate my hunger, I started to smoke for the first time. It developed into a habit that plagued me for the next twenty-two years.

I must also mention that homemade stoves and other utensils the prisoners made from the emptied Red Cross parcel cans were truly remarkably innovative.

The second favorable happening was the improvement of the weather. About early March, it started to moderate. We had sunny days and could get outside to warm our chilled bones. We finally even played baseball. Food and warmth were a double barreled simple combination of basic needs that most of us had never given a serious thought about before our incarceration.

Once a week, we marched about a half a mile to a shower building accommodating about fifty men. Our clothes were left outside for fumigating while we were locked naked in the partitionless building, one shower spigot to each man. We were given a small bar of soap, and on a signal got hot water for one minute, during which we soaped vigorously, and then we got one minute of cold water for the rinse. Incidentally, these were the same shower buildings that Hitler had ordered to spew gas instead of water to eliminate prisoners. I do believe the only saving factor was that the German guards saw no future in that, considering the imminent end of the war and the possibility that they might be held responsible. After the shower, we redonned our debugged clothes which were reinfested once we climbed back into our nondebugged mattresses and blankets later.

I made several friends while housed at Stalag Luft III. One was an infantry second lieutenant who told me the only way to get off of "the line" was to get killed, wounded, or captured. He was weary and said that most of his comrades hoped for a minor wound, the lesser of evils that would facilitate them being sent back from the front. Because of their experience, they had learned that their superiors' talk of rotation was only a dream.

Another friend, George Ross, was a B-17 co-pilot from California. He told me how he had romanced the girls before the war by telling them he was in the movies. He would mention an obscure scene in a popular movie and tell them that he was an actor. Naturally the girls wouldn't remember the scene, even though they'd seen the movie. And him being the "Tom Selleck" type, the girls would gobble up the bait. I mention this now because our basic hunger and warmth requirements being finally "off of zero," we spent much of our time talking about home, food, and women.

The Rescue

The days continued to drag on and our estimate of the length of the war lengthened. One morning in early April we heard the sound of cannon fire in the distance to the east. Each day it drew nearer. Our ranking officers came up with a plan to take over the camp in order to preserve order, and protect our meager food supply. About two weeks later we arose and couldn't find one single German in the camp. The guards had vanished! We immediately put our plan into operation. It was a good thing too because we did have an attempted raid on the larder.

The next day, at about noon a Russian tank column rumbled up to our front gate. What a sight as the tanks were interspersed with an assortment of other vehicles, including horse drawn carts filled with hay, and Russian soldiers (men and women) carrying rifles and a loaf of bread under their arm. They were a solemn, intent group obviously battle and travel weary, as they eyed us unemotionally. To us, they looked like Santa Claus arriving with a sleigh full of goodies!

The Russians took over the camp and we learned that they had joined with the American forces ten miles to the west. Our leaders negotiated for our return to the American lines but the Russians refused as they said that they had no trucks to spare. They wouldn't let us walk there because they said that it was too dangerous, considering that their troops were still "mopping up."

The upshot was that the Russians would send us to Moscow for processing, and then we would be sent home southward from the Black Sea. Each morning, our numbers dwindled as more and more of us sneaked out at night and attempted to find our own way back to the American lines. The Russians didn't tolerate this and they soon set up guards around the camp.

The Russian commandant was a sight to see, strolling around with a young German girl following five paces behind him like a puppy dog. Every evening scores of German women would flock to the front gate, asking us to spend the night with them. When we asked the women what was wrong with the Russians, they said, "Nothing," but apparently the Russians would leave them alone if they were with an American. Otherwise, a parade of Russian soldiers would traipse through their bedrooms all night long. Apparently, [sex with] one American was less grueling to the women than it would be with ten or twenty Russians.

We also observed one compound that housed teenage German prisoners. Every morning they were let out to exercise by marching around the barracks. In addition to this, we also got to see the Russian quarters, which were adorned with beautiful, colored religious scenes on the walls. Where the Russians got the materials and how they made their paint is still a mystery.

One day my infantry lieutenant friend said that there were Americans at the Russian command post negotiating for our release, and he suggested that we take a look. Parked in front of the post was an empty jeep and a half track with American prisoners milling around them. Some of the prisoners had climbed onto the half track. I didn't hesitate and climbed onto the fender of the jeep. My friend also found a spot on the hood. Soon, both vehicles were completely covered with Americans POWs, inside and out. After about ten minutes, four U. S. officers left the Russian headquarters and squeezed into the jeep and the half track. They were somber and looked straight ahead, completely ignoring our presence. To our surprise, they drove off through the gate with practically *no* visibility over the bodies on the hoods.

The Return Home

I was out of Stalag Luft III and never found out what happened to the comrades I left behind. [Author's note: At least 12,500 American personnel in German POW camps overrun by the Russians were never repatriated. Apparently, neither President Truman nor General Eisenhower ever confronted Josef Stalin about this matter. The situation would be repeated later after the Korean War.]

Simultaneously, during our escape from the camp, the Americans had pulled back to the west bank of the Elbe River so we had about a sixty mile trip instead of ten. Along the way, we saw a column of captured German troops being marched east. In one group, I spotted several of our former guards. At one point, we also had a flat tire and had to call for repairs. While we were waiting, we entered a middle class German home. There were only very old and very young people present. The Russians had come through the home and smashed every bit of China and glassware. The occupants of the house were petrified, wanting to know when the Americans would be coming. My heart was cold and I couldn't muster any sympathy for the Germans even though I knew their fear was justified.

We finally arrived at the American lines after dark and were taken to the mess hall for a good, old G. I. supper. Later that night, I got nauseated because the food was too rich for my condition. The next day, we loaded into trucks for a trip down the Autobahn to Paris, France. I had never seen an expressway before. Arriving in Paris, we were put on a train for a trip the next day to Camp Lucky Strike, a disembarkation center on the French coast. That night, the Parisians celebrated the end of the war in Europe. We were confined to the train and couldn't join in the celebration, but I really didn't care.

After about a week of waiting at Camp Lucky Strike, we boarded a "Liberty Ship" for the trip home, which also took about a week. The seas were rough and waves broke over the bow, inundating the entire deck of the ship and forcing us to stay below playing cards.

Suddenly we were entering New York Harbor and I got my first glimpse of the Statue of Liberty. I don't think any immigrant could have been more impressed. For me, it had a *special* meaning. I had been on the other side of her and knew what was there. Other Americans who had not experienced what I had had only heard and dreamt. My heart swelled as we were met by boats with "Welcome Home" banners, dancing girls, and bands on them.

After one night in New York City, I boarded a westbound train. The next morning, I arrived home at Sixty-fifth Street and California Avenue in good old Chicago. It took only three weeks from the time I left Stalag Luft III, a most remarkable feat as all of you know who are familiar with the ways of the United

States Armed Forces. I've always been grateful for that. Incidentally, the number one song at Camp Lucky Strike had been "Don't Fence Me In!"

Epilogue

To the best of my recollection, that is the way it all happened. Hopefully, it is abridged enough to avoid the reader any boredom. I've tried very hard not to understate or exaggerate. As time passed I tried to forget, but obviously I can't. Only small portions of this tale have been wrung out of me over the years and, usually, only as a response to direct questions. It is a real "baring of the soul," almost like recounting the details of one's wedding night.

Even at this late date, recalling these episodes sends chills down my spine. I can't even count the number of times I should have been killed, and it all happened in less than one year! This is the story of a "loser," but several clichés come to my mind: "It was a dirty job, but someone had to do it," and, "I complained of having no shoes, until I met a man with no feet."

Many of my friends did not come back from World War II. Lou Gehrig probably put it best when he said, during his farewell address at Yankee Stadium, "Some people say I've had a bad break, but today I consider myself the luckiest man on this earth."

Outside of the many bad nightmares and the devastating feeling of assault and infringement on my personal rights and freedom (a feeling akin, perhaps, to that of a rape victim's), I came through the experience mostly unscathed. Through the years it made me impervious to other so-called crises that I brushed off as trivial.

Without getting maudlin, I must say that through it all, I still remain a patriot, along with Patrick Henry, Nathan Hale, and John Paul Jones. However, I am most happy to say that if I am ever called again to serve my country, I will be too old to fly an airplane.

I will close with this plaudit. To my crew chief, my wingman, and the dogged German fighter pilot who relentlessly pursued me, wherever you are, this is your story as well as mine. To my parents and fiancée, who suffered that age-old pain upon receiving *the telegram*, you didn't know whether I was alive or dead, and if I was alive you didn't know the state of my health until after several months of suffering after I went down over Germany. At least *I knew* what had happened and where I was.

To the policeman who stopped me for a minor traffic violation shortly after my return, and said, "Listen, Buddy, just because you're in that uniform doesn't mean that that stuff goes here," you didn't notice me biting my lip or my hands gripping the wheel tightly while I fought back against the *urge to kill!* After what I had been through, it wasn't worth winding up at a court martial over such a *jerk* as you.

To the many bartenders that refused me a drink, even a beer, because I wouldn't be twenty-one for another five months, you are forgiven. You only followed the law for your own protection.

And finally to Dr. Joe Cannon, who trained me, flew with me, and became my life-long friend and consultant. At every opportunity, you all never ceased to remind me that I was the kid who took the easy way out. AMEN TO THAT!

A Fighter Pilot's Story

By William B. "Bill" Overstreet

Bill Overstreet (center with pipe) points to his first *Berlin Express*

Training Days

I was born in Clifton Forge, Virginia on April 10, 1921. On December 7, 1941, I was working as a statistical engineer for Columbia Engineering and attending Morris Harvey College. I wanted to get into the Army Air Corps as a fighter pilot, so I did a lot of talking just to be accepted. By February 1942, I was a private, waiting for an opening in the Aviation Cadet program. After several months, I was sent to Santa Anna, California, for preflight schooling.

Then, after several months of preflight education, I was transferred to Rankin Aeronautical Academy in Tulare, California, where I underwent primary flight training flying Stearmans.

The head of the school, Tex Rankin, was a champion aerobatic pilot and often demonstrated his skills. My instructor, Carl Aarslef, was great too. Aarslef had unusual methods of testing his student pilots. One thing he surprised me with, on the downwind leg of the landing pattern, at 500 feet, was when he would turn the Stearman upside down, cut the engine off, and say, "OK, you land it." Of course that was easy, just quarter roll it into a left turn, line up with the runway, and set it down. I guess the real test was for him to see what your reaction would be. Another maneuver we did was to pull up into a normal stall, walk the nose down through vertical, and then push the nose up inverted into an inverted stall, which I repeated until the ground got close.

Then, I went on to basic flight training at Lemoore, California. The flight training was in the Vultee "Vibrator" which had an adjustable pitch propeller. We would dive down to buzz someone or something and set the prop so it really roared over our target. My next stop was advanced flight training at Luke Field, Arizona. [Author's note: I have a copy of the orders Fletcher Adams received instructing him to report to Luke Field in 1943. Also on this set of orders is a list of the other attendees which includes Chuck Yeager, Robert "R. D." Brown, James "Gentleman Jim" Browning, William "Bill" Overstreet, and others who would eventually become original members of the 357th Fighter Group. Yeager contacted me in 2007 and asked me for a copy of the orders which I sent to him.] The commanding officer indicated that I should go to Williams Field for multiengine advanced training, but I was able to convince the Captain that I *had* to be a fighter pilot. Anyway, the AT-6 was really fun to fly and I was able to check out in a Curtiss P-40 before I got my wings.

Upon graduation, a group of us was assigned to Hamilton Field, California. After that, I was assigned to the 357th Fighter Group, 363rd Fighter Squadron and we moved to Tonopah, Nevada for gunnery and bombing training in the P-39 Airacobra. From Tonopah, the 363rd Fighter Squadron moved to Santa Rosa, California. We were able to fly with experienced pilots and we learned a lot. Flying at Santa Rosa was great. There was enough moisture in the air to leave "streamers" from our wingtips in tight turns. Our goal was to get a flight of four together, fly to the end of the runway, peel up into a tight turn and land before the P-39's streamers had faded. I flew with several flight leaders but mostly with Lloyd Hubbard. He was good. We all thought that we could "buzz" pretty closely, but while we may have been able to "mow the fairway" on a golf course, only Hubbard could "mow the greens!"

A flight of three P-39s "beat up" the runway at Tonopah, Nevada

"Hub" also liked to take a flight of four P-39s to the Golden Gate Bridge and do "loops" around it. You *know* we were having fun! Complaints started coming in and charges were placed. Jack Meyers, our legal officer, told me years later that he was able to hold up action on bushels of charges, and eventually took most of them home with him after the war. We liked to buzz farmers, sunbathers, or anything. Years later I asked Don Graham (our commanding officer) why we got away with so much. He replied, "If you were picking [fighter] pilots for combat, who would you pick? The fellows who flew straight and level or the ones who pushed the envelope and tested the limits of their planes?"

Fletcher Adams lands the P-39 Airacobra *Rolly* during training in California

While in training, we were losing too many pilots and planes because of the P-39s tumbling and going into flat spins. It happened to me in combat training on June 28, 1943. [Author's note: See the previous Bill Overstreet story, "Don't Give Me a P-39!" for more details of this mishap.] We had been practicing aerobatics when my plane started tumbling and I couldn't control it. When I released the doors, they wouldn't come off. The air pressure had built up against them. I finally got my knee against one door and my shoulder against the other and was able to overcome the pressure. When I got out, I pulled my ripcord immediately. The chute opened with a jerk, and the next thing I realized was that I was standing among the prop and cannon shells. Later I visited Hamilton Field and thanked the parachute packer. I still have that ripcord and I believe that I was the first pilot to get out of a tumbling P-39 and live to tell about it.

Another day, four of us were practicing aerobatics and had reformed into formation to return to base. We saw a P-39 diving on us, so we broke as if to start a dogfight. This P-39 started to snap roll right through where our formation had been. Later, Ellis Rogers, a nice fellow and a *big* man, came over and said how sorry he was. He had intended to join our formation but his Airacobra had other ideas! Rogers was so big and the P-39's cockpit was so small that he had to lift his legs in order to move the control stick from side to side. He must have wished for a much larger plane.

My father brought my 1938 Buick convertible to California for me. I was able to take him up for a ride in our AT-6. That was a thrill for both of us. With the car, we were able to visit places like Russian River, Bucks Lake and other points of interest.

Bill Overstreet and his 1938 Buick

Soon, my squadron moved to Oroville, California. We were still gaining experience flying the P-39, and learning all the time. One mistake we made was to have all four of us meet over a field from the north, south, east and west. Then we would split-ess to the field, cross below the control tower, pull up and reform. We got a radio message from control stating, "The visiting general wants the four P-39s who buzzed the tower to land immediately!" We obeyed, but chose to land at another base. We didn't feel welcome at our home base at the time. More paperwork.

Our squadron's next move was to Casper, Wyoming. I received a short "leave" to take my car home. I took Dave Kramer to Missouri and "Muscles" Molday to Ohio on the way home. Then, I hitched a ride in a B-24 from Washington, D.C., to Wyoming. I remember getting a free meal at the hotel in Casper because one of our pilots had killed an antelope and donated the meat to the hotel during meat rationing. Another time I rode with Don Graham to pick up pilots from the local nightspots and to bring them back to the base. I didn't know it was possible to get that many bodies into a Lincoln coupe, and I will never tell where we found some of those fellows!

We were declared "combat ready" and boarded a train to Camp Shanks, New Jersey in November of 1943, where we prepared for shipment overseas. Although we were supposed to be confined to the base, we went to a nightclub in New York City. I have a great picture of a bunch of us at that club. Soon we were loaded onto the *Queen Elizabeth* to cross the Atlantic. I remember Bill "Obie" O'Brien kicking his B-4 bag up the gangplank. He suffered a .45 caliber wound in the arm in an accident. [Author's note: For more on O'Brien's accidental shooting see the preceding story "I Had a Little Help."] He told me later that the Royal Air Force decided to ground him and ship him back to the States. Doc Barker, our flight surgeon, overruled them when Obie promised him that he would be able to fly.

Leiston, England

We landed in Scotland and went on to Raydon Wood, England as part of the Ninth Air Force. We arrived to a sea of mud and no airplanes. By then, the P-51s were becoming available and the Eighth Air Force wanted them for long range bomber escort duty. So the 357th Fighter Group was traded to the Eighth Air Force for a P-47 Thunderbolt outfit at Leiston, England. While in Raydon in all of that mud, we were required to "dress" for dinner. War *is* hell!

After moving to the base at Leiston, we found that there was more paving and less mud. Also, we started getting P-51 Mustangs. What a *great day*! I got to fly a P-51 for the first time on January 30, 1944. As the inventory of planes increased, it seemed they hoped for us to get at least ten hours in the new plane before we were sent into combat. On February 8, 1944, Lloyd Hubbard flew with another group to get some combat time and experience. Unfortunately, while strafing a German airfield, Hub was hit and killed. That left Peters, Pascoe, and me to be shifted to other flight leaders. I flew with several of them until I was assigned "tail-end Charlie" to Bud Anderson's flight. From then on, I tried to fly with "Andy" whenever possible. I thought then, and still do, that he was the greatest. His record sure proves it.

I named my first plane *Southern Belle*. However, a few weeks later, when another pilot was flying it, they failed to return from a mission. [Author's note: One of the great mysteries surrounding the names of the 357th's Mustangs was the name of Fletcher Adams's P-51B that was lost with him the day he was shot down and murdered by German civilians on May 30, 1944. In a letter to his wife, Adams wrote that he had considered naming his Mustang *Ye Ole Faithful,* and later, *Louisiana Lullaby* (the author's favorite), but he refused to name the plane after his wife Aline because, he said, "I just can't see my wife's name going into combat." Later Adams wrote to Aline again, and this time he told her that another pilot in the group had named his P-51 *Southern Belle* but that something had happened to the plane and the pilot wasn't going to put the name on his next fighter because he considered it bad luck. The upshot of this is that the "other pilot" said that Fletcher was welcome to use the name on his ship, and at that time Adams's Mustang was officially named "***The** Southern Belle*" (spelled and punctuated exactly as it is in Fletcher Adams's letter). In a phone conversation with this author during the writing of this book, Bill Overstreet said that he remembered giving the name to Fletcher Adams in 1944.]

The only known photograph of *The Southern Belle* which the author found with the help of Merle Olmsted in 2006. In the image above, Fletcher Adams and his P-51B Mustang are seen returning from a mission during the spring of 1944.

By then, in early March, we had begun flying missions to Berlin on a regular basis, so I named the rest of my P-51s *Berlin Express*.

On March 6, just after the first Berlin raid, the 357th Fighter Group showed what our training and teamwork could do. Our combat training and the entire group working together produced tremendous results. Here is a quote from our first citation:

On 6 March 1944 the newly operational 357th Fighter Group provided target and withdrawal support to heavy bombardment aircraft bombing Berlin, which was the deepest penetration of single-engine fighters to that date. The 33 P-51 aircraft went directly to Berlin and picked up the first formations of B-17s just before their arrival over the city. They found the bombers being viciously attacked by one of the largest concentrations of twin-engine and single-engine fighters in the history of aerial warfare. From 100 to 150 single-engine and twin-engine fighters, some firing rockets, were operating in the immediate target area in groups of thirty to forty as well as singly. Each combat wing of bombers was hit as it arrived over Berlin and although they were sometimes outnumbered as much as six to one, flights and sections of the 357th Group went to aid each combat wing as it arrived over the target, providing support in the air for over thirty minutes. Upwards of thirty enemy aircraft at a time were attacked by these separate flights and sections, and driven away from above and below the bombers. Some of the P-51s left there formations to engage enemy fighters below the bomber level in order to prevent them from reforming for further attacks. Though fighting under the most difficult conditions and subjected to constant antiaircraft and enemy aircraft fire so skillfully and aggressively were their attacks on the enemy fighters carried out that not a single aircraft of the 357th Group was lost. In driving the enemy fighters away from the bombers, twenty Nazi fighters were destroyed, one probably destroyed, and seven others damaged. On withdrawal, one flight of P-51s strafed a large enemy airfield in central Germany, damaging three twin-engine and single-engine aircraft on the ground and killing fifteen to twenty armed personnel before regaining altitude and returning to the bombers.

Not long after this, I had a freak accident. I think it was a mission to southern France. While over enemy territory, a burst of flak cut my oxygen line. Since I was at 25,000 feet, I soon passed out. The next thing I knew, I was in a spin, and my engine was dead since the fuel tank it was set on was dry. Somehow, I recovered from the spin, changed fuel tank setting, got the engine started, and dodged the trees that were in front of me. Then I looked at my watch. Ninety minutes had passed that I had no memory of. I had no idea where I was but I remembered where I had been headed and so I reversed it. I was able to find the coast of France and headed for Leiston. By this time, I was so low on fuel that I was forced to land at the Fourth Fighter Group Base. The officer I talked with was Captain Mead, who had lived a couple of blocks from my home in Clifton Forge, Virginia. To top it off, the mechanic who repaired my plane was "Hot Cha" Tucker, a former schoolmate, also from Clifton Forge. I still have a picture of Tucker and me with a P-47. Many weeks later, this story got a lot of publicity-Lowell Thomas on the radio, newspapers and even *Time Magazine*. So that is my claim to fame. I hope that I did do a little bit that was productive.

Oxygen Out, Pilot Flies 90 Minutes With Mind a Blank

AN EIGHTH MUSTANG BASE, May 23—For an hour and a half, 1/Lt. William B. Overstreet Jr., a P51 pilot from Clifton Forge, Va., flew his Mustang fighter over enemy territory and didn't know a thing about it, his mind a perfect blank.

Flying into France, Overstreet's oxygen system failed at 22,000 feet. His plane dropped out of formation and his squadron leader couldn't reach him over the radio. For 90 minutes the Virginian, subconscious from lack of oxygen, apparently flew his plane by reflex action alone and only regained his senses when the ship slipped into a spin, the denser air at 7,000 feet reviving him in time to recover and fly home.

At the hospital, where flight surgeons said he was all right for combat again, it was explained that Overstreet must have dropped from 22,000 feet for his 90 minutes of blank flying, because he probably would have died in the rarified atmosphere of that altitude without oxygen.

During this period I was flying more with Andy Anderson, while Charles "Daddy Rabbit" Peters and Herschel Pascoe were flying more with Jim Browning. My crew chief was "Red" Dodsworth and "Whitey" KcKain was his assistant. Whitey was soon promoted. He and I became good friends in spite of one incident. One snowy day, the visibility was so limited that Whitey was riding on my wing to the runway. At the runway, I motioned for Whitey to get off, but he thought that I wanted him to come to the cockpit. I was watching Andy and he gave it the gun to take off, so I did the same. Poor Whitey was blown right off of the wing, but was wrapped up so well he wasn't hurt. I was very glad of that. I never knew about this incident until many years later. Whitey was riding with me and told me at the time he had promised himself never to ride with me again. He *did* ride with me to Oshkosh several times and we had a ball.

Another mission that didn't turn out as expected was one when I had a sinus infection. When we chased the German fighters out of position to attack the bombers, and they dived away from us, we would sometimes chase them down to the deck. This time, I was chasing an Me-109 in a power dive from about 30,000 feet. Suddenly, my eyes swelled shut! I was able to keep flying by feel (the pressure of the controls). I called for help and Charles "Daddy Rabbit" Peters said he could see me. He got on my wing, took me back to the base and talked me through a straight-in approach and landing. It was days before the doctors could relieve the pressure and I could see again.

On April 11, 1944, I was flying with Andy Anderson, Henry Kayser, and Eddie Simpson. While we were escorting the bombers, a large group of 109s started to attack the heavies head on. Andy led us into the fight, trying to break up their formation and keep them from getting to the bombers. Maybe they didn't like being shot at but they scattered all over. When most of them had dived away, Andy led us down after three Messerschmitt 109s.

Henry "Kay" Kayser

At about 5,000 feet, Kayser got into position and clobbered one of them. It broke apart and Kay (rhymes with eye) had to dodge the debris. At about 3,500 feet, Eddie Simpson closed on another 109 and got two good bursts to its nose section. The Hun rolled over and went straight in.

Eddie Simpson

I was busy with another Me-109 who tried to get behind Simpson. Andy Anderson was turning with another 109 in a tight turn. Andy couldn't hold a lead inside his turn, so he reversed his turn and came in almost head on. As the Me-109 came apart, the pilot bailed out. That took care of the 109s, but Andy spotted an He-111K flying close to the ground. Anderson hit him good but directed all of us to make a pass, too. We all got hits and then Andy came back around, hitting the 111 from nose to tail. The He111K tried to crash-land, hit a pole tearing off the left wing, and then started burning. As it slid along, the crew jumped out and I believe they were all track stars. They were in a *hurry*! Andy insisted upon sharing credit for the claim, although he easily could have kept the victory all for himself. He would rather give us some experience and training.

During May, 1944, Colonel Graham ordered side arms to be carried at all times. There was an alert about German paratroopers. On May 12, I destroyed a JU-52 on the ground. Andy got another Me-109 in the air. With Pierce and Michaely, we also destroyed a locomotive, railcars and some barges.

Joseph "Joe" Pierce

D-Day and the Invasion

On June 6, 1944, the Invasion began. We took off at about 2:00 a.m. in horrible weather. Our element and the others had to climb about 20,000 feet in order to break out of the overcast. It was beautiful when I got to the top. The moon was bright, and as the planes would pop out of the overcast, they were in different altitudes from the long climb on instruments. We never did find our assigned flights, so we just formed up into various flights of four. We went to France to make sure that no German fighters could bother the Invasion force, and to prevent reinforcements from being brought up. After six hours, we came back to the base to refuel. The 357th Fighter Group flew eight missions on the day of the Invasion. Smaller flights had different objectives.

During the days following the Invasion of Normandy the Group claimed trains, rail shacks, boxcars, trucks, lorries, barges, and other targets of opportunity. I also remember that June 29 was a good day for me. I got behind a Focke Wulf 190 and when I started getting hits, he flipped over and bailed out. I used only forty rounds of ammunition the whole day. General Kepner issued another commendation for the 357th Fighter Group and the 361st Fighter Group. We destroyed forty-eight enemy aircraft without losing a single bomber.

On July 29, 1944, I chased an Me-109 to the deck and had a wing in the grass when he blew up. He must been trying to get to his base because we were close to a German airfield. My wingman, Harold Hand, and I made a pass and destroyed another 109 and damaged a DO-217. I went back and got another 109 but then I found that I was alone. I asked Harold where he was and he replied, "I'm giving you top cover." Hand was a smart fellow.

On August 6, we started out on our famous "shuttle mission" to Russia. I was leading a flight with Cleland, Pearson, and Fennel. Jack Cleland was a New Zealand Royal Air Force pilot who had flown two tours in Spitfires and then came to us to get some long-range mission experience. On his previous tours in Spits, no mission had exceeded two hours. What a mixed flight-Cleland and Pearson. Pearson was an American who had gone to Canada, joined the Royal Canadian Air Force, then transferred to the United States Army Air Force and the 357th. About seven hours later and after several dogfights along the way, we landed on a grass field in Russia.

The 357th had sent some mechanics as gunners on the bombers so that they could service our planes. The trouble was, the bombers landed at a different field and subsequently, the mechanics never got close to our P-51s. The Russian crews put the wrong octane fuel in some of the P-51s and this caused a lot of trouble. [Author's note: Due to this mistake, the 357th lost one aircraft on takeoff after it experienced engine failure and bellied in and another Mustang barely made it into the air. The Russian officer in charge at the scene ordered the man responsible for the fueling of the plane to be brought to him. When the young man was located, the officer produced a pistol and was going to execute the soldier on the spot until members of the 357th were able to talk him out of it. Eventually cooler heads prevailed and the Russian responsible for the "snafu" was allowed to live.] I was assigned a cot in a tent that came complete with a black snake in the bedding! When I saw a P-39 on the field, I asked if I could fly it since I had a lot of time in the Airacobra. Not a chance. The Russians wouldn't let me get within a hundred feet of it.

We flew one escort mission out of Russia. This gave me enough time to find some beet vodka. We thought it was better than potato vodka and decided that we should take some home with us. I offered to leave my ammunition behind in order to make space for the vodka. That was fine until we ran into some 109s on our way to Italy. Naturally, we went after them, but they turned tail and ran away. However, we did get close enough to the last one and he rolled over and bailed out. Since I was the closest plane, I could have claimed the Messerschmitt, but I did not want to claim the only enemy plane destroyed with *vodka*! Now all I had to worry about was making a smooth landing in Italy in order to safeguard my precious cargo.

Our mission from Italy was a real thrill. We escorted C-47s to Yugoslavia to pick up downed Allied airmen who had been collected by Tito and brought to a small airfield. The C-47s took turns landing and picking up a load of men, then taking off. The amazing sight was as the fellows jumped into the C-47, they were throwing out their shoes, clothing, etc., for their rescuers. I guess everything was in short supply in Yugoslavia, and our airmen wanted to help out those who had helped them. All that was left of the shuttle mission then, was to return to England. That took about eight hours. How do you think Cleland, whose Spitfire missions had not exceeded more than two hours, felt by then?

I also remember many more exciting missions. On one, an Me-109 blew up when I was following too close. Pieces of the 109 came into my cockpit and landed in my lap! I still have that extremely light, but strong piece of metal. On another occasion, I saw a 109 in a shallow dive after the pilot had bailed out. It crashed into the side of a factory, and then the Messerschmitt's engine came out of the other side of the building and slid down a street. On still another mission, a 20mm cannon shell came through the side of my canopy. The shell took the canopy, my oxygen mask and helmet off, and gave me a haircut and a bad burn on my neck! Everyone knows that you can't hit a fighter with a ninety-degree deflection shot very often, so I still wonder who that German was shooting at. At least I knew why my canopy was missing. Kit Carson lost his Mustang's canopy on a mission and was angry at his crew chief until the chief took him over to *Nooky Booky* and showed him the bullet holes that had caused the canopy to come off. Kit had had no idea until then that he had been hit.

**This photograph was taken minutes after Carson
returned to Leiston Field sans cockpit canopy**

On September 3, 1944, Ed Hiro and I went to a base where a B-24 had been stripped down and loaded with explosives. The pilot of this Liberator had to take off, fly the bomber in the direction of its target, and then bail out shortly after the B-24 had been switched over to "radio control" by another pilot in a "Mother Ship." This *flying bomb* was then flown by remote control into German submarine pens and then it would blow up. The sub pens were located under thick rock formations that had hitherto resisted bombing attacks from the air. But when the explosion occurred *inside, under* the rock cover, significant damage was achieved. My mission log for this day is marked "Secret." [Author's note: President John F. Kennedy's oldest brother, Joseph Kennedy, Jr. was one of the B-24 "flying bomb" pilots in this top secret experiment. He was killed during one of these missions when his Liberator, stuffed full of high explosives, exploded just seconds after he switched the plane over to "radio control" by the mother ship. The 357th Fighter Group was assigned to escort some of these secret missions until the project was canceled. I have not been able to ascertain whether or not any of the Yoxford Boys were escorting Joe Kennedy's plane when it exploded, killing both him and his copilot, but I will continue to research this.]

Around this same time I was asked by the OSS (the Office of Strategic Services was the United States military's WWII equivalent to today's Central Intelligence Agency) to fly for them. They were already operating an almost regular airline service for the Free French behind enemy lines. My job was to pick up Allied airmen downed behind enemy lines, collect intelligence, and to provide supplies to the Maquis. Soon after this I was grounded and ordered back to the United States.

The "Gash-Hound's" Tale

By Oliver Boch

Oliver Boch

I will never forget my second mission as it sticks in my mind to this day. I was flying a "radio relay" mission and my element leader was flying one of his last sorties before going home. We were supposed to loiter over Brussels, Belgium while the rest of the 357th Fighter Group went deep into Germany or Czechoslovakia. After takeoff, we entered overcast at 500 feet and we kept on climbing until, at 37,000 feet we finally reached the top of the clouds. My Mustang was indicating 150mph and that was at full rpm and manifold pressure, with a very severe angle of attack just to maintain altitude. It was very cold at that height but otherwise comfortable, without pressurization. When speaking to Control on the radio telephone only about two words would come out before I would have to take a deep breath again.

Boch in the cockpit of his Mustang

We flew for half an hour in one direction and then did a 180 and flew another half hour in that direction. After five hours of this, you would think that I would know what I was doing and that I would become a great navigator, but oh no! I was in a jet stream with 100 to 150mph winds and it blew my element leader and me off course. As it was not a good day (weatherwise), the bombers and fighters that had strayed were all trying to contact Colgate, the fixing station in England that could more or less pinpoint a plane's location through triangulation.

I finally reached Colgate and they gave my element leader and me a heading of 355 degrees and ninety-five miles to Leiston Airfield. Several minutes before we got under the clouds, the DF (direction finder) at Leiston gave us a heading and we found that we had drifted south. After what we calculated to be ninety-five miles, we descended and broke out of the clouds at 500 feet, and there was the shoreline and the North Sea, but it looked different. After flying up the coastline and seeing strange territory and an airfield full of bomb craters, we were still unsure of our position and, by now, we were down to 300 feet because of the weather. I looked over at my element leader for an instant and thought that I saw flames coming from his engine, but then I immediately realized that they were tracer bullets and other nasty things flying around. I yelled at my partner to hit the deck, which we both did, while wondering who in England would be shooting at us. Were we flying up the Thames estuary? Our being low on fuel by this point made that bombed out airfield look pretty good to us.

Oliver Boch flew forty missions in this P-51 Mustang named
Gash-Hound **(note the cartoon dog under the windshield)**

We then flew north still pondering where we were when I saw a large billboard advertizing Dubonnet wine. Well, this gave us a *big* clue as to where we were. France! The call sign for the emergency field in France was either "Domestic" or "Messenger" and I remembered that it would be sheer luck to call them at 300 feet. Much to my surprise, they came booming through the radio giving us a heading of ninety degrees left. I was a bit wary of this steer because I had heard that the German controllers had talked enemy planes into landing on Nazi fields and where they were then captured. I looked to my left and they were firing mortars from the emergency airfield so that we could find it in the bad weather. A few B-17s and B-24s were in the landing pattern, so that reassured us a good bit.

We were at Merville and it hadn't been too terribly long since the field had been occupied by the Germans. There were graphics on the walls in Deutsche. With such a large amount of aircraft using the emergency field, it took three days before our home base at Leiston was reached and informed of our status. Just as soon as they would let us go, we were off and flying back to Leiston, making a detour around the "bad guys" at Dunkirk that would have liked to have another shot at us, for sure.

When we arrived back at Leiston Field, the guys were not too happy to see me as they had to give back some of my uniforms and my mattress which was a rare commodity. Our Intelligence Officer didn't rest until he rousted a Colgate controller from bed and found out what had happened. It was then that he found out the discrepancy. The controller said that he had told us that we were ninety-five miles from the *French* coast, which NEVER HAPPENED!

Another Godfrey and Gentile

By John W. "Jack" Dunn

Jack Dunn

At the risk of overdoing it, I will take advantage of this opportunity to put down on paper, for the first time, a bit of my personal experiences with the 357th Fighter Group. I was there.

Perhaps humorous, definitely not heroic, my experiences are very likely typical of a great many of us who were fortunate enough to be there at the time, ready and eager to perform the missions. You have probably scanned the books written over the years about the 357th Fighter Group in order to see if I am mentioned in any of them. I am not.

I arrived in England in September of 1944 and returned to the States a year later in September of 1945. As far as air combat is concerned, I think the best

216

way to express it is that, basically, when the enemy was up, I was not! Or if they were up, I was escorting someone home, as on the date of December 24, 1944. I was Dollar Blue Two, flying John Kirla's wing and was assigned to escort Chuck Weaver who had a rough engine, back to our base thirty minutes or so before the group got into a big rat race with the Germans. Or I was screwing up, as on the biggest day of them all, January 14, 1945, when the 357th Fighter Group got a record 55.5 air victories.

Chuck Weaver in his (nameless) P-51 Mustang which sported a comely nude on the nose

On that January 14 mission, I flew someone else's Mustang, which had a record of aborting on its two previous missions because of excessive fuel usage. I had a thing about never aborting, and consequently I never did. Since I had not seen an enemy aircraft on so many previous missions, I thought we would not see any on January 14, so I, very studiously, kept my fuselage tank full so I would have plenty of fuel and not have to abort if and when the squadron was ordered to drop its external wing tanks.

On that day, as on most days, I flew with my flight commander John Kirla on his wing. He had me convinced that we were going to become another *Godfrey and Gentile* team. George Behling was element leader with Jim Gasser on his wing in the number four position. Behling would be shot down and become a POW that day. Kirla got four victories and Gasser got two on *the Big Day.*

John Kirla

On his first turn into the enemy aircraft, John Kirla lost me, his "hotshot" wingman, as I snapped uncontrollably out of the action. You really can't fly a P-51 with a full fuselage tank and make high G turns at altitude without snapping. The amount of fuel in the fuselage tank affected the center of gravity of the Mustang. After my snap and dive, there seemed to be no one in sight except the enemy 109 that had worked its way into firing range on my tail. This of course, with my attitude, gave me a *sure* victory! I felt that I had him all to myself. To snaps later, I was on the treetops with full mixture and the throttle firewalled in order to burn off the excess fuel in my fuselage tank. My Me-109 apparently had some positive feelings about me too, because he was still in my relative position. Suddenly, a flight of four Mustangs dropped in on the German's tail, in front of me, and shot *my* victory out of the sky.

There is one more point of interest from this day. I then proceeded to fly up the bomber stream to see what I might do to help our *Big Friends.* Incidentally, there were smoke and debris all over the place on the ground from the many aircraft that had gone in. Upon reaching the bomber stream and otherwise being alone, my vision began to "telescope." Something was wrong! My oxygen supply was somehow decreased from all of the violent snap rolls, or perhaps more likely, I was suffering from hyperventilation. I don't know which, but the next thing I *did* know, I was again at treetop level. I had passed out at 28,000 feet and recovered in level flight just above the ground. Lucky boy!

At this point, I picked up my average course for home and proceeded to fly out across the English Channel, very much disgusted with myself. En route, I did a couple of rolls at a few hundred feet above the Channel, feeling that if the P-51 and I went in, so be it. Then I emptied my guns at various wave tops along the way and returned to Leiston-Saxmunden, our home base, where victory rolls were being executed it seemed by everyone else but me. Jack Dunn did not participate.

Ten days or so later, the group gathered at the Post Theater to see the gun camera film of the great mission. In about the middle of all of this, and after showing John Kirla's film of him gloriously downing four positive victories, and Jim Gasser getting two kills, came the part of the movie with the heading, "J. Dunn, First Lt." I would have left if I could. Someone shouted, "Hey, it looks like he must be getting one in the clouds!" Next, it was obvious that I was firing into the waves. So you see, all was not heroic, but in fact, at times it was simply frustrating.

D-Day

(A Year before the Big Bang)
By Ted Conlin

**1st Lt. Raymond "Ted" Conlin, Crew Chief Sgt. John Warner, and Armorer
Cpl. Jewel Williams (on wing) with their P-51 Mustang *Olivia De H***

There was electricity in the air as we went about the business of running the war on June 5, 1944. Our base at Leiston, England, had been shut down earlier that morning. No one was permitted to enter or leave the field from 08:00 hours on. The rumor was that the Invasion was imminent and all of England was alive with activity.

At 20:00 hours (8:00 p.m.), everyone was assembled in the hall to hear an address from General Eisenhower, who informed us that, indeed, the Invasion of Europe was only hours away, and that 06:00 (6:00 a.m.) the next morning was designated as "H" hour, the actual time that the Allies' troops would hit the beaches. The general told us that this would be the most important mission that any one of us would ever take part in, and that our job was to protect those brave guys that were going to execute the landings. Our primary aim was to prevent any action by the enemy that would endanger the lives of those men of ours participating in the operation.

**General Dwight D. Eisenhower speaks to the troops
shortly before "H" hour and the invasion of Europe**

Following the speech by General Eisenhower, we were briefed by Colonel Donald Graham, our base commander, as to the specific areas each of our squadrons were to be assigned to patrol and then we were given takeoff times for each squadron. I was in the 362nd Fighter Squadron and our takeoff time was given as 05:00 (5:00 a.m.) and our patrol area was at 27,000 feet over the Jersey and Guernsey Islands, which were just off of the west end of the Normandy coast. Following this, our squadron leader Captain Joseph "Joe" Broadhead assigned the flight leaders, element leaders, and all of the various wingmen. I was assigned to fly Captain Broadhead's wing.

I don't think anyone of us got a decent bit of sleep the rest of the night until we were awakened by the Charge of Quarters and reported to the flight line operations room for a tasteless breakfast and flight preparations prior to takeoff.

Promptly at 05:00 hours, the captain and I roared down the runway and ran smack into a low, heavy overcast, which extended almost to the deck. We went on gauges at once. This was weather with a capital W! After about forty minutes, we broke out into the clear air and arrived on station and on time. It was now very close to "H" hour.

When we were getting ready to go, I had to go (urinate) too, but decided that I would wait until we arrived at our designated area. At that time, I would avail myself of the relief tube that North American had so thoughtfully provided for such an emergency. As we settled into our patrol formation, I started to undo all of the straps, belts, and zippers in order to accomplish my objective. It was at that exact moment that the captain called to inform me that he and I were going to go down to take a look at the invasion. Egad! That meant five miles down on the gauges and then five more miles back up.

Well, *orders is orders,* so down we went. Just as we broke out of the overcast at 2,000 feet near the west end of Omaha Beach, we heard over the R/T (radio/telephone) that two enemy 109s had made a strafing pass from west to east. We just missed engaging them by a few seconds. After several minutes of "stooging" around, we headed back up to join the rest of the boys.

Of course, with all the excitement and the trip down to the Invasion beaches, I forgot all about my personal problem, which wasn't resolved until we returned to base some three hours later!

Round Trip to Leiston

By Tom Morris McKinney

Tom McKinney in his P-51B Mustang

"Round Trip"

I must inform the reader that the following story was taken from an interview with 364th Fighter Squadron pilot Tom McKinney and as such it has resisted my attempts to edit it properly. For this reason I must apologize for the way the story "jumps around," and I hope that my readers will forgive me for my lack of editorial success. It is very difficult to edit some interviews into a smoothly flowing story and it is certainly not the fault of Mr. McKinney or the interviewer. The following is the result of my mostly ineffectual efforts, but I present it to the reader anyway and hope that it is intelligible

"My father and two sisters moved to Simpsonville, South Carolina, after the death of my mother. I was nine years old. I lived in Simpsonville during my remaining teen years. I graduated from Simpsonville High School and volunteered for the Army Air Corp in March of 1941, in Greenville, South Carolina.

My first assignment was to Mechanic Trade School in New Orleans, Louisiana. I graduated two weeks after the attack on Pearl Harbor. Following my graduation, I was assigned as a mechanic on B-24 Liberators in the Thirtieth Bomb Group, Twenty-first Bomb Squadron, stationed at Muroc, California. The Rogers Dry Lake Unit then moved to March Field at Riverside, California, early in 1942.

I applied for flight training and was accepted. I was assigned to Luke Field and graduated as a Flight Officer in Class 43C. Following my graduation, I was assigned to the 357th Fighter Group, 364th Fighter Squadron, and sent to Tonopah, Nevada. While there, I learned all about the P-39 Airacobra and accrued 500 hours of flight time in this aircraft. The P-39 required respect and a *soft touch* and would *bite back* if mishandled. Too many pilots in our group "bought the farm" in the Airacobra.

After training at subsequent airbases around the western United States, the 357th Fighter Group finally set sail for Scotland aboard, I'm sad to say, the *Queen Elizabeth*. The North Atlantic was wet and stormy, but I avoided becoming seasick during the five-day crossing. Upon leaving the *Queen* aboard a ferry, I was shocked by the size of the ship. It carried some 20,000 troops. [Author's note: My research shows that the ship carried about 15,000 troops per voyage.] No wonder it was fair game for the German U-Boats!

We then traveled by train from Glasgow, Scotland, to England. Our first base was Raydon Wood. It was all new with plenty of mud but no aircraft. Our stay there as part of the Ninth Air Force was short and we soon transferred to the Eighth Air Force at Leiston, England. There, we saw our Mustangs for the first time, all five of them. They were P-51Bs, and each pilot flew for five hours around England in them. The Mustang was a dream to fly compared to the P-39 Airacobra. It was a superb fighter and did what it was intended to do. Just ask any bomber pilot or crew member who saw them in action over Berlin, Germany. Even Goering was in awe of the *Little Friends* when he first saw them escorting the bombers over Berlin. After the war, he reported that he knew then that the war was lost. An Me-109 POW on our base in Florida after the war stated that, "a (German) pilot would be willing to make the supreme sacrifice in the Mustang."

After flying long missions from Leiston, I "retired" to a double bed I had bought out of a showroom window with the first English pounds I spent. I had the comforter and all of the accessories. When I left the group to go Stateside, I offered it to my squadron mates at a terrific discount, but got no takers at any price. Later, I learned that John Storch claimed my bed. I hope he slept as well in it as I did. I suppose my second purchase was "fish and chips." That was the extent of my purchases with English currency. The British pound always seemed inferior to the American "greenbacks" to me.

I flew a total of seventy-four missions (301 hours) in the B, C, and D Model Mustangs. All were flown in *Round Trip* and *Round Trip Jr*. These names had been selected by my ground crew and me. I cannot remember ever flying any other Mustang other than my *Round Trips*.

McKinney, his Mustang, and crew, Sergeants Hood, Bazer, and Burleson (with their squadron's mascot Jamaica on the nose of *Round Trip Jr.*)

One time, my plane was down for an engine change, after another pilot borrowed it and used "war emergency boost" and blew the stacks off of the engine. I never "broke the wire," but I've always thought that it had more "boost." My previous mechanic training and work on B-24s taught me never to abuse the Merlin.

During combat, I suppose all of us had guns that jammed in the B Models. On my first encounter, while all alone dogfighting one on one with an Me-109, I lost three out of four of my guns during three head-on attacks. The commanding officer of the 363rd Fighter Squadron called me off of the 109 and ordered me to escort him back to England because his Mustang was barely flying after taking several 20mm rounds from an enemy fighter. Our top speed was only 140mph, the slowest I had ever flown on a return flight. His P-51 had been "vented" really well along the fuselage from cockpit to tail. After I broke off, the Me-109 trailed us for miles, and I am sure he was asking, "What is going on with these two pilots?" I was worried that I had only one gun with which to protect the shot-up Mustang.

Finding myself in a formation with fifty other P-51 Mustangs crossing the North Sea and knowing almost every one of the other pilots by name before going into combat against the Luftwaffe was one of the most memorable of all of my experiences during WWII. It also is a memory that I am extremely proud of. I was flying with fellow pilots who knew that some of us would not be returning home that evening, and yet they were still willing to forge ahead and offer their overwhelming support to each and every other member of the group. They also were ready to pitch themselves headlong into a dogfight in support of their group mates even if this meant that they might end up being the one that didn't get home to Leiston that night. To witness another 357th pilot or friend going down was the toughest thing for me to cope with personally. Some other pilots could not handle it very well either, but a trip to the Officers Club or a nearby pub seemed to help.

One of my most memorable combat missions was one during which I sighted several Focke Wulf 200 "Condors" taking off from an airfield in France. Our Group was returning from a bomber escort mission into southern France, when my flight leader, Glendon Davis, spotted enemy aircraft taking off from a German base 8,000 feet below us. Our flight consisted of three P-51s and I was flying as the number three element leader. The sky was almost solid overcast as we dived down through a small hole in the clouds. Just then, we saw Me-109s below us at 5,000 feet and I was told to engage the enemy fighters. When I broke out of the dive, the 109s flew into the overcast and disappeared. I waited, but they did not reappear. Why, I never found out.

At about the same time, the three Me-200 Condors were shot down and were burning near the airfield. Several others were parked around the aerodrome and we considered targeting them, but when the ack-ack came into play, we pulled up and away, circling a few times before we headed back toward Leiston. I had seen my first enemy planes that day-big ones! The Condors had been guiding the German U-Boats to our convoys in the Atlantic. Maybe an Allied convoy was saved that day because of our actions. What a show for my first enemy encounter!

Later, I saw Messerschmitt 262s on one of our escort missions. I saw them purely as a "demonstration" though, as they were flying much higher and faster than we were, and fortunately made no passes at the bombers that day. I still remember the long contrails they left in the sky above us. The unusual contrails lingered much longer than the ones made by our bombers. Another German "shocker" was the V-1 Buzz Bomb. My ground crew saw one crash near our base at Leiston Field.

Sometime during the war, the Germans developed a delivery system that could carry atomic weapons to England and the aircraft designers at Messerschmitt even built a bomber that could fly all the way to New York City and Washington, D.C., and then return to France. This "top secret" airplane made a flight from Europe to New York and then returned to the Continent undetected. Thanks to the Eighth Air Force, Norwegian saboteurs, and the Royal Air Force, Germany's attempt to create an atomic bomb was derailed a number of times. This prevented us from having to deal with these weapons that later devastated Japan. It was, in my opinion, a very close call.

While flying combat missions over Europe, most often, I flew with members of my flight and the 364th Fighter Squadron. Our first flight of four pilots was composed of Glendon Davis, the flight leader, T. L. (Lil' Red) Harris, the number two man (wingman to Davis), Tom McKinney, the number three element leader, and Morris Stanley, the number four "tail-end Charlie" (wingman to McKinney).

Most of my combat flying was with our own squadron's pilots, and I knew them all, as well as the names of their Mustangs. It was a great feeling to join a bomber or fighter when I was returning to England alone. I found myself alone twice for a short time, and it was a great feeling of relief when I saw other Mustangs as I was out of ammunition on one of those two occasions. (What a mistake, I never let it happen again!)

Once, while alone, I spotted *Hurry Home Honey* and Pete Peterson, and we flew in a storm for some distance before reaching England. It seemed to me that the snowflakes were moving past us on a horizontal plane, but Peterson missed the snow scene as he was flying on gauges in solid IFR (instrument flight rules) conditions.

D-Day

Upon entering the Briefing Room on June 6, 1944, we were told that the paratroopers were jumping into France at that very moment and that this was the "big push." We took off from Leiston before dawn expecting to enter into the largest air battle ever fought. We were in total shock when no enemy aircraft showed up to fight! Why?

Some years later, an Me-109 pilot told me that his unit was stationed at Calais, France, awaiting orders that never came. It was strange that they had all day to fly a short distance to Normandy for the "show," yet the Germans chose to sit this one out. This German pilot used the alibi that they believed that the attack on Normandy was only a "decoy" and that the main attack would be in the Calais area. If the Luftwaffe had looked for us, I'm sure that we could have been found since all of our planes were "zebra striped" for easy identification. We returned to our base after a long day only to learn that Leroy Ruder of the 364th Fighter Squadron was the only pilot lost during the missions flown by our group on June 6, 1944. Once again, my friends and I had another empty bunk to cope with. After D-Day was over I had flown two missions.

During my time with the 357th Fighter Group, I flew with all of our pilots on escort missions including Glendon Davis, John Storch, Tommy Hayes, Tom (Lil' Red) Harris, Ray (Sparky) Sparks, C. D. (Speck) Sumner, Mark Stepelton, Ben Elliot, Henry (Hank) Pfeiffer, George Fandry, Morris Stanley, Jack Warren, Richard "Pete" Peterson, Leroy Ruder, Clarence "Bud" Anderson, Charles "Chuck" Yeager, Glen Hubbard, Henry Spicer, George Currie, Ed

McKee, and Bill Reese. My faithful ground crew consisted of Crew Chief Bill Hood, Assistant Crew Chief Irv Bazer, and Armorer Sergeant Burleson. As a result of their efforts, I flew seventy-four missions without one abort due to mechanical problems.

To my ground crew and to all of the 357th Fighter Group pilots, I am proud to have been a part of the most dedicated and patriotic group of men I have ever known. Thanks for letting me be a member. It was a great honor to have served with you.

The Death of Captain Jim Browning

(February 9, 1945)
By Donald Bochkay and Merle Olmsted

"Gentleman" Jim Browning

I was flying wing to Captain Browning who was leading Cement spares on an escort mission of B-17s to Leipzig, Germany. We were doing nicely on our escort job at 26,000 feet crossing over the bombers and holding a very good formation. At 1115 hours around the Fulda area of Germany, four Me-262s were called in by one of our flights under us at about 4,000 feet heading toward the bombers. We dropped our tanks and Captain Browning dove to the left for an attack. The four 262s broke up, with two diving to the right and two diving to the left. Captain Browning never did get within range of those going left.

I climbed, balls out, keeping the Me-262s in sight as well as covering Captain Browning. I climbed to 28,000 feet and leveled off. Just as I leveled off, the two 262s broke right into a steep climbing turn.

I called Captain Browning and told him that I was cutting them off. Then, I dove my ship in order to gain more airspeed. The sun was in my favor and I believe the pilots of the 262s did not see me. I came in on the lead 262 and broke hard to the right, coming out on the second jet's tail at a very good range of 300 yards. I fired a long burst as he was pulling away from me, but I observed some very good hits around the canopy and right engine. That really slowed him down. The lead Me-262 headed straight down, and the one I hit broke to the left in a gentle turn, so I opened fire on him again at about 400 yards and kept firing all of the way in on him. I saw many strikes all over his ship; his canopy shattered and large pieces were flying off of the enemy aircraft. I broke to the right in order to keep from running into him. As I passed very close to the German jet, the pilot was halfway out of the cockpit. His ship then rolled over onto its back and the pilot fell out. He never opened his chute and his plane went straight in. I then pulled up into a climbing left turn to rejoin Captain Browning, but we got separated because of so many P-51s in the area with the same colored tails. I found myself alone, so I set off to join up with someone from our own bunch. Jim Browning did not return from this mission and no one saw what happened to him.

Jim Browning and his P-51D Mustang *Gentleman Jim*

Gentleman Jim Browning

(A True American Hero)

Captain James W. Browning, of the 363rd Fighter Squadron, was one of the "gung-ho" types, who had come back to the Group for a second combat tour. Gentleman Jim, an ace with five victories before he departed to the Zone of the Interior (U. S. A.) in mid-year, returned near the end of 1944 and scored two more victories.

The mission on February 9, 1945, was the usual heavy bomber escort, with the 357th Fighter Group providing sixty-two Mustangs divided into two groups led by Colonel Dregne and Major Peterson. The Luftwaffe opposition was in the form of the formidable Me-262 jets, one group of three, which used their superior speed to evade Greenhouse Squadron.

Fifteen minutes prior to this encounter, at 1140 hours, Cement Squadron (363rd Fighter Squadron) engaged nine Me-262s. From the mission report, the following can be found: "The Squadron dropped tanks and dived on the jets which broke into elements of two and scattered. The lead jet, although under attack, turned into the bomber formation and made an attack through the box, one of our elements in pursuit. The remainder were driven away from the bombers with above results." (This refers to Me-262s destroyed by Bochkay and Carter, and a "probable" by Foy.) The mission report also states: "One NYR (Not Yet Returned), Captain Browning, last seen in the vicinity of Fulda."

Captain Bochkay was flying Jim Browning's wing that day, both however, were spares and were not required to accompany the Group on the mission. Both being eager fighter pilots, they pressed on regardless. Bochkay later said in a statement: "At 1145 hours, Captain Browning was on the tail of two Me-262s and was chasing them. I was covering Captain Browning at the time, and continued to cover him until it was in our favor for me to be the attacker. I then called Captain Browning and told him that I was cutting him off and for him to cover me. As I was making my attack on the last Me-262, Captain Browning called me and told me to keep going as he had me covered. That was the last I heard or saw of Captain Browning. This happened at 24,000 feet over Fulda, Germany. There were a large number of P-51s in the area at the time." So there the matter rested, and there was no further information forthcoming about the fate of Jim Browning. He simply disappeared.

There are German documents attached to Browning's MACR (missing aircrew report) in the National Archives, but they merely indicate: "1140 hours, one Mustang shot down three kilometers southwest (of) Wueger, twenty kilometers southwest (of) Limburg after fighting with German day fighters. Pilot James William Browning, serial number 0-740361, and aircraft totally burned."

The Army Air Force's efforts to identify and recover the remains of its dead were very thorough and painstaking. Investigating teams had fanned out throughout Europe even before the end of the war. German police and town officials were interviewed and many statements of eyewitnesses were taken. After complete analysis a board then decided if the remains were recoverable, and if so they were located and removed, and then sent to one of several American Military Cemeteries in Europe. Then, if requested by the next of kin, the remains were disinterred and returned to the Zone of the Interior (the United States). The investigation into this case did solve the mystery of what happened to Jim Browning.

In a statement dated August 5, 1947, one Adolf Keller, the burgermeister of the town of Woersdorf, Germany, states: "On February 9, 1945, at noontime, I saw a dogfight in the vicinity of Wuerges, besides a German fighter which was engaged in the fight, there were several other planes in the air. The German fighter rammed an airplane and both of them caught fire and crashed down." Keller found the site of the wreck and recovered several items, including a gold ring, an identification tag (dog tag) with Browning's name on it, a photograph with his name on it, and some currency.

The following comments were extracted from a statement dated August 6, 1947, by one Wilhelm Manrer: "I am a railway employee. On February 9, 1945, I was in my office when I heard firing from (the) weapons of a plane, followed by an explosion. I went outside and saw a cloud of smoke about 600 meters from the station. When I was relieved at 1800 hours, I went to the place of the crash. There I saw the wreckage of a plane scattered over an area of 400 meters. I could not recognize the plane's type. On one part I found printed letters 'Zanke' [Zarnke]. The plane was burnt. I did not see any remains or parts of a body. Approximately 600 meters from the place of the crash, a German plane had crashed. I, however, did not see that crash."

The "Zanke" reported was undoubtedly the canopy rim and the name was "Zarnke," since Jim Browning was flying Glen Zarnke's P-51 *Junior Miss II* on that date. At some point then, after Bochkay had taken the lead in the attack, Jim Browning collided with one of the jets, and as a result, both pilots died in the manner described.

Of interest is the high rank and title of the German pilot. His name was Freiherr Riedesel. (Freiherr means "baron.") My contacts in Germany and in the United States have identified Riedesel as the commander of KG(J) 54, and he was flying an Me-262 with the Werk Nr. (serial number) 500042. His unit was a former bomber gruppe (same as our *wing*), as shown in the "KG" designation, which had been re-equipped as a fighter unit "J" at the time when the Luftwaffe needed fighters much more than they needed bombers. KG(J) 54 lost five Me-262s on this date to the Seventy-eighth and 357th Fighter Groups.

Jim Browning knew the risks he was taking by returning for a second combat tour, and he could have remained in the States, but he came back to "the old outfit" (as many soldiers have a way of doing). The odds caught up with him, however, and now, after more than fifty years, we know what happened to him.

In May of 1949, Headquarters, American Graves Registration Command, Europe, issued a synopsis of his case, and recommended that his remains be declared "non-recoverable." He is one of twenty-six "unrecovered" in this area of Europe as of this date.

Because there were no recoverable remains, James Browning's name is listed on "The Wall of the Missing" at the American Military Cemetery in Luxembourg.

The Saga of Kenneth Hagan

Ken Hagan was an original member of the 357th Fighter Group (362nd Fighter Squadron) and the best friend of Fletcher Adams. Hagan and Adams married around the same time while in training in the Zone of the Interior and they, along with their wives, Bonnie Hagan and Aline Adams, lived together in the same boarding house before the men went off to war. Less than three weeks after Fletcher Adams was shot down over Tiddische, Germany, and murdered, Ken Hagan, by then the assistant operations officer of his squadron and one of the 357th's most respected fighter pilots, went down over Occupied France on June 17, 1944, after his Mustang *My Bonnie* suffered engine failure. Luckily, Hagan was quickly picked up by the French Underground and they were able to help him evade and return to his unit.

The following story was sent to me by Kenneth Hagan's nephew, who shares the same name as his uncle. It was written by Andre Rougeyron, a member of the Marquis during World War Two. I have borrowed it from his book, *Agents for Escape*. Historian Stephen Ambrose wrote the following description of Rougeyron's book and the sacrifices he made in assisting Allied airmen to escape the Nazis during WWII:

> "*War brings out the best in some men, the worst in others. We see both in this splendid memoir of a French Resistant who helped dozens of British and American Flyers, shot down over France, to escape German-occupied Europe. Rougeyron paid a terrible price for his courage-Arrested in 1944, he was sent to Buchenwald, where his suffering at the hands of the Germans was immense. He described his experiences in straightforward, simple prose that captures the spirit of the time and puts one inside Occupied Normandy and later inside the concentration camp. It makes for fascinating, if not always pleasant, reading.*"

**Ken Hagan (center) and crew in front of his
P-51B Mustang *My Bonnie***

Here is the story of Kenneth Hagan as written by Rougeyron and later translated by Marie-Antoinette McConnell:

On June 17 a motorcycle stopped at my door. It was Dr. Ledos, who announced, "An Allied fighter plane has crashed into a wheat field. The pilot has escaped unharmed and has found temporary shelter on a farm. We must get him out." I replied, "Of course." We opened the survey map and located the site. It was the James farm at La Grande-Corbiere in Tinchebray. We planned our strategy: we would take the direct route there, then return with a detour through Yvrandes to avoid the Germans, who were everywhere. The doctor left to notify Madame James. Bobby jumped on Totor's bicycle. I told Duffy and Joe that a third American was coming, and they were very pleased. At last we would know exactly what was going on on the other side of the lines. Two hours passed by, three, then relief: here they were. My new guest was all smiles, sitting on the frame of the bicycle, carrying under his arm a little khaki bundle . . . his military clothing. He came in. Joe and Duffy rushed toward him and they engaged in an excited conversation whose flow could not be checked. I brought out a bottle of wine to celebrate.

Our new boarder was Captain Kenneth E. Hagan from Lincoln, Illinois. He was the pilot of a Mustang. After engine failure four miles away, his aircraft had hit the ground violently, turned over, and split in half. Kenneth escaped with nothing more serious than a scrape on his forehead. He set fire to his plane and took off. Bobby told us he had gone to the site to take a photograph of the Mustang. This explained the delay in their arrival. On the way, they had passed German soldiers; the aviator had never seen any before.

The captain's uniform was hidden away in a safe place where we had already stored many compromising items: maps of parachute drop sites, photographs, coded messages, the cipher I used when I was a transmitter, a series of articles written in 1943 in cooperation with a Paris attorney, Maitre M. Philonenko, for the underground press, liaison signals, and so on.

I took care of Kenneth's outfit. He had been given some good clothes at the James farm, but we had fits of laughter at the large V shaved right in the middle of his brown hair during a recent hair cut. This mark had to be kept hidden at all costs, and I gave him formal orders never to remove his Basque beret.

Finally, we made his identity card and other required papers. Duffy had become Adolphe Vilmont, adjuster, Joe was Joseph Portier, mechanic, and Kenneth would become Max Haigan, carpenter. All three were residents of Caen. Since Kenneth's arrival, we had details on the scope of the invasion and on the awesome weaponry of the Allied forces. We were more confident than ever in the rapid conclusion of the operations. The Allied front slowly developed, with the American and British troops progressing toward the east.

On June 20, Bobby received orders to return to Caen with the airmen if they wanted to attempt to rejoin the Allied front. The airmen agreed, and their departure was imminent. A photograph was taken of all of us, and we spent the evening preparing the supplies for their trip. Despite their protests, Jeanne and I insisted that they take along certain provisions.

**This is the picture taken of Ken Hagan (center back row) and his Maquis
friends shortly before they left for Caen**

*On June 21, at dawn, Jeanne and I watched the road as four shadows faded out of
sight, headed toward their destiny. The house seemed strangely empty, and the dinner table
too large. I wondered, "Will they get through? Will they make it?"*

*To guard against any eventuality, Jeanne and I installed a bed in the former "night
residence" of our airmen. The inhabitants of the areas close to the battles were leaving
and going south; this was the beginning of a lamentable exodus that would increase each
day. At night the convoys rolled incessantly, and there was much aircraft activity; we were
getting used to all the uproar and machine-gun fire, which was more and more frequent.*

May 1945

*We were liberated on August 15, 1944. We returned to our house, but it had been
terribly ransacked. This was the month that marked the Victory of Right over Oppression.
It was spring, and the birds were singing. Jeanne and I received two letters, which we
opened eagerly. One came from America, the other from England.*

Kenneth (Max) wrote:

> *You have surely been told what happened to us and how we were
> liberated. I'll briefly narrate the details: On August 2 you left us in the
> care of two men who led us to the home of a Frenchman in Domfront.
> His name was Andre Rougeyron. We spent the night in his chateau
> built on the side of a bluff overlooking part of the city. Early the next
> morning, Andre was arrested by the Gestapo. The four of us fled his*

home. One of the men that were left, Rene Leray, led us to a little village a few kilometers southeast, where we were met by Raymond Alexandre Guesdon. From there we immediately went back to Domfront, crossed the city, and headed toward Granville. Shortly afterward, we turned toward the hills southeast of Lonlay l'Abbaye. At this point Raymond Guesdon left us (Joe, Duffy, Jacques/Edward, and me) in the care of Rene Leray to look for a route that would allow us to cross the lines and rejoin the Americans. We stayed in a little hut (for bread-baking) near a village and enjoyed some tranquility and sun for three days. The sounds of battle were getting closer. On the third day, August 7, Raymond Guesdon came back after having spent a night with the Americans. He said he was going to take us across the lines, but first he wanted me to go with him to Lonlay l'Abbaye to survey the situation and obtain information likely to interest the Americans. When we arrived in Lonlay, we heard that six Germans were holding the city and that ten hostages were going to be shot because someone had killed two soldiers during the night. They were also going to set fire to the town. We decided to join the Americans immediately to see if they could take Lonlay right away, before a tragedy took place. We returned to the place where Joe, Duffy, and Jacques were hiding; then we walked the twelve kilometers to the American lines. I gave all the information to the American commander, who told me he would try to save the people of Lonlay. Then we were evacuated to a safe location, so we never found out what happened. Do you know if the people of Lonlay were spared? We spent the night of August 7 at the Air Force General Headquarters. On August 8 we went by jeep-via Saint Lo-to an Air Force camp off the coast of Brittany, from there we were flown to England by transport plane. Joe, Duffy, and Jacques flew to the United States on August 20; I stayed with my squadron until the end of the month . . .

After returning to the United States, Kenneth Hagan was assigned to duty at Tyndall Field at Panama City, Florida, which later became Tyndall Air Force Base. On December 12, 1946, Ken Hagan was found dead ten miles from the base. Hagan, one of the heroes of the 357th Fighter Group, was twenty-three years old. He died under extremely mysterious circumstances and the truth behind his demise is still in question today. Ken's nephew contacted Colonel Arval "Robie" Roberson shortly before Roberson passed away. Roberson had been an original 362nd Fighter Squadron member and had been friends with Ken Hagan since July of 1943. In an email to Hagan's nephew, Robie described the circumstances surrounding his uncle's death. The following is Colonel Roberson's account of the tragedy as retold by Hagan's nephew, Ken Hagan:

Ken Hagan was found hanging in a tree. The area and the sapling had been burned previously. He also elaborated that Kenny had no char marks on his pants. When a colonel tried to climb the same tree, he could not climb it without getting any marks on his pants and he tried three different times! Very unusual! The rope used was the kind used to tie down airplanes. Roberson said that the area around the base was thought to have been owned by Al Capone or some of his gang members. Arval said that there was some thought that Kenny had picked up a hitchhiker (as many soldiers did) but it is still unknown. Roberson did not have a theory or knowledge about what happened. He said that the official report stated that Ken Hagan "died at his own hands or at the hands of others." The authorities never really explored the case very much. Arval said that they didn't think too much of the police force around Panama City.

In 2009 I attempted to investigate Hagan's death. I contacted Tyndall Air Force Base, the Bay County Clerk of Court's Office, the Panama City Police Department, and the Bay County Coroner's Office. No one that I contacted ever replied to my request for information. Ken Hagan's family can rest assured, though, that I have not forgotten my pledge to them to continue my efforts to solve this mystery. I will continue to "rattle the cages" of the powers-that-be in Bay County, Florida until I am satisfied that I have extracted all of the historical information involving this case.

So Long for a While

Lt. Walter N. Perry, Jr.

There's a saying over here that if one returns from a mission he is doing fine. That tells the story 'cause I'm still here. This life is positively one chapter I would not miss even if it costs me my life. You know the rules; a guy's talking to you in the morning and to God at night, but it's just part of the game. So says fate.

You tell me all the good things, I'll tell you all the good things, and we'll both save that other stuff for Adolf. So long for a while, Walt.

The letter from which this quote was taken has been lost forever. Only one page of it still exists, and although it contains no date or even an addressee, Walter N. Perry, Jr., its author, makes his point "in spades." Walter Jr., the oldest son of Mr. and Mrs. Walter N. Perry Sr. also had a kid brother and six sisters, and they all grew up happily and peacefully in Raleigh, North Carolina until December 7, 1941. On that day, the Japanese forced the United States to choose sides in the largest and bloodiest conflict in the history of civilized man, and Walter Jr.'s future would be sacrificed as a result.

The young man volunteered and joined the Army Air Corps, but since he was still a minor, his father, Walter Sr., had to sign a waiver before he could be inducted. Being a father with a son the same age, I can only imagine the doubt that Mr. Perry must have felt about doing so, and I'm sure he questioned that decision after he learned that his oldest boy had been killed in action two days before Christmas while flying another of his many combat missions with the 357th Fighter Group. This story was not uncommon during the brutal war we now call World War II, but for Walter Perry Sr., his wife, and his remaining seven children, it certainly *was* unique and it altered their lives forever in many ways. Surprisingly, one positive thing was born from this tragedy. It compounded the Perry family's undying love and deep respect for Walter Jr., and these emotions still burn in their hearts and minds like the warm, comfortable, afterglow of a beautiful sunset. Walter lives on forever through their love for him.

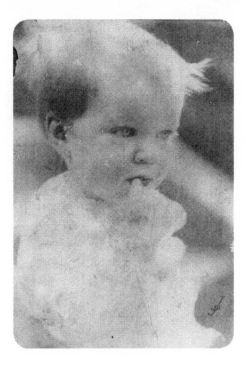

Walt Perry

Captain Walter N. Perry, Jr. also lives on in history books. Having proved himself as a successful fighter pilot in a P-51 Mustang, he also stood out as a hero and an inspiration to the other pilots and crewmen in the 357th Fighter Group (one of the greatest fighter outfits in the history of military aviation) even after his untimely death at the age of twenty-one. Yet do not weep for this young man, for he will never be forgotten or go unloved. It is for this very reason that I am telling his story now.

Walter Perry joined the highly esteemed 357th Fighter Group (362nd Fighter Squadron) during the summer of 1944 and after a short stint in the group's "Clobber College" he began flying combat missions over Europe in July of that year. He quickly rose in rank due to his outstanding performance as a seasoned fighter pilot and on December 22, 1944, the day before his demise, he was promoted to captain.

Perry in the cockpit of his P-51 Mustang

Perry was one of the most upbeat and enthusiastic members of his squadron and his positive attitude still shines through in the letters he sent home to his family some sixty-seven years after they were written. He faithfully wrote not only to his mother and father, but also to his siblings, regardless of their ages, and this author has decided to include several of these letters in this story.

"Dear Mom,

All is fine and dandy with me. I am now doing what I've wanted to do since I first left home. Yes, I'm fighting the Jerrys with P-51s and it's a cinch. It's just about as safe flying here as it was in the States.

We have a wonderfully organized Air Force here, everything is well planned and we get the best possible treatment. Even the English civilians who don't have too much are making it very pleasant for us. The girls are different, but they do their best to please us with dances, parties, etc.

I only wish you could be here to enjoy all the historical sites and study the customs and habits of the people.

You wrote of the beach-I would like to be there and get a little sun; an item that is rationed very much here.

Captain Don Gentile, now in the United States, was recently here and made a great record as a P-51 pilot. There are lots of other high-ranking "aces" here and I'm aiming to join them as soon as possible.

If you don't get too many letters from me, don't worry; they hold them up sometimes for security reasons. Just remember, don't worry a bit, 'cause I'm in there punching and I'd like to come home just as much as the next guy, and will as soon as this thing is over.

Just to prove that we're not being starved, I now weigh 165 pounds and am in very good condition, as I have been doing weight lifting for about a month.

So long for a while, Walt. "

Soon after arriving in Leiston, England, Walter Perry was assigned his first ship, a P-51B (serial number 43-6637) with a "Malcolm hood" which had formerly belonged to Alden Smith and carried the name *American Girl*. As soon as Perry took possession of the Mustang he renamed it *Rubber Check* but it still carried its old code "G4-K." Lt. Perry would fly this ship for several months, scoring 2.5 victories (and one damaged enemy aircraft) in it before it was finally destroyed by fire in a crash on an icy runway at Leiston Field on December 2, 1944.

Walter Perry on the tail of Clifford Anderson's
P-51 *Buddy Boy*, code G4-G

    Lt. Perry's first victory occurred on August 18, 1944, when he shared a "kill" with the 362nd Fighter Squadron's leading ace Johnny Brook England after the pair caught two silver Me-109s "with their pants down" and destroyed one of the enemy ships.

8-23-44

Dear Dad,

I have some pretty good news for you this time. Yes, I got my first victory over an enemy aircraft just recently. He was the first Hun aircraft I had ever seen in the air.

We were out on an escort job, and I was leading the element in green flight. I spotted a "bogie" at 10 o'clock high, and called him into my flight leader, who executed a steep "balls out" chandelle to get into firing position if the "bogie" turned out to be a "bandit." Well, it was a "bandit"—an all white Me 109 with black crosses. My flight leader fired a burst at 60° deflection, and got a coupla strikes on the Jerrie's wing, but due to his low airspeed he stalled out when firing. The 109 executed a split "S", and that was my chance. I kicked in full bottom rudder, and started lining up on the Hun, who was now going "balls out" down the hill. I gave him a squirt, which knocked his hydraulic system out and caused his undercarriage to drop. He immediately started evasive action — he had a few tricks all his own, and knew how to handle the ship. The action had started at 15,000', but we were at about 5000' before I could line up for

another burst. I was closing fast
as hell, but got in a good burst,
and his coolant started streaming
out. I had to pull up to keep from
overshooting the Hun, who was
still going for the deck. He was
about 55' off the trees so I closed
up to about 100' feet and cut loose.
I got a lot of good strikes which
started him smoking, and knocked
parts off his ship.

That did it. he pulled up to
about 200' and hit the silk. His
ship hit & burned, and as I was
getting ground fire I had to
get out of there. I joined my flight
and we headed out.

The day before I got the Jerry
ship, I got two direct bomb hits

on a German locomotive, and I got two trucks by strafing.

This fighter flying is really the stuff, but I'm sure glad I'm not doing it for the Huns. They are really on the wrong side, and it is my personal opinion that they know it.

I'm glad to hear that everybody is O.K. I'd sure like to dig into some good old watermelons, and some of those apples from the farm. I wonder if you and Butch have had a chance to put out some grapevines, and pecan trees.

So long for a while,

Walt

Perry's first Mustang, the P-51B *Rubber Check* and its crew

Then, on the eighteenth and nineteenth of September, 1944, Perry scored two more victories. For the benefit of my readers, I have included both of those encounter reports in this book.

2nd Lt. Walter N. Perry, Jr. 0-821770

A. Combat
B. 18 September 1944.
C. 362nd Fighter Squadron, 357th Fighter Group
D. 1500 B. S. T.
E. Vicinity of Nijmegen, Holland
F. Slight haze
G. Me-109
H. I was flying number three position in Dollar Blue flight when we spotted a gaggle of forty plus Me-109s at ten o'clock and 2,000 feet above. We climbed up and bounced them. I broke left into one enemy plane which was tacking on to my wingman. I fired several short bursts, observing clean strikes around his wing roots and cockpit. At about 2,000 feet altitude I poured in a long burst from close range, getting strikes which caused parts to fly off the enemy plane and started him smoking. He went into a spin, hit the ground, and exploded. I did not see the pilot bail out.

I claim one Me-109 destroyed.

I. 900 rounds

    Enemy casualty: pilot

2nd Lt. Walter N. Perry, Jr. 0-821770

A. Combat

B. 19 September 1944

C. 362nd Fighter Squadron, 357th Fighter Group

D. 1705 B. S. T.

E. Vicinity of Ijsselstein, Holland

F. Hazy

G. Me-109

H. Pilot

I. I was flying wing to Flight Officer Jenkins in Dollar White flight. We were heading south when, at about 10,000 feet, I spotted a fight between Me-109s and P-51s at twelve o'clock and slightly low. I dropped my tanks, and as we approached, two 109s headed to the right and out of the fight. Jenkins took one and I took the other. Both split-essed to the deck. I followed my 109, catching him at 5,000 feet, and firing a short burst from 500 yards. He pulled out on the deck and started turning. I closed to about 200 yards and fired several short bursts, observing strikes all over his canopy and wing roots. He started burning and the pilot jettisoned his canopy. However, he did not get out, as his ship hit the ground and exploded. I fired a long burst into the wreckage to get a picture.

I claim one Me-109 destroyed.

J. 380 rounds

Walter Perry, Jr.'s fourth and final encounter with the enemy occurred on October 6, 1944, during which time he witnessed a large group of Me-109s and FW-190s attacking a box of B-17 bombers 20 miles northwest of Berlin, Germany. Perry singled out one of the Focke Wulf Butcher Birds (190s) and as its pilot split-essed in a desperate attempt to evade the pursuing Mustang, Walter latched onto his tail following the Jerry through two rolls before closing to 200 yards. Perry then loosed a burst from *Rubber Check's* four fifty caliber guns striking the fleeing FW-190 in the engine and lower wing roots. Fortunately for the German pilot, the Mustang's guns jammed and Walter Perry was forced to break off the engagement. Back in Leiston that evening, he put in a claim for one Focke Wulf 190 damaged. Between the rest of October and the end of November, 1944, Perry went scoreless and then the harshest winter in decades descended over Europe.

During December, 1944, the 357th Fighter Group's Mustangs were grounded 42 percent of the month due to the bad weather. Fog, snow, and icy conditions kept the pilots from flying missions on thirteen of the thirty-one last days of 1944. The brutal weather was to blame for the fact that during the first six days of the month, only two missions were flown by the group, one on the second and one on the fifth of December. Although Walter Perry, Jr. did not fly the mission on December 2, someone else borrowed his Mustang. And upon this pilot's return to the base that day he managed to crash-land *Rubber Check* on the runway at Leiston. The result of this crash was that within minutes the P-51B was consumed by fire and completely destroyed, leaving Walter Perry without a fighter to fly.

Luckily the group had just received a brand-new P-51K. This Mustang had been delivered to the Eighth Air Force in England on November 12 and arrived at Station AAF-373 (Leiston Field) on November 26, 1944. After spending a few days being outfitted and repainted, the fighter became available to the next 362nd Fighter Squadron pilot in need of another mount and that was Walter Perry, Jr. [Author's note: It is also possible that Walter Perry, Jr. had been given the new P-51K before the demise of *Rubber Check* on December 2 as it was not uncommon for more experienced pilots to receive new aircraft when they arrived at the base. These pilots then passed their older planes on to lesser experienced pilots. Eventually the older model Mustangs were labeled "war weary" (which was painted on their tails) and passed on to the newest 357th Fighter Group pilots, who flew them in the group's "Clobber College," where the experienced Yoxford Boys put them through a "crash course" in weather flying and dogfighting techniques before sending the replacement pilots into combat.] Perry named his new P-51K (tail number 44-11689) *Toolin Fool* and the name was painted onto the nose of the Mustang.

For decades Perry's family has believed that Walter borrowed this plane from another pilot when he flew his last mission on the twenty-third of December, but this author believes that this was not the case. During my research for this chapter of the book, I received a batch of letters that Perry wrote during 1944. In one of Walter's letters home that the family believed was written during November of 1944, he mentioned that he had just received a new aircraft and that he had not had a chance to "test it out in actual combat yet." Since Walter Perry had only flown *Rubber Check* until it was destroyed, with the exception of days that he may have borrowed another Mustang while his was undergoing maintenance, it is almost certain that *Toolin Fool* was his assigned aircraft during the last month of 1944. In fact, when I studied the letter in which he mentioned receiving a new plane, I found a postal stamp that had bled through onto the last page of the letter. The airmail letter had been stamped "Raleigh, North Carolina, Dec. 12, 1944," proving that it had arrived in the United States in the middle of that month. This means that the undated letter was almost certainly written shortly before or after December 2, 1944, and within a few days of the destruction of *Rubber Check*. It is also fairly certain that he was describing the new P-51K Mustang *Toolin Fool* in this letter. Adding to this mystery is the fact that it was later rumored that another pilot in the 357th Fighter Group flew a Mustang named *Toolin Fool* before December, 1944, and that a piece of the wreckage of that plane was found in Germany with that name on it. Even if this is true, the reader must remember that there were several P-51s in the Group that shared the same names at different times, including *Southern Belle* and *My Bonnie*.

On December 23, 1944, after the 357th had been grounded for five straight days due to bad weather, the group put up sixty-five fighters for a mission to Germany. This was another escort mission and the 357th Fighter Group was assigned to shepherd the B-24 *Big Friends* which were bombing communication centers in the Third Reich that day. According to 362nd Fighter Squadron pilot Jesse Frey, in a phone call with the author, he was flying with the group that day and Walter Perry was his flight leader. Frey said that the squadron was in the vicinity of Dahlem, Germany, when Walt Perry called in bogies that had been sighted down on the deck below his flight. After telling Frey and the others in the flight that he was going down to investigate the unidentified aircraft, Perry began a rapid descent toward the bogies. The following, taken from Walter Perry, Jr.'s MACR (missing aircrew report) is pilot Bill Mooney's account of what happened to Walt Perry next:

> *I was flying White Three in Dollar Squadron when we made a pass at some bogies at 1240* [hours] *from 15,000 feet near Prum, Germany. I saw a silver P-51 which was undoubtedly Lt. Perry heading straight down at approximately 15,000 feet. As I watched, it started snapping at approximately 5,000 feet* [and] *both wings came off at the roots. The fuselage dove straight into the ground and exploded. I did not see the pilot bail out.*

The MACR also says that *Toolin Fool's* "wings came off in dive at *compressibility.*" The problems associated with compressibility dives plagued Mustang pilots throughout the war and killed several of the 357th pilots. P-51 Mustangs were notorious for their rapid acceleration in dives and Kit Carson, the leading ace of the Group, was quoted as saying, "The P-51 would accelerate so fast in a dive that it would make you sick, literally."

When in a vertical or near vertical dive, a Mustang fighter would quickly accelerate as it sliced through the thin air at higher altitudes. Then, as the plane neared 5,000 feet and entered the thicker layer of air, it would begin to suffer the adverse effects associated with compressibility. As its speed approached 550-600mph, the Mustang's controls would start to become "heavy" due to the high air pressure building up on the elevator, ailerons and rudder. Remember that the P-51 Mustang had no hydraulic control system and that the stick was connected to the control surfaces by pulley wheels and cables. This meant that the pilot had to utilize his upper body strength in order to operate the ailerons and elevator at extreme speeds. During these high speed dives, some P-51 pilots claimed that it felt like the control stick was "set in concrete" and that it took all of their strength to move it in any direction. As the plane's speed increased and it accelerated closer to the state of compressibility, the opposite would occur according to many of the Mustang pilots I spoke to. At this extreme airspeed, the air would begin to build up or "compress" in front of the wings of the P-51, and when this happened the control surfaces would lose all of their effectiveness. Ted Conlin, a former 357th Fighter Group pilot, told this author in an interview that the stick would act like it had become disconnected and would "just flap around with no effect at all on the plane's attitude whatsoever." The only hope a pilot had when he found himself in this situation was to retard the throttle and hope that the aircraft slowed down enough to allowed the controls to become effective again. If this did not happen, the Mustang would enter the last and fatal stage of the compressibility dive during which the plane would begin to buck violently and then start snapping. In most cases, when this occurred the tail of the aircraft would detach violently from the fuselage and the wings would crumple and/ or shear off of the P-51. There is little doubt that this is what happened to twenty-one-year-old Walter N. Perry's *Toolin Fool* two days before Christmas on the afternoon of December 23, 1944.

As a tribute to Walter, his sister Anna Mae Perry Beachem wrote the following story about her oldest brother, and I think that it well worth including here.

(Back row) Walter Jr. with Gaston on his lap; Dorothy with Anna Mae (Muff) on her lap, and Celeste, (front row) Kathleen (with pixie grin) and Jean (showing off her watch)

My personal memories about Walter are that he was tall, good-looking, and had blue eyes. He was a good person. I particularly remember that he treated my younger sister Carolyn and me with great kindness and tenderness. Carolyn, when three years old, was a poor eater and he used to try to get her to eat by playing games with her. Walter had a grayish (peppery) sweatshirt and he told us that it was his "salt and pepper" shirt. Also, he would do things like hold a carrot in his two hands and bite a piece off and eat it and say, "This is the way a rabbit eats."

He used to drive us to Sunday School when we moved from the farm to Boylan Avenue in Raleigh and on Christmas Eve, Walt would take Carolyn and me to "see the Christmas Lights" and we would have a nice time. Of course, in the meantime Santa Claus was getting out toys to get them ready for Christmas morning! I also recall hearing that once on our farm, Daddy was building a dam at a creek (with Walter's help) when Walter got caught up in some quicksand. Daddy tied a rope to the tractor and used it to pull Walter out.

The Perry home in Raleigh, North Carolina

Walter graduated from Broughton High School in 1940. He enrolled in North Carolina State College. At that time, there were already rumors going around that the United States might wind up going to war. Sometime after Pearl Harbor, December 1941, Walter joined the Army Air Force, but because of his age Daddy had to sign for him to be able to enlist. He trained to be a fighter pilot and did very well. My brother was sent to England to fight in the war in Europe and was one of the "Yoxford Boys." I remember the last time I saw Walter. He was standing in the foyer at the front door of our house getting ready to depart for England. Then, he wore the brown uniform of the Army Air Force. He was so strikingly handsome in that uniform. My brother, Gaston, remembers that at the same visit home he and Walter walked together down Main Street in Raleigh and Gaston said that he felt like he was ten feet tall walking next to Walter in that uniform. Walter was Gaston's hero, as he was for all of us.

Walter was stationed near Yoxford, England, and flew his P-51, Rubber Check, *out of Leiston Airfield. Before the 357th Fighter Group became operational, the Allies were in big trouble during the war because they could not get enough of their bombers through to bomb the airplane, tank and ammunition factories as well as the roads, railways and bridges in Germany. Before the Mustangs began flying with the bombers, the other fighters could accompany them only so far over Europe and then they would have to return for more fuel. By the time Walter got involved in World War Two, the P-51 long range fighter had been developed. I can tell you now that those Mustangs definitely turned the tide of the war in favor of the Allies. Those fighter planes could accompany the bombers much farther and shoot down the German fighters that were trying to knock out our bombers. Then, the Allies' bombers began to get through and devastate the German targets. Walter was also involved in strafing German ammunition trains. In fact, I understand that he and his fighter group were instrumental in stopping one German ammunition train and as a result of having no ammunition the Germans lost an important battle.*

At one point while Walter was in England, he wrote me a letter. Inside, he addressed it to "Muff" and "Hibbie" (the nicknames for me and Carolyn). He spoke warmly about the English children and their animals. He also told us that the English children would run up to the American pilots and say, "Any gum, Chum?" Daddy mailed Walter a big box of candy and chewing gum, which Walter gave out to the children, much to their delight! Walter also wrote to his older sister Dorothy and told her that no matter what happened to him he wanted the family to know that he was doing what he wanted to do and was fighting to protect our country.

By September of 1944, fighter pilots had to fly 270 hours of combat time before they would be able to come home. During the "Battle of the Bulge" in December of 1944, Walter was almost finished with his combat tour when his plane went down. His date of death is listed as December 23, 1944. He was twenty-one years old at that time and I was 10. One of his fellow pilots, Lt. Mooney, said that Walter's plane went straight down and began breaking up before it hit the ground. Walter did not get out. When we got those telegrams-the first saying that Walter was "missing in action" and later that he was "killed in action"—well, this was the only time that I ever saw my father cry. My mother just about lost her mind with grief for a while. After the war, Daddy was contacted by the War Department as to whether or not he wanted Walter's body sent back to the United States for burial or buried in a military cemetery in Europe. Daddy felt that bringing Walter's body back would just reopen everything for Mother and would devastate her again, so he made the decision to bury Walter Jr. at the American Military Cemetery in Hamm, Luxembourg. I visited his grave in 1968 along with my mother and a nephew. Recently the Broughton High School Band was in Luxembourg for a celebration of the fiftieth anniversary of the liberation of that country and they played "Let There Be Peace" at the cemetery. Afterward a small contingency from the Broughton Band walked to Walter's grave and laid a wreath on it along with the yellow and red checkered emblem of the 357th Fighter Group.

One thing can be certain, and that is that there was never any question as to what these young men gave their lives for. Can you even imagine what this world would be like today if Adolf Hitler had taken over? No one would even want to think about that. And when all of those little Jewish children were being herded up and killed off, you and me and the rest of the American and English children were being kept safe by the young men like my brother, Walter, and all of the thousands of others like him on the land, sea, and in the air. There is nothing that I or anyone else can ever say that could possibly pay full tribute to these courageous young men who fought so valiantly and paid the ultimate price.

Thank you and God bless you all!

Combat Diaries of the 357th Fighter Group

The Diary of Captain Fletcher E. Adams

Captain Fletcher E. Adams

Beginning on October 30, 1943, Fletcher Adams kept a war diary chronicling his day-to-day experiences with the 357th Fighter Group. He was faithful to this diary until May 22, 1944, just days before his murder. For the sake of history, this diary is preserved intact and complete:

October 30, 1943: Aline and I went hunting today. Just she and I. Killed one water bird and one large greenhead mallard. Am planning to cook it but don't know where.

October 31, 1943: Bonnie sure pissed us all off today. Hagan took a sip of whiskey and boy did she get mad. Sure am glad my wife isn't that bad about it.

November 1, 1943: Payday today but Hagan wouldn't pick up my check. Aline getting ready to go home. A very sad deal. I am thinking the car is in shape to make the trip, though, I think.

November 2, 1943: Aline leaving tomorrow morning. Had squadron party last night. Howling success. Aline crying all the time. It makes me want to but shouldn't. It's as hard on me as she.

November 3, 1943: Today my better half left for home. Much to my regret. Haven't tried to sleep. Think it would be an impossibility. Broadhead left me my room. Everyone thinking we leave November 8.

November 4, 1943: Another day as a single man, it's hard to take. Think I'll live through. Beal moved back on the post. Got my first wire from Aline. Making good time toward Louisiana.

November 5, 1943: The first promotions came in today. All but mine and Beal's. Hike called off because of shots and colds. Thanks to Doc Snedden, wisdom tooth pulled today.

November 6, 1943: Again the hike was called off. Good news. Aline arrived home 4pm. PSI "B" and "Cs" overseas / So orders read. Leaving for POE on Tuesday. Hike again called off.

November 7, 1943: Slept till noon. Ate large steak at mess. Wire from Mother (50 dollars). Beal received first lieutenant. Packing clothes for loading on train. Disliking Maj. Broadhead more each day. I love my wife.

November 8, 1943: Last day at PAAB. *Thank God.* Heard from A. W. King. Found my hat. England had it. Went to town to have a few drinks with the boys. Was a good boy.

November 9, 1943: After day on train, I am very sleepy. Made poor time. Am lonesome as hell. I love her more each day. Not a bit of drinking. Surprised.

November 10, 1943: Married five months today. Still riding this darn train. Am writing a continued letter to my darling. Won a little playing blackjack. Haven't been off of the train yet. Getting awful tired.

November 11, 1943: Still in route to POE. Somewhere in southern Canada now. EM [enlisted men] had fight on train. Rode in caboose for a while. Am more in love. Missing her awful.

November 12, 1943: Finally arrived at Camp Shanks, NY. Restricted to post for unknown time. Trip OK. Unable to write my darling. Hoping for a pass and a trip to the big city.

November 13, 1943: Confined to post. Passes maybe tomorrow night. Going to New York if so. Buying candy and gum supply for overseas. New gas mask. Training starts tomorrow. Dental Inspection. Drew new gas mask. Bed at 10:30pm.

November 14, 1943: Still no passes. Hopes of getting one tomorrow. Gas chamber. Drew partial payment. Everyone has become crap shooters. Won $30 myself. Went to show. Northern Pursuit. Am really missing my little woman.

November 15, 1943: We finally are getting passes to go into New York. Reads 6pm to 6am. Beal and I are going together. First am getting a great big steak. Then shop for Aline's X-mas gift. I really miss Aline.

November 16, 1943: Sure feel sorry for Beal. He misses Barbara so much. Certainly wish Aline could have been with me last night in town. Saw beautiful sight from RCA building. Had my steak at "Salombo's." Returned to camp by bus at 6:00 a.m. Formation at 9am. Was I tired. I really love [Aline].

November 17, 1943: My second trip to the big city. I do wish I could get in during the daytime to see the town. But no hope. Are to be alerted tomorrow everyone thinks. Home earlier tonight at 3:30 a.m.

November 18, 1943: Again am going to town. Am not going to drink much if any though. Am going shopping for Aline a present. A raincoat or fountain pen. Do hope I can find one to send her. Am going to write her from town.

November 19, 1943: Just returned from taking EM [enlisted men] to show. They aren't allowed to leave barracks. Am completely fed up with outfit. Am asking for a transfer overseas. Packed and almost ready. Maybe tomorrow will be the day. I hope.

November 20, 1943: Am packed and ready to go to the boat tomorrow. Am still lucky about catching details. A lucky few gets to go. Squadron doesn't leave till Monday night. Ship sails shortly afterward. Heard from Aline today.

November 21, 1943: Am now aboard the *Queen Elizabeth*. The largest passenger ship afloat. Quite some ship. Wish we were underway. Haven't heard from Aline. Squadron comes aboard tonight.

November 22, 1943: Polish prisoners came aboard at 6pm. Mace and I had troops to load in cabins. Awful cold in this ship. Squadron came aboard at 12pm. Scheduled to sail sometime tomorrow.

November 23, 1943: Sailed this morning for England. Had first emergency muster this morning. Only two meals per day. Very short meals. Wrote Aline today. Sent her an English pound worth $4.

November 24, 1943: Received two letters today from my wife. They were brought aboard by the group. She had spring fixed. Also said Jerry was getting fat.

November 25, 1943: Several fellows are already sick. So far am OK. Doing nothing but eat, sleep, and play blackjack. Beal is awful lonesome. Am more than ever in love.

November 26, 1943: Sailing over rough water and it's awful hard to sleep. Still not seasick. Had emergency muster today. Storming in ocean. Ship leans almost to water.

November 27, 1943: Nothing new. Just plenty water. Saw two escort planes today. PBYs American. Have awful cold. Am taking cold tablets. Unable to write in diary. Officially, I mean.

November 28, 1943: Due in Glasgow tomorrow morning at 7:30am. Set watches back for fourth time today. Had meeting in lounge. Bought some English money today.

November 29, 1943: Dropped anchor in River Clyde in Northern Ireland. Just off coast of Scotland. Unloading this afternoon to board train for airbase just east of London.

November 30, 1943: Arrived at Air Base this morning at 11:30. Camp is new. No planes. Whole Group is to be here. Blackout begins at dusk. Bombed every night. Am writing my love.

December 1, 1943: Just returned from my first visit to an English town. Colchester, 12 miles from camp. All black[ed] out. Hard to find your way around it is so dark. Rode GI trucks in and out. Nothing like America.

December 2, 1943: Second visit to Colchester. Same as before. Money hard to count. Spent $7 tonight and $.75 last night. Cars drive on left hand side of the road. Shows almost the same as U.S. Wrote Aline. No letters yet.

December 3, 1943: Spent the night writing letters. Slept till noon today. Not going to town again until I can go to London. Can hardly wait to hear from Aline and Mother. No mail as yet. Planes due in ten days. P-51s. I love my darling wife. Had lots of fun burning farts—first—Ha Ha. Obie let one and made 8-inch flame.

December 4, 1943: Today marks the beginning of our squadron. We we[re] put into flights that we fly into Combat. Am in Perron's flight. Mace is his wingman. Vogel is mine. Am well satisfied. Wrote Aline again today. Didn't go to town. All fellows went to town tonight. Lichter came and we had Bull session.

December 5, 1943: Today our new pilots came into the squadron. Seem to be a fine bunch of fellows. Am glad though that I have an old fellow flying my wing. The fellows in my barracks are still in town. They must be really hanging one on. Have been gone since yesterday morning. Certainly glad I didn't go in as I started. Am sure I couldn't have knocked down the temptation. Am continuing to write my darling wife. I love her.

December 6, 1943: The party finally came to an end. Ground school started and to continue hereafter. Lichter and I are going to London tomorrow afternoon. Hope to find some of those Battle jackets and some new Ninth Air Force insignia. No changes in flights. Pyeatt is still trying to get on my wing. Hope he does in a way. Planes due to start coming in this weekend. One thing for certain I can say truthfully. I am really true to my wife. Am more in love every day.

December 7, 1943: My first trip to London which made a very bad impression on me. All the women want to do is take your money. But none of mine. Was true to my wife I am proud to say. London is a long way behind the USA. You don't know how much you appreciate the States till you leave them. Hotels see Americans coming and charge them two prices for rooms. Nothing to do but go to shows which are years old. Am loving my wife more than ever.

December 8, 1943: Back from London and going to school now. Am learning German planes only now. No mail as yet. Some of the fellows heard from home in 7 days. Good time. Saw show in Colchester. Pictures are dull. Unable to see or hear them. Supposed to ferry back planes Sunday or Monday. Food in London was very poor. But good for you I guess. Writing Aline in just a few min[utes].

December 9, 1943: Am finally living with some clean clothes and things I really need. Our footlockers came in today. Wrote Aline a card and also letter this afternoon. Leaving on Sunday to go to Wing for some kind of school and lectures. Weather still very bad. Fog all day long and also too night. Can't get over situation in London. Am thoroughly disgusted with it. Second week's supplies from PX. Am more in love than ever.

December 10, 1943: *Married 6 months today*. Our first raid since arriving ended minutes ago. Not very bad. At least no bombs fell close to our camp. Wonder how London came out. All attack seemed in that general direction. No mail from home yet. Am certain Aline is writing. Moved beds around barracks to make more room around stove. Major Egenes returned from London. Washed some clothes this afternoon. Wrote Aline a letter.

December 11, 1943: Nothing new around this Bloody dump. No mail. No planes. Just plain nothing. Am I pissed off. Lonesome as hell on top of all that. Hope it is much different when we get started flying. Even local. Would be better than sitting around. Wrote Aline two V-mail[s]. Today was payday. Am out of debt in Squadron now. No raid. Bought dance ticket but didn't attend. Gave it to Rice. Am slowly but surely going nuts.

December 12, 1943: Still have a bad cold. After visiting Eighth FO we had discussion of our beliefs on war situation. Everyone thinks that it will last much longer now. After seeing what we saw today. German Defenses are pretty dam[n] good. No mail today. Am really getting pissed off about the whole dam[n] thing. If I don't hurry and hear from Aline am really going to get mad. But can't help but love her more each day.

December 13, 1943: My second trip to London and am safe to say it is my last one. A costly one at that. It cost me my GI watch. I could wring the person's neck who stole it. Saw the part of town that received most of the bombs. Perron, Brown, and myself came almost to having fight with some of these English soldiers. Am safe in saying I am really in love with Aline, my wife.

December 14, 1943: Back at camp early tonight. No mail as usual. Can't understand why I have not heard from Aline and Mothe[r]. Am certain they have written a number of times. Saw a good show in Colchester. Am writing Aline.

December 15, 1943: Finally the mail came in. Received 6 letters from my darling wife. Was about time. Planes due [a] week from today. Due for navigation trip around England tomorrow. Wrote Aline a long letter tonight.

December 16, 1943: Two more letters from Aline today. Ground school is still taking most of each day. Had lecture today by some P-47 pilot that was forced down here today. Wrote Aline again today. Navigation flight tomorrow.

December 17, 1943: Nothing much happened today. No mail from Aline. Am writing her though. Raining like hell. Am good and tired of England and their backward ways. Be glad for invasion to come.

December 18, 1943: Went to Colchester tonight. Still raining hard. Rode in English truck. Had pretty good time at Officers' Club. Brought our radio from town. No mail but I love her.

December 19, 1943: No mail yet. Wrote Aline and Mother. Bad check returned from Pocatello. Made the navigation trip today. Saw many different kinds of planes. Group got 6 planes today.

December 20, 1943: Letter from Aline. Card from Miss Cope. Wallen, Hagan, Lichter, and I went to Ipswich. Nothing to do there either. Squadron got two planes today.

December 21, 1943: Planes almost ready to fly. Waiting on radios to fly planes. Went to Colchester. Saw show "Stormy Weather." I love Aline. Most of fellows are on 48 hr. pass.

December 22, 1943: Still no flying. Radio[s] not here yet. All ready except for that. B-17 landed with flak holes all over it. Crew was wounded. 5 bailed out. No mail from Aline. Am more in love.

December 23, 1943: Beal and I went into Colchester tonight. Was pretty drunk out too. Not too drunk though. First flying today. Maj. Broadhead and Lingo flew. Tomorrow is the day, so they tell us.

December 24, 1943: X-mas Eve and everything is still nil. No, I haven't checked out yet. Going to town tomorrow night. Everyone went in tonight. I had to bring Pyeatt home.

December 25, 1943: Had turkey dinner today. Perron checked out in P-51. Letter from Aline, Barlow and Mr. and Mrs. Yancy. Still haven't checked out. Everyone staying in tonight. Am still in love with Aline.

December 26, 1943: Another good dinner today. Wonderful tasting steaks. Fog has grounded all the aircraft in the Group. Sure am anxious to fly this ship. Squadron adopting an orphan. Still no mail. Sent Barlow some gum.

December 27, 1943: No mail today. Several more fellows were checked out today. Me tomorrow. Went to town tonight. Perron and Beal went with me. Perron had Pyeatt's boots. Hope he didn't steal them. Still in love with Aline.

December 28, 1943: Today was the happy day for me to fly the P-51. Really a sweet flying ship. Had bout with C-47. Mail hasn't come in yet. Anxiously looking forward to flying again. Really miss Darling Aline.

December 29, 1943: Had a helluva lot of fun today. Out on an escape practice. Stealing GI trucks, etc. Vogel, Junior were together. Took us all day to get back. Beemer was shot at by MP coming through the gate. Package from Aline.

December 30, 1943: Leaving today for someplace on Irish Sea for an airplane. Bringing it back with several more fellows. Stopping overnight in London. Be back tomorrow or next day. No mail from home.

December 31, 1943: *Happy New Year.* Next year with Aline and Jerry. Just returned from party at Officers Club on post. Wonderful time. Stole Granbaca's hat. Everyone tight. No mail from my lovely wife. I really love her. The major seems much more human now.

January 1, 1944: First day of the new year but doesn't seem like it to me. No mail from Aline. Didn't fly today. Cold as the devil. Everyone went to town except 4 of us.

January 2, 1944: Norris and I are staying in the barracks tonight drinking our wine. Most of the fellows are in town as usual. Still looking forward to going after plane.

January 3, 1944: Really pissed off at Williams, Perron, and Brown. Took my flight away from me twice. Staying at home tonight. Nothing doing at all. Aline has heard from me.

January 4, 1944: Went into Colchester tonight. Took show at Red Cross. No mail from Aline. Pugh and Obie was tight. Am writing to Oscar tonight. Still in love with her.

January 5, 1944: Another visit to Colchester, England. Went to show. Saw Betty Grable in Sweet Rosie O'Grady and Henry Gets Glamo[u]r. People sure like westerns. Ruin good music. Love Aline.

January 6, 1944: Spending evening writing Dave, Aline, and Mother. Lichter and I going to London tomorrow. Buying a pair of fleece lined boots. Three letters from Aline. K. borrowed the car.

January 7, 1944: In London now. Had awful time finding a place to stay. Hotels and RC clubs completely filled up. Staying with an ole Polish flier and his wife. Going to show.

January 8, 1944: Spent the day shopping in London. Bought my weekly candy, cig, and gum ration. A pair of boots and pair gloves. Hagan ordered boots. Saw vaudeville show.

January 9, 1944: Came back to post today. My anti-G suit was here for trial. Very secret. Only 3 in Squadron received them. Major says try them tomorrow. 5 letters from Aline.

January 10, 1944: Married 7 months today. Got to fly in P-51 today. 36,000. Pretty good ship alt. Wrote Aline a letter. Got one from Aline. Played darts in barracks all evening.

January 11, 1944: Issued 5 eggs today plus one orange. Had fried eggs in GI mess hall tonight. Sure were good. Staying home for some time. I love Aline.

January 12, 1944: Today was Katherine's seventeenth birthday and I didn't send her a darned thing. Will make it up on graduation though. Haven't flown in several days. One letter today.

January 13, 1944: Sitting around playing darts and drying my clothes in barracks. No mail today. Weather bad. Some went on low altitude navigation trip.

January 14, 1944: Fog set in at 4pm. Ships grounded at 4pm. No flying for me. Two letters from Aline. Wrote her one. No mail from Mother. Good chow in mess. I love Aline.

January 15, 1944: Field still closed. Flying Circus came in our field consisting of two Typhoons and two Spits. Took my day off. Slept till noon Sunday. No more mail. Wrote Aline.

January 16, 1944: Another day and no flying. Didn't even go down to the line. Had turkey for chow and certainly was good. Was supposed to have show but called off. Played poker in hut.

January 17, 1944: Fog still around and no flying. Saw film on Anti G. Also Jane Eyre in the Officers Club. Chow terrible tonight. Beat Beemer 4 games of darts. I love Aline.

January 18, 1944: Went to Colchester. Had shower at Red Cross and saw English film. Didn't enjoy it one bit. Still no mail. Getting completely fed up with this [unreadable] outfit.

January 19, 1944: [Unreadable] is correct. No more promotions until 75 percent openings. Major made Lt. Col. Can't make myself be satisfied in the squadron anymore. Would like a [unreadable] outfit.

January 20, 1944: Some of the fellows were able to fly a couple of hours today. Weather improving gradually. Lots of pilots went to London. No mail yet.

January 21, 1944: Went into Colchester tonight. Saw a show Gentleman Gangster. Saw same show in U.S. a year or more ago. I love my wife.

January 22, 1944: Flew today trying my new secret suit out. Works pretty good. No mail as yet. Was given another bottle of wine today. Major E. [Egenes] went on combat mission.

January 23, 1944: Pete and all the other boys in the other barracks got drunk. Ankeny, Pete passed out. Hagan drunk too. No one wheel landing today, Roughgarten?

January 24, 1944: Received several letters today. All were old though. One was from Miss Cope and Bonnie. Capt. Giltner missing in combat mission today. Beemer sent to ferry command for a while.

January 25, 1944: Flew all today with suit. Pretty day all day till 5pm and it is raining now and cold as hell. Am writing two letters to Aline. Junior is rushing WLA girl.

January 26, 1944: Nothing of importance. Flew two hours today. No mail from Aline. Everyone but me in town tonight. Rumored we move to a new field in a few days.

January 27, 1944: Brown and I are now in Kiblington, England. Brought Oxford to have it fixed. RAF base. Nice for officers. The NZ [New Zealand] boys are tops with me now.

January 28, 1944: The fellows from Canada and New Zealand will trade, sell, or give away anything they have. Really have some nice souvenirs from them. Boots, etc.

January 29, 1944: Mail today from King, Miss Cope, but none from Aline. We are to move to new field Monday. Back from RAF station. Am really lonesome for Aline.

January 30, 1944: Went into town tonight. Had a pretty good time. Moving to Leiston Monday or Tuesday. Right on the coast. No more planes in squadron till now. No mail.

February 1, 1944: Today we were supposed to move or ones to fly were. Weather held us up. Nothing to do but sit around and be lonesome for my Aline. A letter today.

February 2, 1944: What a disappointment we had today when we landed at our new base. Muddy as hell. Good living quarters however. Good club too.

February 3 1944: Lots of mail today from Dave, Aline, and Kathryn. Made a walk to mess today. All pilots worked on it. Going off on ferrying job tomorrow. Wrote Aline.

February 4, 1944: Another trip called off. Haven't found my cap someone stole a couple of days ago. No mail. Wrote Mother and Dad. Hopes of flying. We have 25 planes now.

February 5, 1944: Johnny Rice and I went into town tonight to see what was there. Not going again. One show (made in 1900). Have my own plane now. Thackering crew chief.

February 6, 1944: Captain Lingo went on Op. mission today with the 354th [Fighter Group]. Came out OK. Col. Graham damaged 190. Received my artificial tooth today. Looks OK. One letter from Aline.

February 7, 1944: Heard today we go on first mission Wednesday. Won 17 pounds today. Am going to send Aline a couple hundred. Are going to have pretty swell pilots 'room.

February 8, 1944: Mission for tomorrow scrubbed. Capt. Hubbard of 363rd [Fighter Squadron] killed strafing German field today. Hard to realize we are so close to this thing but will find out soon.

February 9, 1944: Again mission scrubbed because of the weather. Practice missions also called off. B-17s forced down here. Maybe tomorrow we will be able to get off. No mail from home.

February 10, 1944: Really hit the jackpot on mail. Twelve letters today. Heard from NL, Kathryn, Mom, and Aline. Lost a few pounds in the club tonight. Went to bed pretty early for the mission tomorrow.

February 11, 1944: Our first group mission today. No action however. Flack came close to me. Three German planes followed us a ways. No one lost and no trouble. No mail.

February 12, 1944: Another mission today. I now have two missions to my credit. A total of four hours forty-five minutes. Two V-mail letters from Aline. Stationery from Mother. I love her.

February 13, 1944: The group's third mission today but I didn't get to go. Expect some excitement on tomorrow's mission. R. W. Brown bailed out in the Channel. Broke both legs.

February 14, 1944: Nothing of importance today. Valentine's Day and I didn't get one card. Heard from Aline, Mother, Lillie, and Carrie. No mission today.

February 15, 1944: Saw Dave today. As big and happy as ever. Only spent a couple of hours with him. Big mission tomorrow. Everyone thinks to Berlin.

February 16, 1944: Rained like hell all day. No flying at all. We got rumors as we are getting new group CO. Sent Aline $150.00 today. Plan to send another $100.00 payday. Letter from Kathryn.

February 17, 1944: Made trip to Wing Hq. today. Boy, what a trip. About 7 hour ride. Hope we don't have to go again. One letter from Aline. Wrote Barlow and Randal.

February 18, 1944: Still grounded for weather. Nothing doing all day long. Going to Colchester tomorrow. I think Junior and I. Wish we could go on a mission.

February 19, 1944: Spent night in ARC Colchester. Had a[n] awful hard place to sleep. Rock train to and from. One letter from Aline. Didn't write though.

February 20, 1944: First big mission for group and I had to be on pass. Willy scored the first victory over Me-109 today. Ross from group is missing. No mail.

February 21, 1944: Snowed all day long today. Two letters from Aline. Went to show at post theater. Saw Judy Garland [in] Introducing Mrs. Mandy or something. No mission today.

February 22, 1944: Today will always be remembered by me all my life. My first German plane. Scored victory over Me-109. Rode his tail for 3 min. and shot hell out of him.

February 23, 1944: No mission today. Lichter is no longer with us. Bailed out over Holland yesterday. Two letters from Aline. Mailed her the change of insurance beneficiary.

February 24, 1944: Today we lost our first member of the Sad Sack Shack. Sure seems lonesome without Rice. No one knows what he did. Forgot to write Aline today.

February 25, 1944: This has got to come to a close. Another member of the Sad Sack S[h]ack went down today. Beemer bailed out over Germany. Miss him more than Rice. Sqdn. got 5.

February 26, 1944: Seems to be a jinx on 362nd. Four pilots are already on Honor Roll. Kerrer [Kehrer] got it today. Think he was killed. Rec'd box of candy from NL. Sure was good too.

February 27, 1944: Our Squadron Victory Party tonight. Boy what a time had by all concerned. It was really lots of fun. Carson may move back in with us. Too much vacant space for comfort.

February 28, 1944: Snowed all day today. Suppose nothing could have happened because everyone slept almost all day. Wrote Aline tonight but got no mail.

February 29, 1944: Payday today. Am sending about $100 out of [$]150 I was paid home I think. No mission today either. Went to the [flight] line in the evening.

March 1, 1944: Our first mission in several days. Played poker at club till 10:00pm. Came home but news of another mission sent us to bed.

March 2, 1944: Today we went to Bernberg, Germany. Not much excitement though. Junior flew my wing. We looked but couldn't see a thing.

March 3, 1944: The first mission to Berlin but was scrubbed before reaching the target. As usual, I didn't get to go on a good mission.

March 4, 1944: Second mission to Berlin. Started but had to abort. Wallen shot down FW-190. Came all the way back home on the deck with no canopy.

March 5, 1944: A long mission to Bordeaux, France today. Obie shot down FW-190. I didn't even see E/A. No mail on Sunday. Still haven't got money orders.

March 6, 1944: Today I took my first pass for almost two months. Went to London. Spent the night in Red Cross. Saw two shows. Going shopping tomorrow.

March 7, 1944: Bought me a watch and pr. [of] gloves today and thinking about going to see sights on RC convey tomorrow morning. Wrote Aline.

March 8, 1944: Came back from pass today. Perron got three ships over Berlin yesterday. Group got 21 ships. ETO record. Two letters from Aline. One from Bill.

March 9, 1944: Dave and Baker made Capt. Everyone says all 43E promotions went in today. Also mine. I doubt it like hell. Two letters from Aline. Wrote one.

March 10, 1944: Have been commissioned one year today. Also married nine months. Am asking for transfer in one month if promotion doesn't come in.

March 11, 1944: Two new additions to the shack today. Smith and Hill. Think they will be OK. Obie went on pass. Also Jr. and Pyeatt haven't flown for 5 days now.

March 12, 1944: Still haven't went on mission. The weather is bad though. Bombers went over today. Five letters from home today. One from Barrett.

March 13, 1944: England flew my ship on spotter mission and had to land somewhere in Southern England for some reason. No mission yet. Flew locally for 1 hour.

March 14, 1944: Still no mission and no promotion. Am thoroughly pissed off too. J. J. Bell was by to see all the fellows today. No mail from home.

March 15, 1944: Went down to Colchester with Pugh and Norris. Spent the night in Red Cross. Saw several old friends of mine. Nothing much happened while gone.

March 16, 1944: Back from pass and group out on a mission. Pyeatt was lost today. No one knows what happened to him. Also lost Meyer. Both in my flight. Four letters from Aline.

March 17, 1944: Was on alert today but fog was on the ground so couldn't fly. Did nothing but play ball. Wish I were home with the wife. Certainly do miss her.

March 18, 1944: I knocked down my second German. Another Me-109. This time just north of Paris, France. Coon was with me. No mail from Aline. No drinking this time."

March 19, 1944: No mission and nothing to do. Haven't done a thing all day but sleep and try to write letters. Wrote Mother and Aline. Two letters from Aline today.

March 20, 1944: Ankeny's promotion came in today and boy did I raise hell with Broadhead. Says mine should be here any day now. Hope so or I'm going to transfer.

March 21, 1944: No mission today. Played volley and baseball all afternoon. Rode bicycles part of the day. Wrote some letters and retired.

March 22, 1944: Again I am on alert but no mission. So just sit around the Pilots' Room waiting for weather to clear up. But to no avail. Heard from King.

March 23, 1944: Finally my promotion came through. Had to abort from mission with rough engine. Three packages from Aline and Mother. Wrote Aline a letter.

March 24, 1944: Almost took off on another mission today but weather held us up. Sitting around eating Mother's fruitcake and cookies. Wrote Aline on her blue stationery.

March 25, 1944: First Group party tonight. Pretty good time had by all. But didn't have much drinking because of thinking we have big mission tomorrow.

March 26, 1944: No mission today. No one knows why not because most beautiful day we have had in the ETO. All ships to be painted yellow with big red checks on it. No mail.

March 27, 1944: Long mission south of Bordeaux, France today. No one saw a thing. 5 ½ hours. Three letters from Aline today. Nothing much happening here.

March 28, 1944: Went to Colchester. Spent night in the ARC. Junior bailed out over France. Egenes crashed on German Airfield in France. Brown and Starkey dow[n] a Mosquito.

March 29, 1944: Three boys in Group spin out of overcast going out. Broadhead gets 109. Tomorrow I am leading a flight. Sure seems like something is on fire.

March 30, 1944: No mission. That is we climbed through overcast to 27,000 and still in it. Lost two pilots today Perron and Rydberg.

March 31, 1944: Searching mission for Dave but no one saw a thing. Not much hope for them now. Today was payday. Not allowed to take furlough."

April 1, 1944: Am either to be flight leader or Asst. operations officer. My first break in this squadron. Am going to make the most of it too.

April 2, 1944: Obie and Norris left for Scotland today but Pugh and I are not getting to go now. Next week tho[ugh]. We hope. Won some money playing B[lackjack].

April 3, 1944: Weather very bad lately. No mission for three days now. Got package from Aline today. Candy was in it. Most 43 E promotions came in.

April 4, 1944: Still no mission. Lecture and show today. Saw "What a Woman." Good show. Two letters from Aline. Am thinking of buying a bike.

April 5, 1944: Made weather hop over France today. Certainly was terrible weather. Had hell of a time getting back down through the soup. Two letters today.

April 6, 1944: Weather still bad. Letter from Aline saying Baby would be born on 24th or 25th of this month. Can hardly see myself a father.

April 7, 1944: Another milk run today. No one saw a thing in southern France. Came home and had two letters from Aline.

April 8, 1944: Had mission today but I didn't go. Group got seven victories today. 4 in our squadron. Very bad weather all over England.

April 9, 1944: Again I fly another milk run but not to France. To Germany proper. Had three letters from Aline and one from mother.

April 10, 1944: No one flew today. Weather was very bad so we all slept in all morning long. Went to chow at 12:00. Wrote Aline a long letter.

April 11, 1944: Today I scored a double victory by getting two Me-109s. One and didn't fire a shot at him. He spun in trying to follow me.

April 12, 1944: Pugh and O'Brien both got their second ones today. But I didn't get to go. Didn't want to as for as that matter[s]. I love my wife.

April 13, 1944: Today I got a letter from Aline telling me that she had been going to the doctor all the time and is OK. Can hardly wait till the thirtieth of April.

April 14, 1944: Just 11 or 12 more days and I'll know whether I have a daughter or a son. I hope it is a son. But a girl will be OK too.

April 15, 1944: Getting ready to go to Scotland Monday. Pugh and I are going together. Just 11 more days. No flying because of bad weather.

April 16, 1944: Still no flying so we all sleep in each morning. Am certainly counting the days till the twenty-sixth or twenty-seventh. Aline wants to name the girl Rebel Yancy.

April 17, 1944: Wrote Aline not to name the girl Rebel Yancy. Hope she isn't mad at me for it. But don't give a damn what she names it. Just as long as she has a boy.

April 18, 1944: Rec.'d Air Medal today and spent the day riding train to Scotland. Aline sure will miss my letters while in Shreveport too.

April 19, 1944: My first day in Scotland. Really a swell place. Almost like home. Swell people. Friendly and think the world of Yanks.

April 20, 1944: Have really been resting up. Sleeping most of the time. Been seeing some swell shows. Sure would like to mail Aline a letter.

April 21, 1944: Went to visit an old palace today of Queen Mary of Scotland. Real old and beautiful. Bought Aline a beautiful paperweight.

April 22, 1944: Am missing Aline more every day up here. Seems so much like USA. Saw old castle and all the city today in tour.

April 23, 1944: Back in camp and awful tired from riding trains all the night. Had 10 letters from Aline. Sure enjoyed them.

April 24, 1944: Scored a triple victory today. Jumped 20 Me-110s and 6 of us destroyed 13 of them. Really had a picnic. Wrote Aline.

April 25, 1944: Another mission today to France. But didn't see a thing. Had a long 5-hour ride. Really sweating Aline and the baby.

April 26, 1944: Today the baby should be born. Am looking for a wire from Aline. Gosh I sure wish I could be there with Aline. But just impossible.

April 27, 1944: Another milk run today to France. Have made last five in a row now. Two of them today. One early morning and one late afternoon.

April 28, 1944: Big event came off. Jerry was born either 23 or 24. Got wire from home just after returning from my sixth straight mission.

April 29, 1944: Slept in today. First mission I miss they go to Big "B." But no one saw a darn thing. A milk [run] to Berlin. No mail from Aline in two days.

April 30, 1944: Another milk run to S. France. Am going on pass tomorrow. Had group Party at Officers Club. Everyone had a good time.

May 1, 1944: Went to London. Picked up Jr.'s Battle jacket. Too small for me. Also got some underwear and socks. The piece came out in S. & Stripes today.

May 2, 1944: Another raid to Berlin but weather scrubbed it. Heard from Mother and Bill. Both say Aline and Jerry doing fine.

May 3, 1944: Weather terrible today and it is expected to be this way for several days. Everyone slept till noon. Sent [$]150.00 to Aline.

May 4, 1944: Another letter from Mother about Baby and Aline. Flew up to see Dave today. Sure was glad to hear news about the baby.

May 5, 1944: Hagan and England made captain today. Mine went in about the same time. Hope to get [it] soon. No flying today because of the weather.

May 6, 1944: Heard from Randall today. Doesn't like Alaska. Wish I could hear from Aline and hear from her about our Jerry.

May 7, 1944: A trip to Berlin today. Couldn't find the bombers. Went almost to Sweden. Came back over North Sea. No one saw a single German ship.

May 8, 1944: Another trip to Berlin. Complete overcast and no German fighters. Sixty-fourth ran into some coming home. No mail from Aline yet.

May 9, 1944: Again target is Berlin but very few fighters seen. No one shot any down. Sure would love to see Jerry and Aline.

May 10, 1944: No flying today. Another day of rest. Engine change on my ship. Should be ready tomorrow for flying.

May 11, 1944: Test hopped my ship. Didn't go on today's mission to France somewhere. Becker's Capt. Came in today. Mine should soon.

May 12, 1944: Escort bombers to Germany today. My luck I miss it. Baker gets his first one today. Also Norris gets two.

May 13, 1944: Today the longest raid of war. Poland. Also made captain today. Sure surprised me too. No one but 364th saw anything on raid.

May 14, 1944: Mother's Day and no flying. Everyone slept in all morning. Went to show tonight. P-51 breaks record for X-C coast to coast.

May 15, 1944: A milk run to France. A two-hour mission. Nothing seen. Letter from Barlow, Mother, and Aline. Raining all day long. Also when we landed.

May 16, 1944: Nothing brewing today. Rained all day long. No mail but wrote Barlow, Mother, Aline, and NL. Hoping to fly tomorrow.

May 17, 1944: Today the group went to Berlin. No one saw a single E/A. But another group really went to town and mopped up on GAF.

May 18, 1944: Another milk run to Berlin. Getting pretty bad when [we] go to Berlin and no opposition. Several letters from Aline today. Two from Aline.

May 19, 1944: Roberson and I shared a 109 today. One more dead German. He really blew up pretty. Came home and found a package from Kathryn. Candy.

May 20, 1944: Listening to German news broadcast. Corney [sic]. No mail to whole squadron today. Maybe tomorrow. No mission today. Wrote Aline.

May 21, 1944: Group lost three pilots today, straffing [sic]. Pierce, Reese, and Michalley. Two were definitely killed. I wasn't on mission. Our squadron didn't lose any.

May 22, 1944: Saw Red Cross show tonight. It was pretty good. Good crowd. Mission today was to Kiel, Germany. No E/A seen. Am really lonesome tonight.

The entry on May 22, 1944, was the last one made by Fletcher Adams in his diary. Pages for May 23 through May 30 are empty, with the exception of a single line drawn through each page.

The Diary of Harry Ankeny

May 19, 1944: Another mission to Berlin. Our job was to escort seven boxes of B-17s into the target, the railroad yards of Berlin. I flew as element leader in Captain Williams's Red flight with Lt. Holmberg, [a] Kansas boy, on my wing. Just before takeoff, a whole group of P-38s flew in here to refuel. Evidently, they were based in southwest England, part of the Ninth Air Force. We took off about 11:15 a.m. and headed out on a heading of seventy-seven [degrees]. That took us up above the mainland and we flew along the Frisian Islands until we rendezvoused with the bombers near Kiel. We then headed southeast to Berlin. About fifty miles above Berlin, some of the Big Friends were attacked by a large force of Me-109s. Our particular flight didn't get in on the engagement; we kept covering the bombers, flying at 28,000 feet. I did see a couple of dogfights and was quite sure I saw a 109 being chased. I peeled off once on a ship but by the time I dropped my belly tanks, he had disappeared in the clouds below. [There was] not much happening, so we turned and headed for home. Captain Adams, Lt. Roberson, and Lt. Harris shared a 109 together. The group score was ten destroyed, and we lost one pilot—not from our squadron. Everything went pretty smooth but it was a tiring mission, logged around five hours. We did a very nice job of missing flak today. They did put up quite a barrage for the bombers over Berlin.

May 21, 1944: Started engines at 1029 [hours] for a fighter sweep. The area we were to hit was north of Berlin near Rostak. Started out as element leader in Captain Hagan's Green flight with Lt. Starkey on my wing. Soon after we reached the enemy coast, Captain Baker pushed his engine up to forty inches manifold pressure and I just couldn't stay up. Lt. Starkey and I dropped back and planned to cut off the squadron. Everywhere was completely overcast going in and we caught a lot of flak. We finally met the squadron at Hannover, and the flak got so bad the whole squadron split up again. Lt. Conlin joined up with Starkey and myself and we continued on toward our strafing area. Hit the top of the Reich around Wismar, circled around and I saw an airport out on a peninsula near Wismar, Germany. Decided to give it a try. Went southeast about ten miles, dropped to the deck at 375mph and headed across the bay right on the water. Pulled up slightly as I neared the field and fired a long burst at a He-111K. I thought at the time it was an Me-110 but the films showed it to be a He-111K. Lt. Starkey shot up an Me-110 and damaged a Ju-52. Lt. Conlin fired into a hangar. We joined up over the water again and headed back. We had just got inland around Lubeck at 12,000 feet and got in the middle of a flak barrage—it was terrific. Ordinarily flak appears black in large puffs but these were so close you could see orange flashes and see the fragments bursting around the flame. I never thought we would all get out but we did. A 354th group boy joined us and we headed back home over the North Sea. I didn't want to go near land. Navigation worked perfect, and we arrived home in good time.

May 24, 1944: Bomber escort to Berlin flying Captain Hagan's White flight with Lt. Starkey on my wing. Starkey is really an eager boy, he'll try anything. Took the bombers into Berlin, missing flak barrages pretty well. Our withdrawal fighter support came in and we headed home. About that time the bombers were severely attacked by a large force of Jerries but we couldn't help them. We cruised on home, dodging cities. They, the bombers, hit the rail yards in Berlin, Germany.

May 25, 1944: Another bomber escort to the middle-eastern part of France; Metz and Neuers. I flew as element leader in Major Gates's Green flight with Lt. A. E. Smith on my wing. We picked up the bombers on time, [and] escorted them over the target and clear back to the English coast. Saw the bombing very clearly. Our particular box missed the rail yards, their target in Metz.

May 27, 1944: Our job today was to provide escort for the bombers while they bombed the rail yards at Stuttgart, Germany, 50 miles below the Ruhr (Happy) Valley. Stuttgart and surrounding towns are large industrial localities. Started out as spare in our Squadron. Got almost to rendezvous when around 100 fighters tore through the bomber formation. Just then Lt. Sehl had to return with a bad engine and I had to escort him back. We got back OK but missed the big fight. Our Squadron got six planes, the group score was twenty-one. The group lost four pilots, including Captain R. D. Brown from our squadron.

May 29, 1944: Bomber escort to Posen, Poland again. Someone screwed up the times because we rendezvoused with the bombers over Zuider Zee. We stuck with them and took them clear into and past the target until the red-nosed P-51s picked them up. I ran both drop tanks dry and my main fuselage tank but didn't have to sweat gas much. My oxygen ran low but not serious. Major Broadhead did an excellent job of navigating coming home and we never hit a bit of flak. I flew as element leader in his flight with Lt. Starkey on my wing. Logged 5.50 hours, a long drag. Total time to date:146 hours combat time. Bombing results were excellent, really lowered the Focke Wulf aircraft factories.

May 31, 1944: Lt. Pugh led the squadron and did a very good job. We started out for Strasbourg down in southwest Germany. Lt. Starkey flew on my wing in Major Gates's White flight. We crossed in OK but the weather continued to get worse. Picked up the bombers OK but they decided to bomb their second alternate target, an airfield a little south of Brussels. A short mission but it worked out OK. We escorted the heavies clear back to the English coast near Manston and came on in.

June 2, 1944: Captain England led our Squadron and we were to support the bombers over an airfield near Lille, France. Lt. Roughgarten flew on my wing in Captain Hagan's Blue flight. We went out at noon and returned at 2:30 p.m. Didn't see a thing.

June 12, 1944: Just returned from a week's rest at the rest home near Alton, England. A swell deal. Went there with Lt. Wallen. Lt. Roughgarten flew my wing in Major Gates's White flight. We went on an area support just east of the beachhead, east of Le Havre. Started engines at 06:38 [hours] and landed at 11:05 [hours].

June 13, 1944: Flew as element leader in Captain Hagan's Green flight with Lt. Coon on my wing. We were escorting bombers to bomb an airfield near Rouen, France, fairly near the beachhead. All went well. I have been noticing a single Me-109 flying high above the formation around 35,000 to 40,000 feet. It has been going back and forth over us, probably a German spotter ship.

June 14, 1944: Area support east and south of Le Havre clear down to Paris. I flew as element leader in Major Broadhead's Red flight with Lt. Badger on my wing. An early morning mission starting engines at 05:50 [hours] and returning at 09:20 [hours]. Some of a flight of the 364th ran into a pack of FW-190s near Paris. They shot two down and lost one man. The Germans are getting very crafty and have been bouncing flights and smaller [groups] straggling around. We have been sticking close together to avoid such attacks. Five P-47 fighter bombers were shot down just off of the enemy coast and there have been similar incidents. All pilots are really watching out from now on.

June 16, 1944: Started out and I was breezing down the runway [when] my left gas connection on my droppable tank broke and really started shooting out gasoline. I left a vapor trail all around the pattern and on landing the other gas connection broke on my right droppable tank.

June 17, 1944: Flew as element leader in Captain Smith's White flight with Lt. Sehl on my wing. We were to escort the bombers to an airfield just north of Paris. The bombers got all screwed up and finally went on and dropped their bombs on an empty airfield. Instead of weaving back and forth across the bombers we would fly alongside them for a while [then] turn 180 [degrees] and go to the rear, repeating the procedure. In my opinion, I couldn't see this method. It makes the boys in the rear pull too much mercury. We got kind of messed up on the takeoff and I took a flight through overcast. We finally found Smith. As we were returning, Captain Hagan's ship quit on him dead and he glided down and tried his best to make the beachhead. He made a crash landing just about 10 miles south of Caen, probably right in the midst of two German panzer divisions and one infantry division. It certainly was a terrific blow to the Squadron since he has been Assistant Operations officer and an excellent pilot. In my opinion we lost the most valuable man in the squadron. We have slight hopes that he may work his way through the lines. My total combat time including this mission is 166 hours and 10 minutes.

The Diary of William Foard

Again, I have been literarily challenged while trying to record this for prosperity. I have attempted to edit the following diary entries by Will Foard and want to make the reader aware of the fact that this is *not* a literal version of Foard's diary. The following is an edited version of his account:

By 1945 most of our missions were as high altitude escorts for B-17 and B-24 heavy bombers. This late in the war there was very little German fighter opposition, as they were short of fuel, aircraft, and pilots. Consequently our main concerns as pilots were the weather, engine trouble, and flak.

February 21, 1945 (five hours, forty minutes): Nuremburg rail yards, 1,000 bombers at 32,000 feet. I flew Red number two position on Captain Murphy's wing. This mission was a "milk run" with only a little flak. I mostly saw only the side of Captain Murphy's plane because I didn't want to goof up and lose him.

February 22, 1945 (six hours, ten minutes): South Germany diversion and then north to Bera-Leipzig-Strasburg rail yards. We lost the bombers in the clouds. Then we climbed above the weather and kept climbing to 42,000 feet, mushing along nose high. A break in the clouds revealed mountains! The clouds were full of rocks! (Must have been the Alps.) Heading north while hunting for the bombers we got into a mess of flak. I landed back in England with fifteen gallons of gasoline left. I flew on Green number two on Captain "Shorty" Hatala's wing. (He was an old guy at twenty-one.)

February 27, 1945 (five hours, thirty-five minutes): Leipzig rail yards. This was a milk run. I flew Green number two on Shorty's wing.

March 2, 1945 (four hours, fifty minutes): Leipzig rail yards. We hit some Me-109s and FW-190s east of Magdeburg. (Group lost three planes.) Our group shot down some of them and then did some ground strafing. I flew Green number two on Shorty's wing. My "reckerlection" of this melee was of everybody rolling over and heading down and dropping wing tanks. While all of the group was funneling down on the Krauts, all of the wing tanks appeared to be flying *up* at me. As I was dodging sing tanks, I lost Shorty Hatala and I then noticed my airspeed going past the 500mph "red line." After I managed to level out, I noticed that I had not dropped my own wing tanks! I spent the rest of my time trying not to get run over by all of the P-51s. I finally found a building to try and drop my wing tanks on.

March 3, 1945 (four hours, fifty minutes): Rail yards southeast of Hannover. A lot of flak. I saw some "blow jobs" Me-262 jets. I flew Red number two on Lt. Col. Storch's wing leading the squadron.

March 5, 1945 (four hours, forty-five minutes): Target oil depot northeast of Dresden. I flew White number two on Shorty's wing. When we joined up with the bombers near the Rhine, I noticed that my oxygen switch had been on 100 percent setting since we took off using that high rate. I switched it off to conserve as much as possible as we climbed. When we got above 12,000 feet, I switched to auto feed. We were getting into the target area when my oxygen mask "sucked in" so I called "Sortie" and said that my oxygen was gone and I was headed down. I let down into the hazy under cast at 32,000 feet and my gyro spilled but I could keep my bearings by the sunspot shining through the haze. I broke out under the clouds at 10,000 feet and humbugged west with a lot of miles to go to get out of enemy territory. Later, while I was feeling lonely while "scootin'" across Germany, I saw a spinner (lookin' like a 109's) behind me, way back. Williams, who was flying White number four, had been having some engine problems and had left the flight to go home with me. He finally got me on the radio and asked, "Fer Christ's sakes, Foard, slow down!" We got back to the base about an hour before the rest of the group.

March 10, 1945 (three hours, forty-five minutes): Rail yards in the Ruhr Valley. It was a milk run with some flak. I flew Green number two on Shorty's wing.

March 11, 1945 (four hours, five minutes): Submarine bases at Hamburg. Another milk run with some flak. I flew Green number two on Shorty's wing.

March 12, 1945 (five hours, fifty minutes): Oil and docks at seaport north of Stettin. I flew White number two on Captain Moore's wing. Lil' flak.

March 14, 1945 (five hours, zero minutes): Oil depot south of Celle. Lotsa flak! I flew Green number two on Shorty's wing. We were told about a big flak "fun" installation on a hill in the area and that it twarn't healthy a'tall to go near it. Doggone if we didn't run right over it! (When you see black puffs of smoke, that ain't good. When you can hear "Boom!" with black puffs, you done messed up-and that ain't talkin' about your navigation. When you also hear sounds like gravel hittin' a tin roof, numerous things happen, and not just to the plane!) When all of that stuff exploded around us, our four planes went in every possible direction. My first reaction was to glance at the coolant temperature gauge. (If you get a leak and lose coolant, the engine will overheat and shut down in a short time.) The gauge pointer was at the bottom of the scale which meant that I would be on the ground in a few minutes. I blacked out from fright, I guess; it was only seconds but it seemed like a long time. Then I realized that the plane I was flying that day had the coolant temperature gauge and the outside temperature gauge in swapped positions and it was cold outside with snow on the ground. When I got back to the base, there was no hydraulic fluid for the flaps. I shook the wheel down until I felt them lock and then waited for the entire group to land on the short runway. Using the long runway, coming in "hot" with no flaps, I was able to slow down with the little reservoir for brakes. The hydraulic lines all along the coolant and fuel lines had a crease cut them!

March 15, 1945 (five hours, twenty minutes): Rail yards north of Berlin. Lots of flak! I flew Red number four on Wasylyk's wing in Colonel Dregne's flight, leading the group.

March 17, 1945 (five hours, fifty minutes): Aircraft factory north of Leipzig. I flew White number four on Weber's wing in Shorty Hatala's flight. Bad weather.

March 18, 1945 (five hours, thirty minutes): Rail yards in Berlin. I flew Major Foy's wing.

March 22, 1945 (three hours, fifteen minutes): Fighter sweep around and north of the Ruhr Valley. I flew Green number four on Weber's wing in Shorty's flight.

March 23, 1945 (four hours, twenty-five minutes): Rail yards and other installations in the Ruhr Valley. Another "milk run" with the bombers. They really clobbered the targets.

March 24, 1945 (four hours, twenty minutes): Patrolled area northeast of the Ruhr Valley during Rhine crossing to stop any German fighters from getting to the ground troops. We jumped about twenty Me-109s heading for the front. We wiped 'em out. Shorty got two and Wasylyk got one. I flew Blue number four on Wasylyk's wing in Shorty's flight. My recollection of the wild affair was that Wasylyk and I got separated from Hatala right away. Wasylyk was chasing a 109 in a left turn. I was behind and off to his right covering for him, when another 109 came swooping down from the left heading in on Wasylyk. I called, "Wasylyk, there's one on your ass!" as I pulled over to give him a "squirt." The Me-109 rolled off to the right and headed down overrunning Wasylyk. Wasylyk peeled off to the right behind him and got a good shot but had to pull up because the ground was getting close. (We were at full throttle.) I saw the Kraut hit the ground and spatter, so I was able to confirm Wasylyk's kill. (I never did get around to go over to the photo shop to see if I got any of my shots close enough to scare the Kraut! When Steger and I transferred to the 339th Fighter Group to go to the Pacific, I didn't go to pick up what little film I had. I remember feeling "What the hell, it don't make a durn bit o' difference an' I'd jes as well fergit it. Now I'm curious!)

March 27, 1945 (three hours, thirty minutes): I escorted British RAF Lancasters to bomb the rail yards at Paderhorn east of the Ruhr. Flak! I flew Blue number two on Moore's wing.

April 3, 1945 (four hours, ten minutes): Submarine pens and docks at Kiel. I flew Red number four on Weber's wing in Colonel Dregne's flight leading the group. The target was clobbered, and we encountered little flak.

April 4, 1945 (four hours, fifty-five minutes): Patrolled around two rescue launches in the North Sea north of the Frisian Islands. North 53 55' East 04 38' heading west for England. I flew Teamwork number four on Weber's wing.

April 9, 1945 (five hours, fifteen minutes): Munitions depot and airfields near Munich. The bombers clobbered the target. A little flak. I flew Blue number four on Wasylyk's wing in Ed Fry's flight.

April 10, 1945 (five hours, ten minutes): Airfield northwest of Berlin and some strafing. I flew Yellow number four on Wasylyk's wing in Fry's flight. The bombers clobbered the target.

April 16, 1945 (six hours, fifteen minutes): Rail yards southeast of Munich. I flew White number four on Wasylyk's wing in Captain Maxwell's flight. I was flying *Buzz Buggy* and the engine was running rough. I kept running up the RPMs to clean it out for smoother running. (I was using extra fuel at higher RPMs.) I left the Group with three other planes having problems and headed home. When we got to the North Sea, we were at 10,000 feet for insurance. My engine quit! (Wow! I never heard such *quiet*!) I turned back, lookin' for some solid ground but I only see some trees stickin' outta the water in a flooded dyke. (Dykes in Holland had been opened up to flood the land in order to restrict troop movement.) It did not look good to go down in the North Sea cause the water would "do you in" if you weren't picked up in a half an hour. After going through all of the procedures I could think of, the engine sorta started running halfheartedly. I headed south mushing along nose high into a thick haze just barely holding altitude. At our briefing that morning, we were told, with much emphasis, *not* to land on any Ninth Air Force bases and muck up their runways, put it down in the dirt. The Ninth Air Force was making lots of sorties in support of the ground troops. I got a steer for a repair base in Belgium and started running into the bomber stream headed home. I couldn't see in front of me with the nose high and the thick haze! I was seeing bombers go by above, below and on both sides of my Mustang. After dropping down below all of that hardware, I lost contact with the repair base. After some time, while watching each of the fuel tanks go empty, I saw an airfield off of each side of the plane. About that same time, the tanks went dry and my engine quit! I rolled over into a glide toward the nearest field and hit the runway just right. *Buzz Buggy* rolled to the middle of the runway, stopped, and I climbed out feeling *so* proud. All of the sudden lights were flashing and a jeep with a bunch of guys hanging all over it hollering at me while blowing the horn was bouncing across the field toward me. At the same time A-26s came roaring over the field peeling off to land on the same runway where I was sitting feeling fat, dumb, and happy. We pushed *Buzz Buggy* off of the pavement just as the first A-26 touched down. I spent a couple of days there at Lyon, France, getting in the way of a couple of mechanics who were unfamiliar with the Rolls Royce Merlin engine. They never did get it to run right. I think the problem was with the wiring harness on one side of the V and it was causing it to short out so only half of the engine would run. A B-24 stopped at the base, so I bummed a ride back to England. The crew was very friendly since they didn't normally have any close contact with us "Little Friend" pilots. The pilot of the Liberator let me sit in the left seat and steer all the way back. After we got over England, a B-26 passed below us. Without giving it any thought, I racked back up on the left wing and headed down to make a pass using the formation flying stick to the left of the wheel. There was a lot of noise on the intercom and the pilot came up suggesting that he take over since we were getting close to the base. I got a ride back to Leiston in the back of a truck. A P-51 with a new engine was assigned to me so I got to name it *Swamp Fox.* (My home county of Marion is swamp fox country. The ironic humor of the *Swamp Fox* being in England was lost on the locals. Those folks are just not up on their Revolutionary War history! The British never could catch American General Francis Marion because he would disappear into the swamps around the Pee Dee River. The British called him the Swamp Fox.)

April 21, 1945 (five hours, twenty-five minutes): Target airfield east of Munich. I flew just about everybody's wing. Half of the Squadron aborted and the weather was poor. The Mustangs were getting "war weary" as well as everybody in the group. This was my last mission. In a way, it was a letdown because I'd just gotten a really good plane and I had a feeling that all of that training hadn't accomplished anything. But looking on the bright side, I was still in one piece.

May 13, 1945: A great, big flyover of London by all of the planes that the Eighth Air Force could get into the air. It was a spectacular show!

May 29, 1945 (six hours, twenty-five minutes): A fantastic group mission at low altitude to Antwerp, Strasburg, Munich, Nuremburg, Frankfurt, and the Ruhr Valley where we ran into a big weather front. We broke up into elements and went on instruments for an hour it seemed. It was interesting to circle the bombed-out areas at low altitude without having to look over your shoulder.

This is Westminster Abbey

By Apple

Next time you're in London, tear yourself away from Picadilly Circus (if you can) for a couple of hours and stroll down to Westminster Abbey. That's the place you've heard so much about during school days, remember? It's the famous old church where all the great personalities in English history are buried—poets, statesmen, scientists, military and naval heroes, educators, kings and queens, the British Unknown Soldier. You walk in through the portals, removing your officer's cap, and immediately you're impressed with the great silence, a slight musty smell as of great age, a queer sensation of insignificance and of smallness, for all at once you realize that yourself (a wonderful person around whom the earth revolves) doesn't amount to a hill of beans. But you are glad, nevertheless, that such a memorial does exist. It has recalled to your mind great men and the deeds they performed. It has inspired you a little, for you become acutely aware that though man's flesh may decay, his spirit lives on, communicated through other men, men of younger generation, men like yourself.

This Pilots' Room is Our Westminster Abbey

But unlike the original, it recalls fellows with wings who are not necessarily dead—though some of them are. Those knife carved nudes upon the wall, for example, were done by a handsome kid named Beemer who is a prisoner of war in Germany with a couple of broken legs. He intended to decorate every panel, but a bunch of Me-109s upset his plans shortly after we went operational. The ashtrays made out of practice bombs (which you so frequently don't hit with your butts) are the handiwork of husky Lt. Connahgan, a guy who didn't smoke himself. He had a midair collision with an Me-110 over Munich. The linoleum on the floor was produced by a high-strung fellow named Broadhead. He became our CO and a major, finished his tour and went home to the good old states. His ship was christened "Baby Mike" and it turned out to be a sweet baby. Athletically built Lt. Mace did the Mustangs on the wall and cut the swastikas.

288

We had several awfully good days and Mace got discouraged trying to keep it up to date. Jerries were getting shot down faster than his knife could carve. Californian Captain Becker did most of the work on that fireplace in the back. (His shell-shattered windshield is resting over the mantelpiece, a souvenir from one of our early "Big B" raids.) And in case you were wondering how that classy snack bar ever came into existence, here's a synopsis—Lichter, a prisoner of war, who bailed out over Holland, did a great part of the bricklaying, along with Rodney (Mosquito Mauler) Starkey and Obee (Shanty Irish) O'Brien. Junior Drollinger, the lad who evaded Jerry with the help of the French Underground and came back, laid the top. And Captain England, our high scorer and operations officer, painted the darned thing. The card tables materialized through Captain Dave Perron, a triple-killer boy, who spun in one day when the overcast was so thick the birds were walking. Of course, everyone pitched in on the interior decorating—Williams, Baker, Lingo, Harris, Adams, Hagan, R. D. Brown, Rydberg, Vogel, even Colonel Egenes. Everybody had a hand in it, that's for sure.

Some of that strange elusive stuff commonly referred to as "money" made the lounge as nice as it is. We chipped in and purchased the radio, the record player, the Begin-the-Beguines and Rock-it-for-Me's and Star-Dust and Beau-Night-in-Hotchkiss-Corners. The Dinah Shores and Fats Wallers and Glenn Millers and T. Dorsey numbers you like to play so much. During the invasion days we flew so often and had cots bunched all around the room, we forgot about music and listened continually to BBC and AFN. That was the only time we kept up with news, for there was little to be seen from the air. Money paid for the bottle of liquor from which each man downed a shot after his first Jerry. Money paid for the enlisted man's wages. It's been convenient as hell to get up late and eat hot cakes, French toast, eggs sunny-side-up, and drink fruit juice and steaming hot coffee before a mission. That's what money is for, though.

Westminster Abbey, we called it, but in a different sort of way from the original. We don't want the place solemn and dark; it should be light and cheerful. We want comfortable chairs and not hard benches. We didn't want sacred hush-hush. But the right to storm in after pitching a good drunk and raise all kinds of hell in our own way. We want those luscious pin-ups on the walls and the pink lingerie which Hollywood studios sent us hanging where we can caress it once in a while. We're young and alive and might as well gather our rosebuds while we may. The guys who have gone would have wanted it that way. That's why they helped to make the lounge, and that's how we want it for you, too.

This room has seen a lot of things in the past, all right, from a pair of Sealyham dogs to General Kepner, from five cats to an Associated Press reporter, from a Red Cross gal trying to kiss bashful Captain Hank Beal after he knocked down a Jerry to Little Johnny Pugh working mighty hard (without success) to get a piece from a beautiful blond around two o'clock in the morning. It has seen lots of fellows nervously putting on their parachutes for their first hop across the Channel, happy and afraid at the same time. It has seen pilots exuberant after a successful day, everybody chattering loudly, going through gestures of combat, doing Immelmans and snap rolls with the hands, dumping the stick or firewalling or dropping flaps to keep from over-shooting all over again. It has seen pilots morose and irritable, browned off because they had to fly in lousy weather or because they had to sit on the ground on a mission to Russia or because their engine got rough and they had to abort; or because another bed in the Nissen hut where they live is empty. It has seen fellows like yourself playing cards, reading mail from home, throwing darts, opening up a can of corned beef, batting the breeze, scuffling around and screeching like a bunch of wild Indians. This place is home—over here.

At first, the new replacements act kinda meek in this room. They are quiet and do a lot of reading and walk up to the area instead of riding and wait for the older guys to speak first. They feel that they will never catch up, that they missed the big show. We're all that way at first.

And then, not long after, they're going on a combat mission for the first time. They come back talking a blue streak, acting a bit more bold as they step up for their fried eggs or yell for the weapons carrier, they've become part of the squadron, you see, and they belong to the room, as it belongs to them. There's a brotherhood about this room.

It's *your* Westminster Abbey too, pal.

Index

The letter i following a page number denotes an illustration.

CPSIA information can be obtained at www.ICGtesting.com
Printed in the USA
LVOW100257250112

265469LV00002B/6/P